label design

College of Arts &
Community Studies

Eastwood Lane, Rotherham S65 1EG
Telephone: 61801

Production Office du Livre

label design

the evolution, design
and function of labels
from the earliest times
to the present day

with 1000 illustrations
chosen and introduced
by Claude Humbert

Thames and Hudson · London

NOTE
The dates given in the captions relate to the
labels' period of use.

Acknowledgments and thanks are due to all the
libraries, collectors, printers, publishers, agencies
and artists who have made material available to
us and thereby greatly facilitated our researches.

PHOTOGRAPHS

J. Henry, Genève.
The Bodleian Library, photographic service,
Oxford:
Oxford University Press collection.
J. R. Freeman & Co, London:
British Museum collection.
The New York Public Library, photographic
service, New York:
New York Public Library collection.
J. Arlaud, Genève: 867, 883, 896, 898, 903.

English translation by Nicholas Fry
German translation by R. M. Ostheimer

First published in Great Britain in 1972 by
Thames and Hudson Ltd, London
© 1972 by Office du Livre, Fribourg

ISBN 0 500 23166 4

Printed in Switzerland

Contents

Introduction

What, it may be asked, is the point of producing a book devoted entirely to labels? However, if we try for a moment to imagine a world without labels, we quickly realize the extent, to which they dominate our daily lives.

This is no accident, for the label plays a unique informational role in the field of graphic design, as it has done since its first appearance. Its evolution has been largely governed by the exigencies of production (of the commodity to which the label is applied) and the perfecting of manual and mechanical methods of reproduction (of the label itself). These different elements are examined in the following brief study, which precedes a visual presentation of a thousand different labels covering the 17th, 18th, 19th and 20th centuries.

Some of the examples present striking similarities or contrasts, and the illustrations have been chosen with this in mind, rather than classified according to product, country or period.

This volume should therefore be regarded not as a dictionary but as a handbook which, to the receptive eye, will provide a vast reservoir of creative ideas which can be used in a variety of different ways.

Introduction

Pourquoi, nous a-t-on demandé fréquemment, et pour qui, éditer un livre concernant exclusivement l'étiquette?

Essayez donc d'imaginer un monde sans étiquettes? Très rapidement vous prendrez conscience de la place prépondérante que l'étiquette occupe dans notre vie quotidienne.

Ce n'est pas un hasard: dans le domaine de la création graphique, elle est seule à remplir une fonction d'information absolument indispensable. L'étiquette fait partie du design auquel elle a appartenu dès son apparition. Les impératifs de production et le perfectionnement des procédés manuels ou mécaniques de reproduction sont à l'origine de son évolution.

Ces différents éléments font l'objet de la brève étude qui précède la présentation visuelle de mille étiquettes couvrant les XVIIe, XVIIIe, XIXe et XXe siècles.

Les confrontations sont parfois étonnantes, et c'est dans cet esprit que les illustrations ont été réparties, sans distinction de produit, de pays ou d'époque.

Ce volume n'est donc pas à considérer comme un dictionnaire, mais comme un instrument de travail qui livre, à celui qui sait regarder, une source immense de possibilités dans le domaine de la création, quelle que soit la forme par laquelle elle se manifeste.

Einleitung

Weshalb, fragte man uns oft, und für wen, ein Buch herausgeben, welches sich ausschließlich mit dem Etikett befasst?

Versuchen Sie es doch, sich eine Welt ohne Etikette vorzustellen! Sehr schnell werden Sie sich darüber bewußt werden, welchen vorherrschenden Rang das Etikett in unserem täglichen Leben einnimmt.

Das ist kein Zufall; auf dem Gebiet des graphischen Schaffens erfüllt es allein eine informative Funktion, die ganz und gar unentbehrlich ist. Das Etikett ist Teil des Design, dem es seit den Anfängen angehörte. Die Produktionserfordernisse und die Vervollkommnung der handwerklichen oder mechanischen Reproduktionsverfahren bilden den Ursprung seiner Entwicklung.

Diese unterschiedlichen Einzelheiten sind Gegenstand der kurzen Studie, die der visuellen Vorstellung von tausend Etiketten aus dem 17., 18., 19. und 20. Jahrhundert vorausgeht.

Die Gegenüberstellungen sind manchmal erstaunlich, und in diesem Sinne haben wir die Abbildungen verteilt, ohne besondere Rücksicht auf das Produkt, das Land oder die Epoche.

Dieser Band ist also nicht als Wörterbuch zu betrachten, sondern als Arbeitsinstrument, das demjenigen, der zu beschauen weiß, eine unermeßliche Quelle schöpferischer Möglichkeiten bietet, welches auch immer die Ausdrucksform sein mag.

The Label: its Evolution, Function and Composition

We live in a world in which everything is labelled—products, streets, houses, cars, trains, air-flights, days, hours, individuals. Clearly, the label plays a major part in the social life of the 20th century.

The label originated from the simple, practical necessity of identifying the contents of an opaque container or indicating whom it belonged to. It would be hard to imagine earthenware amphorae, the pharmacist's porcelain jars or the drawers in a grocer's without some indication of what they contained.

The information given on the label has been amplified over the centuries, until now it not only identifies the contents, but also tells us about their quality, the date of manufacture, the latest date for consumption, the quantity, value, origin and often the method of use. Thus the label has a well defined and indispensable informational role (fig. 1, 2, 3, 4 and 5).

While the label has always fulfilled this essential function, its visual element has undergone a considerable evolution. The changes which have appeared over the years are due to three factors—the development of reproduction techniques, the taste of different periods and its effect on the letter-forms and ornaments used, and lastly, over the past half century, scientific market research, which has

L'étiquette: évolution, fonction et structure

Nous vivons dans un monde où tout est étiqueté: les produits, les rues, les maisons, les voitures, les trains, les vols aériens, les jours, les heures, les individus. C'est dire à quel point l'étiquette joue un rôle prépondérant dans la vie sociale du XXe siècle.

A l'origine, l'étiquette est née d'une simple nécessité pratique: identifier un contenu enveloppé dans une matière opaque, ou en indiquer l'appartenance. Il est en effet difficile d'imaginer des amphores en terre cuite, des pots de pharmacien en porcelaine, des tiroirs d'épicier, sans une indication des produits qu'ils contiennent.

L'information que donne ainsi l'étiquette s'est complétée au cours des siècles. Elle permet actuellement, non seulement une identification, mais elle renseigne sur la qualité, la date de production, la date limite de consommation, la quantité, la valeur, l'origine et, souvent le mode d'emploi. L'étiquette remplit donc une fonction d'information bien définie et indispensable (fig. 1, 2, 3, 4 et 5).

Si l'étiquette a toujours rempli cette fonction essentielle, elle a par ailleurs visuellement beaucoup évolué. Trois facteurs sont à l'origine des modifications apparues au cours des ans: le développement des procédés techniques de reproduction,

Das Etikett: Entwicklung, Funktion und Aufbau

Wir leben in einer Welt, in der alles etikettiert ist: die Waren, die Straßen, die Häuser, die Wagen, die Züge, die Flüge, die Tage, die Stunden, die einzelnen Menschen. Dies zeigt, welche hervorstechende Rolle das Etikett im sozialen Leben des XX. Jahrhunderts spielt.

Ursprünglich entsprang das Etikett einer einfachen praktischen Notwendigkeit: einen in einem undurchsichtigen Material verpackten Inhalt zu kennzeichnen oder dessen Herkunft anzugeben. Tonkrüge, Porzellantöpfe eines Apothekers, Schubladen eines Kolonialwarenhändlers lassen sich nämlich schwer ohne irgendeine Inhaltsangabe vorstellen.

Die Information, die das Etikett somit liefert, hat sich im Lauf der Jahrhunderte vervollständigt. Gegenwärtig erlaubt es nicht nur eine Identifizierung, sondern es gibt auch Aufschluß über die Qualität, das Herstellungsdatum, den Endtermin der Verbrauchsfähigkeit, die Menge, den Wert, den Ursprung und beinhaltet oftmals die Gebrauchsanweisung.

Das Etikett erfüllt also eine genau bestimmte und unerläßliche Funktion (Abb. 1, 2, 3, 4 und 5).

Wenn auch das Etikett stets im wesentlichen diese Funktion erfüllt hat, so hat es sich andererseits im visuellen Bereich stark

1

2

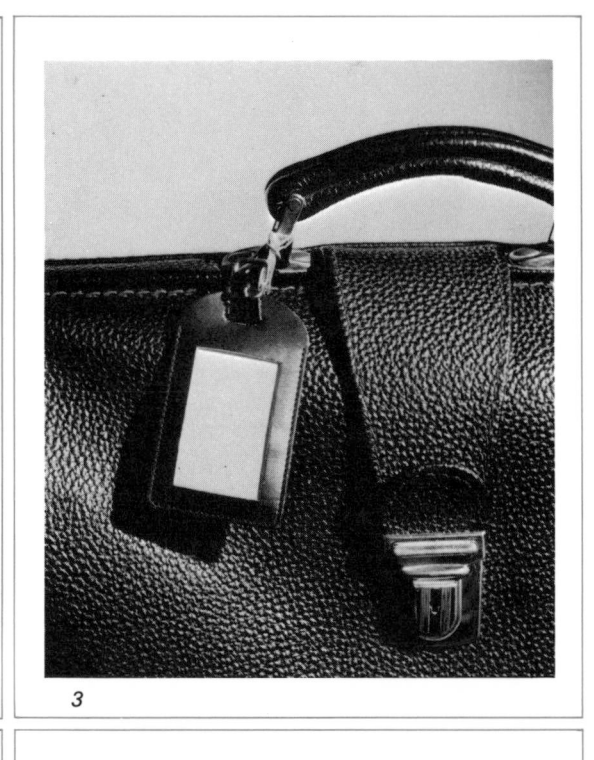

3

1-5. The label plays a predominant part in 20th century life as a means of identification and information. It is only useful in so far as it fulfils these two functions.

1-5. *L'étiquette joue dans la vie sociale du XX*e *siècle un rôle prépondérant d'information et d'identification. Elle n'est utile que dans la mesure où elle remplit ces fonctions!*

1-5. Das Etikett spielt im sozialen Leben des XX. Jahrhunderts vor allem eine Rolle für Information und Identifizierung. Es ist nur insofern nützlich, als es diese Funktionen erfüllt!

4

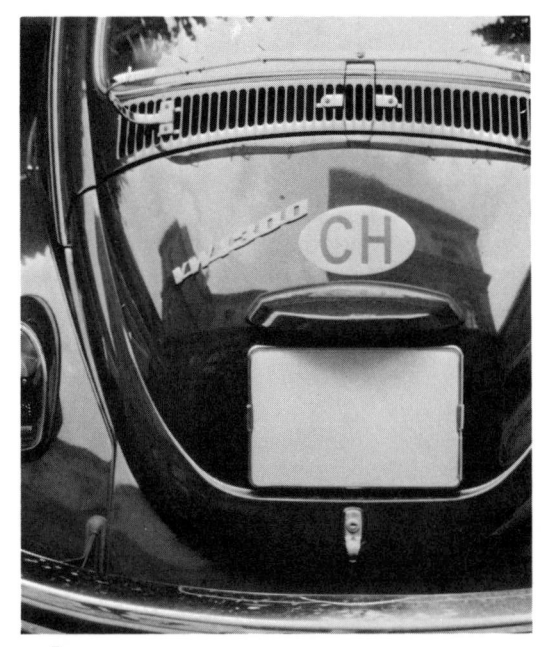

5

added a conditioning factor to the role of the label.

Examining these different points, we can place the labels reproduced in this volume approximately in time. It is also of some interest to look at the evolution of printing, the appearance of which must have created as much of a revolution as did the the appearance of the photographic image.

Over the course of the centuries, the transformation of the means of conveying the information—from handwriting to wood blocks to printing from type—has been matched by a parallel evolution in the materials used for the label itself. Thus stone, clay, papyrus and parchment all preceded the appearance of paper. The latter took nearly a thousand years to reach Europe from China, passing via the Middle East and North Africa to arrive in Spain in AD 1150.

The woodcut, the first process enabling the multiple reproduction of written or illustrated documents, also originated in China, around AD 450. It was not used in Europe until 1390. It is a relief printing process which can be used to produce a fairly large number of copies. However, it lacks flexibility, since the wood block has to be engraved as a whole and can only be re-used as a whole (fig. 22). In the face of this limitation, human ingenuity was led to discover a more flexible process, in the form of movable type. In the East, characters were produced successively in clay (1050), tin (1150), wood (1300) and finally bronze (Korea, 1390), while in Europe Gutenberg created movable type, independently of outside influence, in 1450. It is interesting to note that the material he used—an alloy of lead, tin, and antimony—has remained more or less unchanged ever since. Not unexpectedly, the characters used in the composition of the famous Mainz bible (fig. 6) were still governed by the technical

le style des différentes époques marqué par le caractère typographique et l'ornement qui le complète et, enfin depuis plus d'un demi-siècle l'étude scientifique du marché qui ajoute à l'étiquette un facteur de conditionnement.

Il apparaît opportun de préciser ces différents points qui nous permettent de situer approximativement, dans le temps, les étiquettes reproduites dans ce volume. D'autre part, il est intéressant d'examiner l'évolution de l'imprimerie qui, à son apparition, a dû créer une révolution semblable à celle que créa l'apparition de l'image photographique.

Lié de façon étroite à la transformation de l'indication manuscrite ou gravée jusqu'à l'imprimée, le support a parallèlement évolué au cours des siècles. Pierre, argile, papyrus, parchemin précèdent l'apparition du papier. Sa route, partie de Chine, passant par le Moyen-Orient et l'Afrique du Nord pour aboutir en Espagne en 1150 ap. J.-C., s'étale sur près d'un millénaire.

Quant à la xylographie, premier procédé permettant la reproduction de documents écrits ou illustrés en plusieurs exemplaires, elle est également née en Chine vers 450 ap. J.-C. Elle ne trouvera son application en Europe qu'en 1390. Mais si la gravure sur bois offre l'avantage d'un certain nombre de tirages basés sur le principe de l'impression en relief (fig. 22), elle ne présente aucune mobilité. La planche est gravée dans son ensemble et ne peut être réutilisée que dans son ensemble. Conscient de cette limite, l'homme s'est ingénié à trouver une formule plus souple: le caractère mobile. C'est ainsi que sont apparus successivement en Orient des caractères en argile (1050), en étain (1150), en bois (1300), enfin en bronze (Corée 1390), alors qu'en Europe, sans aucune influence extérieure, Gutenberg créa le caractère mobile en 1450. Il est intéressant de noter que la composition de l'alliage plomb, étain,

entwickelt. Drei Faktoren bilden den Ursprung der im Lauf der Jahre erfolgten Veränderungen: die Entwicklung der technischen Reproduktionsverfahren, der Stil der verschiedenen Epochen, der durch die Druckletter und die sie ergänzende Verzierung geprägt ist, und schließlich, seit über einem halben Jahrhundert, die wissenschaftliche Marktforschung, die dem Etikett einen Faktor der Konditionierung hinzufügt.

Es scheint angebracht, jene verschiedenen Punkte zu präzisieren, welche es uns erlauben, die in diesem Band reproduzierten Etikette zeitlich annähernd einzuordnen.

Darüber hinaus ist es interessant, die Entwicklung des Buchdrucks zu untersuchen, dessen Anfänge eine Umwälzung verursachten, ähnlich derjenigen, die die Anfänge der Fotografie hervorriefen.

In enger Verbindung mit dem Wandel der handgeschriebenen oder gravierten Anweisung hin zum Gedruckten, hat sich das Material im Verlauf der Jahrhunderte parallel fortentwickelt. Stein, Ton, Papyrus und Pergament gehen dem Papier voraus.

Sein Weg, der in China beginnt und durch den Mittleren Orient und Nord-Afrika bis nach Spanien — im Jahre 1150 n. Ch. — führt, erstreckt sich über nahezu ein Jahrtausend.

Auch die Xylographie, das erste Verfahren, das die Reproduktion geschriebener oder illustrierter Dokumente in mehreren Exemplaren ermöglicht, ist in China gegen 450 n. Ch. ins Leben gerufen worden. In Europa wird sie ihre Anwendung erst im Jahre 1390 finden. Zwar bietet der Holzschnitt den Vorteil einer gewissen Anzahl von Abzügen nach dem Hochdruckprinzip, doch erlaubt er keinerlei Beweglichkeit. Die Platte wird als Ganzes bearbeitet und kann ausschließlich als Ganzes wieder verwendet werden (Abb. 22).

6

7

8

6. Gothic type, Mainz Bible, Germany, 15th century.
7. Gothic type, Mazarin Bible, France, 15th century.
8. Reproduction of an etching by Rembrandt, wood engraving, 19th century.
9. Typical 1900 letters and ornaments, England.
10. Renaissance border, France.

6. *Caractères gothiques, Bible de Mayence, Allemagne, XVᵉ siècle.*
7. *Caractères gothiques, Bible Mazarine, France, XVᵉ siècle.*
8. *Reproduction d'une eau-forte de Rembrandt, xylographie, XIXᵉ siècle.*
9. *Lettres et ornements typiques 1900, Angleterre.*
10. *Bandeau Renaissance, France.*

6. Gotische Druckbuchstaben, Mainzer Bibel, Deutschland, XV. Jahrhundert.
7. Gotische Druckbuchstaben, Mazarine Bibel, Frankreich, XV. Jahrhundert.
8. Reproduktion einer Radierung von Rembrandt, Xylographie, XIX. Jahrhundert.
9. Typische Buchstaben und Ornamente 1900, England.
10. Renaissance-Band, Frankreich.

9

10

demands of the handwritten Gothic script. The same type was subsequently used for printing the Mazarin Bible in France (fig. 7). In the fifty years which followed, more than 2000 new blackletter types were created.

It was also in the second half of the 15th century that copper plate engraving, an intaglio process, moved from the purely artistic to the industrial field (fig. 23). In the centuries which followed many combinations of these three processes were used, particularly of woodcuts with movable type. The woodcut and the related process of wood engraving were used for reproducing illustrations up to the end of the 19th century. By this time, wood engravers had become so skilled that they could even reproduce copper plate engravings on wood (fig. 8).

The 'old face' letter—the first of the four great families of roman types—is distinguished by its triangular serifs (fig. 13). It was restored in the middle of the 19th century, but was originally created by the family Elzevir as a type at the beginning of the 16th century as a result of the geometrical studies of Geoffroy Tory in 1529 (fig. 11). These researches also led to the creation of the type known as 'Caractères de l'Université' by Garamond in 1540 (fig. 12).

At the same time, movable typographical ornaments in wood or metal were also developed, and these could be assembled to harmonize with the Renaissance-style characters.

After this, there were few major developments until the late 18th and early 19th centuries, when a creative explosion both in typography and in the development of printing techniques to some extent overthrew the well-established principles of the past few centuries.

In 1780, Didot created the type with hairline serifs which bears his name

antimoine, n'a guère changé depuis cette époque. Comme dans toute invention, les caractères qui ont servi à composer la fameuse Bible de Mayence (fig. 6) sont encore régis par les impératifs techniques de l'écriture gothique manuelle. Le même type sera utilisé en France pour l'impression de la Bible Mazarine (fig. 7). Dans les 50 ans qui suivent, plus de 2000 caractères gothiques nouveaux furent créés.

C'est également dans la deuxième moitié du XVe siècle que la gravure sur cuivre, procédé en creux, passe du domaine artistique au domaine de la production (fig. 23). On verra au cours des siècles suivants beaucoup de combinaisons de ces trois procédés, tout particulièrement de la gravure sur bois et du caractère mobile. La xylographie sera utilisée jusqu'à la fin du XIXe siècle pour la reproduction d'illustrations. Les graveurs, à cette époque, feront preuve d'une telle virtuosité qu'ils iront jusqu'à reproduire des gravures sur cuivre (fig. 8).

Le caractère Elzévir, première des quatre grandes familles d'écriture ronde, se distingue par ses empattements triangulaires (fig. 13). Il fut restauré au milieu du XIXe siècle, mais est ainsi nommé parce qu'il a été créé par la famille Elzévir au début du XVIe siècle, faisant suite aux recherches géométriques de Geoffroy Tory en 1529 (fig. 11). C'est ainsi que sera créé par Garamond, en 1540, le type dit de l'Université (fig. 12).

En parallèle se développent les vignettes xylographiques et typographiques mobiles qui permettent, par leur assemblage, une heureuse harmonie avec les caractères de style Renaissance.

Il faut attendre la fin du XVIIIe siècle et le début du XIXe pour assister à une explosion créatrice aussi bien dans le domaine typographique que dans celui des techniques d'impression qui vont

Sich dieser Beschränkung bewußt, hat der Mensch eine anpassungsfähigere Formel erdacht: die bewegliche Letter. So sind im Orient nacheinander Buchstaben aus Ton (1050), aus Zinn (1150), aus Holz (1300), schließlich aus Erz (Korea 1390) entwickelt worden, während in Europa, ohne Einfluß von außen, Gutenberg im Jahre 1450 die bewegliche Letter schuf. Es ist interessant zu bemerken, daß sich die Zusammensetzung der Legierung Blei, Zinn und Antimon seit jener Epoche kaum geändert hat. Wie bei jeder Erfindung, sind die Drucklettern, die dem Satz der Mainzer Bibel (Abb. 6) gedient haben, immer noch den technischen Anforderungen der gotischen Handschrift unterworfen. Diese gleiche Type wurde in Frankreich später zum Druck der Mazarine Bibel (Abb. 7) verwendet. In den folgenden 50 Jahren wurden über 2000 neue gotische Drucklettern geschaffen.

Ebenfalls in der zweiten Hälfte des XV. Jahrhunderts geht der Kupferstich, ein Tiefdruckverfahren, vom Bereich der Kunst in den der Produktion über (Abb. 23). In den folgenden Jahrhunderten findet man zahlreiche Kombinationen jener drei Verfahren, ganz besonders die des Holzschnittes mit der beweglichen Letter. Die Xylographie wird bis Ende des XIX. Jahrhunderts für die Bildreproduktion benutzt. Zu jener Zeit bringen es die Xylographen durch ihre Fertigkeit bis zur Reproduktion von Kupferstichen (Abb. 8).

Die Elzevir-Letter, erste der vier großen Rundschriftfamilien, ist durch ihre dreieckigen Serifen gekennzeichnet (Abb. 13). Sie wurde Mitte des XIX. Jahrhunderts wieder eingeführt. In der Tat geht ihre typographische Entstehung auf den Beginn des XVI. Jahrhunderts zurück, den geometrischen Untersuchungen von Geoffroy Tory im Jahre 1529 (Abb. 11) folgend. So schafft Garamond im Jahre 1540 die sogenannte Type der Universität (Abb. 12).

11

A B

H I

12

E

13

N

14

Δόξα τῷ Θεῷ! Ἰδοὺ καὶ εἰς σκαρᾶς. Εἶνε ἀψόγως ἐνδεδι νὴν ἀναξυρίδα καὶ μελανὸν
ΣΩΚΡΑΤΗΣ ΕΥΘΥΦΡΩΝ

15

Thibaudeau classified the roman types into four families, according to the shape or absence of serifs. To facilitate comparison of the proportions of the different characters, they have been enlarged to the same measure.

11. Geoffroy Tory's geometrical studies, France, 16th century.
12. 'Caractères de l'Université' type, Claude Garamond, France, 16th century.
13. Elsevier types, Holland, 16th century.
14. Type designed by Firmin Didot, France, 18th century.
15. Greek type, Giambattista Bodoni, Italy, 18th century.

Thibaudeau a établi le classement des caractères typographiques (écriture ronde) en quatre familles, en fonction de la forme des empattements ou de l'absence de ceux-ci. Afin de pouvoir comparer ces différents caractères dans leurs proportions, ils ont été agrandis dans un cadre identique.
11. *Recherches géométriques de Geoffroy Tory, France, XVIe siècle.*
12. *Type «de l'Université», Claude Garamond, France, XVIe siècle.*
13. *Caractère Elzévir, Hollande, XVIe siècle.*
14. *Caractère dessiné par Firmin Didot, France, XVIIIe siècle.*
15. *Grec ancien, Giambattista Bodoni, Italie, XVIIIe siècle.*

Thibaudeau hat eine Klassifizierung der Druckbuchstaben (Rundschrift) in vier Familien aufgestellt, nach der Form der Serifen bzw. deren Abwesenheit. Um einen Vergleich der Proportionen dieser verschiedenen Druckbuchstaben zu ermöglichen, wurden sie in einem Rahmen von konstantem Format vergrößert.

11. Geometrische Untersuchungen von Geoffroy Tory, Frankreich, XVI. Jahrhundert.
12. Type «der Universität», Claude Garamond, Frankreich, XVI. Jahrhundert.
13. Elzevir-Druckbuchstabe, Holland, XVI. Jahrhundert.
14. Von Firmin Didot gezeichneter Druckbuchstabe, Frankreich, XVIII. Jahrhundert.
15. Altgriechisch, Giambattista Bodoni, Italien, XVIII. Jahrhundert.

16

18

17

19a

19b

16. Grotesque type, France, 19th century.
17. Egyptian type, France, 19th century.
18. Drawn copperplate script, litho, France, 19th century.
19. (a). The binary system of the 20th century computer enables its functions to be translated into a 'language' of figures and letters. (b). Adrian Frutiger, who created the Grotesque 'Univers' type and adapted it for photosetting, later improved the design to meet the special requirements of the computer.

16. Caractère «Antique», France, XIXe siècle.
17. Lettre «Egyptienne», France, XIXe siècle.
18. Lettre «Anglaise» dessinée, lithographie, France, XIXe siècle.
19. Avec l'évolution technique du XXe siècle, le computer par sa lecture binaire permet la transcription de sa «pensée» en chiffres et en caractères (a). Adrian Frutiger, créateur de l'Antique «Univers» et de son adaptation à la photocomposition, en améliorera le dessin en fonction des exigences particulières à l'ordinateur (b).

16. «Antiqua»-Druckbuchstabe, Frankreich, XIX. Jahrhundert.
17. «Egyptienne»-Buchstabe, Frankreich, XIX. Jahrhundert.
18. Gezeichneter «englischer» Buchstabe, Lithographie, Frankreich, XIX. Jahrhundert.
19. Auf Grund der technischen Entwicklung des XX. Jahrhunderts erlaubt der Computer durch sein binäres Ablesen die Transkription seines «Denkens» in Ziffern und Buchstaben (a). Adrian Frutiger, Urheber der «Univers»-Antiqua und ihrer Anpassung an die Fotokomposition, wird deren Zeichnung mit Rücksicht auf die speziellen Anforderungen des Ordinators verbessern (b).

(fig. 14). This austerely proportioned type is characteristically French. At the same period, Bodoni was carrying out research along similar lines in Italy, in particular for the printing of texts in Ancient Greek (fig. 15). The 'modern' faces of Didot and Bodoni form the basis of the second of the four families of roman types.

The chance discovery of lithography by Senefelder in 1796 opened up new horizons both for illustration and for printed lettering, which could now be drawn by calligraphists (fig. 18). There was no longer any limit to the reproduction of different shades and colours. The use of half-tone screens for colour separation eventually enabled illustrations to be printed in more than eight different colours. In the USA, labels were produced by this method up to 1935. Only by close examination with a screen-counter can one tell that they have been mechanically reproduced (fig. 24).

Around 1815 two new typographical forms were invented, which gave rise to two new major families of type, according to Thibaudeau's logical classification, which is still accepted today: Grotesque, a regular, sans-serif face inspired by Greek stone inscriptions, and Egyptian, with a more squat outline and rectangular serifs (figs. 16 and 17).

Numerous derivatives of these two types flourished during the mid-19th century— italic, condensed, expanded, shaded, reversed Egyptian, light Egyptian etc. (figs. 20 and 21).

Also in the 19th century, photography made its appearance, discovered by Niepce in 1822. It developed rapidly and by the end of the century was ready to be adapted to photomechanical reproduction methods. Thus offset printing—based on the lithography principle—was invented by various French printers between 1860 and 1880. Its technical development was

bouleverser quelque peu les principes bien établis depuis plusieurs siècles.

En 1780, Didot crée le caractère à empattement filiforme qui porte son nom (fig. 14). D'une grande rigueur de forme et de proportion, ce type bien français détermine la seconde famille de caractères. Bodoni a poursuivi, à la même époque, des recherches analogues en Italie, tout particulièrement pour l'impression des textes de grec ancien (fig. 15).

Due à un effet du hasard, la découverte de la lithographie par Senefelder en 1796, ouvre des horizons nouveaux aussi bien pour l'illustration que pour l'écriture qui sera dessinée par des calligraphes (fig. 18). Il n'y aura plus de limites dans la transcription des valeurs et des couleurs. On arrivera même, par une décalque de trames croisées en fonction des différentes couleurs à en imprimer au-delà de huit. On verra encore des étiquettes ainsi réalisées aux U.S.A. jusqu'en 1935! Seul un examen approfondi au compte-fils permet de déceler la technique manuelle de reproduction (fig. 24).

En 1815 environ, naissent deux caractères typographiques qui détermineront deux nouveaux types de grandes familles, selon le classement toujours admis et logique de Thibaudeau: l'Antique inspirée des inscriptions lapidaires grecques, au tracé rationnel sans empattement, et l'Egyptienne, plus trapue et bien assise, aux empattements rectangulaires (fig. 16 et 17). Ces deux caractères verront fleurir une variété considérable d'adaptations sous le Second Empire: italique, maigre, large, ombrée, Egyptienne italienne, Egyptienne anglaise, etc. (fig. 20 et 21).

Rappelons également qu'en ce début du XIXᵉ siècle la photographie, découverte par Niepce, fait son apparition en 1822. Elle se développera rapidement et permettra déjà en fin de siècle de mettre au point son adaptation aux procédés de

Gleichzeitig entwickeln sich die beweglichen Vignetten in der Xylographie und im Buchdruck, die durch ihre Zusammenführung eine glückliche Harmonie mit den Renaissance-Lettern ermöglichen.

Erst Ende des XVIII. und Anfang des XIX. Jahrhunderts erleben wir eine schöpferische Explosion, sowohl auf dem typographischen wie auf dem Gebiet der Drucktechniken, welche die seit Jahrhunderten wohleingerichteten Prinzipien erschüttern.

1780 schafft Didot die Letter mit strichförmiger Serife, die seinen Namen trägt (Abb. 14). Durch ihre große Genauigkeit in Form und Proportion bestimmt diese echt französische Type die zweite Druckbuchstabenfamilie. Bodoni führt zur gleichen Zeit in Italien ähnliche Untersuchungen weiter, ganz besonders im Hinblick auf den Druck von Texten in Altgriechisch (Abb. 15).

Die einem Zufall zu verdankende Erfindung der Lithographie durch Senefelder im Jahre 1796 öffnet der Illustration neue Horizonte, ebenso wie der Schrift, die von Kalligraphen gezeichnet wird (Abb. 18). Es gibt in der Wiedergabe der Tonwerte und der Farben keine Beschränkung mehr.

Es gelingt sogar, mit Hilfe des Durchpausens gekreuzter Paßlinien, abhängig von den verschiedenen Farben, bis zu acht Farben zu drucken. Derartig hergestellte Etikette sieht man noch bis 1935 in den U.S.A.! Nur eine mit Fadenzähler durchgeführte gründliche Prüfung ermöglicht es, das handwerkliche Reproduktionsverfahren nachzuweisen (Abb. 24).

Etwa um 1815 entstehen zwei Drucktypen, die zwei neue Arten von großen Schriftfamilien bestimmen, gemäß der noch immer anerkannten und logischen Klassifizierung Thibaudeau's: die Antiqua-Letter, die auf die griechischen Steininschriften zurückzuführen ist, mit

TYPE ITALIQUE
Enseignement 4

a

DANRIVAGE
GAUTHIERT 128
GAVARNI
LAFAYE

b

TENURIPUY
MONTUVILLER
JURERO

c

ESTHÉNIALE

d

DARCOLE
GIRANDIE

e

20

20. Variants of Grotesque: (a) the basic form; (b) Grotesque shaded; (c) Grotesque with hairline and three-dimensional shading; (d) open Grotesque shaded; (e) inline Grotesque shaded; France, late 19th century.

20. *Variantes du caractère «Antique»: type pur (a), Antique noire ombrée (b), Antique noire à filet, simple et ombrée (c), Antique blanche ombrée (d), Antique creusée (e), France, fin du XIXe siècle.*

20. Varianten des «Antiqua»-Druckbuchstaben: reine Type (a), Antiqua schwarz, schattiert (b), Antiqua schwarz, umrandet, einfach und schattiert (c), Antiqua weiß und schattiert (d), Antiqua hohl (e), Frankreich, Ende des XIX. Jahrhunderts.

LÉGENDE
Farfadets.5

a

SUCRE

b

GANDVIE
ERUSTA

c

ANOUE

d

THÉATRE FRANÇAIS

e

DUBOLE

b

RALYE
MONLOT
PENOLAN

f

L'ARMÉE PASSE LES ALPES
BONA

g

SUCRE SCULTI
PONT DE LOD

h

BRUIME

i

21. Variants of the Egyptian character: (a) the basic form; (b) Egyptian shaded; (c) Egyptian with hairline and three-dimensional shading; (d) ornamental Egyptian shaded; (e) reversed Egyptian condensed; (f) open Egyptian shaded; (g) reversed Egyptian; (h) reversed Egyptian, open and shaded; (i) reversed Egyptian shaded; France, late 19th century.

21. *Variantes du type «Egyptienne»: type pur (a), Egyptienne noire ombrée (b), Egyptienne à filet et ombrée (c), Egyptienne ornée ombrée (d), Italienne allongée (e), Egyptienne blanche ombrée (f), type primitif (g), Italienne blanche ombrée (h), Italienne noire ombrée (i), France, fin du XIXᵉ siècle.*

21. Varianten der Drucktype «Egyptienne»: reine Type (a), Egyptienne schwarz, schattiert (b), Egyptienne umrandet und schattiert (c), Egyptienne verziert und schattiert (d), Italienne schmal (e), Egyptienne weiß, schattiert (f), ursprüngliche Type (g), Italienne weiß, schattiert (h), Italienne schwarz, schattiert (i), Frankreich, Ende des XIX. Jahrhunderts.

21

begun in 1904 by the American W. Rubel (fig. 25).

Photogravure is hardly used for printing labels since its qualities and advantages are more appropriate to large-scale production of book and magazine illustrations (fig. 26). On the other hand, the very ancient Japanese technique of silk-screen printing reappeared at the beginning of the 20th century, and has enabled labels to be printed on the surface of containers and packaging made from materials such as glass, porcelain, plastic, etc. A large number of bottles and flasks are labelled in this way (fig. 27). This process is extremely flexible, being not only adaptable to the shape of the container but also heat resistant, and avoiding the necessity of re-labelling returnable bottles each time they are cleaned and filled. Silk-screen is also now used for transparent and self-adhesive labels (figs. 28 and 29).

In the development of the label, three different components appeared successively—the wording, the embellishment and finally the illustration. All three of these, as soon as the available techniques allowed, were used to contribute to the impact of the label. At the same time their style was inevitably governed by the fashions of the time (fig. 9).

Initially, the label simply served to convey information. By the 16th century, however, decorative borders were being used to give it a more attractive appearance (fig. 10). From the 18th century onwards, illustrations were widely used to show the quality of the product, the place where it was manufactured, or the size of the concern. This represented the very first attempts to condition the potential user of a commodity by means of the label, a process which developed markedly during the 19th century, to become scientifically based in the 20th century.

Hence there were certain subjects which appeared on labels regardless of the product

reproduction qui deviendront au début du XXᵉ siècle photomécaniques. C'est ainsi que divers imprimeurs français ont inventé, entre 1860 et 1880, l'offset ou roto-calcographie, basé sur le principe de la lithographie. Son exploitation technique démarrera en 1904, sous l'impulsion de l'Américain W. Rubel (fig. 25).

Quant à l'héliogravure, (fig. 26), elle n'est pratiquement pas utilisée pour l'impression des étiquettes, ses qualités et avantages étant tournés essentiellement vers une grande production dans le domaine de l'illustration pour les livres et les magazines. Par contre, une très ancienne technique japonaise, la sérigraphie, réapparait au début du XXᵉ siècle et va permettre l'impression des étiquettes à même les emballages en matière telle que verre, porcelaine, plastique, etc... C'est ainsi que sont étiquettés un nombre considérable de bouteilles et flacons (fig. 27). Ce procédé offre non seulement l'avantage d'une grande souplesse, par son adaptation au volume et sa faculté de cuisson, mais également celui d'éviter, dans le cas des verres repris, les opérations de nettoyage et d'étiquetage à chaque nouveau remplissage des récipients. La sérigraphie est également utilisée couramment pour les étiquettes auto-collantes et transparentes (fig. 28 et 29).

Dans l'évolution de l'étiquette, trois composantes apparaissent successivement: le texte, puis l'ornement et enfin l'illustration. Tous trois également sont assujettis à la mode qui en définit le style (fig. 9).

Si, au départ, l'étiquette remplit simplement une fonction d'information, dès le XVIᵉ siècle, on lui donnera un aspect plus attrayant en adjoignant des encadrements décoratifs (fig. 10). L'illustration sera largement utilisée dès le XVIIIᵉ siècle, pour situer la fabrication, l'importance de l'entreprise, la qualité du produit. On entre ainsi dans une toute première phase de conditionnement,

ihrer rationalen Zeichnung ohne Serife, und die Egyptienne-Letter, die etwas gedrungener und wohlgefestigt ist, mit rechteckigen Serifen (Abb. 16 und 17).

Diese beiden Drucktypen lassen unter dem Second Empire eine beachtliche Vielfalt von Anpassungsformen aufblühen: kursiv, mager, fett, schattiert, italienische Egyptienne, englische Egyptienne usw. (Abb. 20 und 21).

Erinnern wir gleichfalls daran, daß zu dieser Anfangszeit des XIX. Jahrhunderts die von Niepce erfundene Fotografie im Jahre 1822 erscheint. Sie entwickelt sich rasch fort und schon Ende des Jahrhunderts ist die Ausarbeitung ihrer Anpassung an die Reproduktionsverfahren, die zu Beginn des XX. Jahrhunderts fotomechanisch werden, möglich. So kam es, daß verschiedene französische Drucker zwischen 1860 und 1880 das Offsetverfahren oder die Rotokalkographie, beruhend auf dem Prinzip der Lithographie, erfanden. Seine technische Ausnutzung lief im Jahre 1904 unter dem Impuls des Amerikaners W. Rubel an (Abb. 25).

Der Lichtfarbendruck seinerseits wird praktisch nicht im Etikettendruck verwendet, da seine Eigenschaften und Vorteile hauptsächlich auf umfangreiche Produktion im Bereich der Buch- und Zeitschriften-illustration ausgerichtet sind (Abb. 26).

Demgegenüber erscheint Anfang des XX. Jahrhunderts eine sehr alte japanische Technik, der Siebdruck, wieder und macht den Etikettendruck direkt auf Verpackungen wie z.B. aus Glas, Porzellan, Plastik usw. möglich. So werden zahlreiche Flaschen und Flakons etikettiert (Abb. 27). Dieses Verfahren bietet nicht nur den Vorteil einer großen Vielseitigkeit durch seine Anpassung an die Oberflächengestalt und durch seine Kochbeständigkeit, sondern zusätzlich den — im Falle der Gläser-rücknahme —, die Säuberung und

22

23

24

25

26

The different printing processes are classified according to the principle on which they are based: relief, intaglio or planography.

22. Wood engraving (like letterpress printing) is a relief process, i.e. the ink is carried on the surface of the block or type.
23. Copperplate engraving is an intaglio process, the ink being carried in the depressions in the plate.
24. Lithography is based on the principle that grease and water do not mix.   It is a planographic process: the printing surface is flat.
25. Offset printing is also a planographic process, derived from lithography.
26. Photogravure is based on the same principle as copper plate engraving.   Depressions of varying depths in the plate carry a greater or smaller quantity of ink.

Les procédés de reproduction sont classés en fonction de leur principe d'impression: par relief, par le creux, à plat.
22. *La gravure sur bois (de même que la typographie) imprime par le relief.*
23. *La gravure sur cuivre imprime par les creux dans lesquels l'encre est répartie.*
24. *La lithographie est basée sur le principe de la réaction eau et matière grasse qui se refusent réciproquement. C'est un procédé à plat.*
25. *L'offset est également un procédé à plat, issu de la lithographie.*
26. *L'héliogravure découle du principe de la gravure sur cuivre. Dans les creux plus ou moins profonds est accumulée une quantité d'encre plus ou moins importante.*

Die Reproduktionsverfahren werden nach ihrer Druckart eingeteilt: Hochdruck, Tiefdruck und Flachdruck.

22. Beim Holzschnitt (wie beim Buchdruck) drucken die hochstehenden Teile.
23. Beim Kupferstich drucken die mit Druckfarbe ausgefüllten Vertiefungen.
24. Die Lithographie beruht auf dem Prinzip des gegenseitigen Abstoßens von Wasser und Fett. Sie ist ein Flachdruckverfahren.

25. Der Offsetdruck ist ebenfalls ein Flachdruckverfahren, das von der Lithographie ausgeht.
26. Der Lichtfarbendruck ergibt sich aus dem Prinzip des Kupferstiches. Die mehr oder weniger starken Vertiefungen sind mit mehr oder weniger Druckfarbe angefüllt.

27

28

29

27-29. Silk-screen printing is an ancient Japanese process which has been adapted to the demands of the 20th century. It can be used on surfaces of varying shapes and on materials such as glass, plastic or textiles, thereby enabling the label to be printed on the packaging itself (fig. 27). It is also used for self-adhesive and transparent labels.

27-29. La sérigraphie, ancien procédé de reproduction japonais, a été adaptée aux exigences du XXe siècle. Par ses multiples possibilités d'impression sur le volume et des matières telles que le verre, le plastique ou le textile, elle offre l'avantage d'une impression de l'étiquette à même l'emballage (fig. 27). Elle est également utilisée pour les étiquettes autocollantes ou transparentes.

27-29. Der Siebdruck, ein altes japanisches Reproduktionsverfahren, ist den Anforderungen des XX. Jahrhunderts angepaßt worden. Wegen seiner zahlreichen Möglichkeiten, Oberflächen verschiedener Art und Materialien wie Glas, Plastik oder Textilien zu bedrucken, bietet er den Vorteil eines unmittelbar auf die Verpackung druckbaren Etiketts (Abb. 27). Man verwendet ihn auch für die selbstklebenden und durchsichtigen Etiketten.

they were applied to. The female form always played an important part, whether it was to sell matches, cocoa, air transport or books (figs. 30, 31, 32 and 33). Banners, flags and coats of arms gave a feeling of authenticity and tradition (figs. 34, 36 and 37). Real or fake medals became a symbol of quality (figs. 35 and 38). Before the appearance of transparent packaging, labels carried an appetizing picture of the product, especially in the case of foodstuffs (figs. 39, 40 and 41). There are many more significant examples one could mention—they speak for themselves in the pages which follow.

Identification of the product is, however, only one of the label's functions. It also serves to indicate precautions to be taken, the manner in which something is to be used or handled—Danger, Urgent, Not to be opened before Christmas Day, Fragile, Airmail, etc. (figs. 42, 43, 44, 45 and 46). In this form the label is part of an international visual language, which is increasing day by day.

Today the label plays an important part in the selling process, and is closely related to packaging. Like the latter it is one of the stimuli which leads to the act of buying.

Before the label is created, specialists lay down its format, colour, illustration and graphic proportions on the basis of statistical research and without any regard for aesthetic considerations. As a result it scientifically conditions the buyer, often promising him more advantages than the product really offers. However, the consumer is becoming aware of the means being used to influence him, and is beginning to rebel against this restriction of his personal liberty in the choice and quantity of goods he wants.

At the same time, the marketing experts are clearly running out of ideas. After having exhausted all their scientifically based

dont le développement sera apparent au XIXe siècle, pour devenir scientifique au XXe siècle.

C'est ainsi qu'un certain nombre d'éléments se retrouvent sur les étiquettes, quel que soit le produit pour lequel elles sont créées. La femme y joue un rôle important, aussi bien pour vendre des allumettes, du cacao, des transports aériens que de l'édition (fig. 30, 31, 32 et 33). Les oriflammes et les drapeaux, ainsi que les armoiries donnent en même temps un sentiment d'authenticité et de tradition (fig. 34, 36 et 37). Les médailles, réelles ou factices, sont devenues synonyme de qualité (fig. 35 et 38). Jusqu'à l'apparition de l'emballage transparent, on peut voir la représentation appétissante du produit, surtout dans le domaine de l'alimentation (fig. 39, 40 et 41). On pourrait donner un nombre d'exemples important, ils apparaissent d'eux-mêmes dans les pages qui suivent.

Mais si l'étiquette, quelle que soit sa forme, identifie le produit, elle joue aussi un rôle important de mise en garde, elle dicte certains impératifs: danger de mort, urgent, usage externe, ne pas ouvrir avant Noël, fragile, par avion, etc... (fig. 42, 43, 44, 45 et 46). L'étiquette rejoint sous cette forme un langage visuel international qui tend, de plus en plus, à se développer.

L'étiquette joue actuellement un rôle très important dans le contexte de la vente, apparenté étroitement à celui de l'emballage. Comme lui, elle provoque le geste qui déclenche l'achat.

Sur la base d'enquêtes et de statistiques, précédant la création de l'étiquette, les spécialistes définissent son format, sa couleur, son illustration, ses proportions graphiques, sans aucun souci d'esthétique. Par conséquent, elle conditionne scientifiquement l'acheteur, très souvent en lui promettant plus de qualités que le produit n'en possède en réalité.

Wiederetikettierung bei jeder neuen Füllung der Behälter zu vermeiden. Zudem wird der Siebdruck häufig für selbstklebende und durchsichtige Etikette verwendet (Abb. 28 und 29).

In der Entwicklung des Etiketts erscheinen nacheinander drei Komponenten: der Text, dann das Ornament und schließlich die Illustration. Alle drei können durch eine treffende Auswahl, sobald es die Technik erlaubt, zur Gestaltung beitragen. Alle drei sind gleichermaßen der Mode unterworfen, die ihren Stil prägt (Abb. 9).

Wenn das Etikett zu Beginn einfach eine informative Aufgabe erfüllt, so wird man ihm seit Anfang des XVI. Jahrhunderts ein attraktiveres Aussehen geben, indem man dekorative Einrahmungen hinzufügt (Abb. 10). Die Illustration wird seit dem XVIII. Jahrhundert weithin verwendet, um das Herstellungsverfahren, die Bedeutung des Unternehmens und die Qualität des Produktes einzustufen. Man gelangt so in eine allererste Phase der Konditionierung, deren Entwicklung im XIX. Jahrhundert sichtbar und im XX. Jahrhundert wissenschaftlich wird.

So findet man auf sämtlichen Etiketten eine gewisse Anzahl von bestimmten Elementen, wie auch immer das Produkt aussehen mag, für das sie geschaffen sind. Die Frau spielt dabei eine wichtige Rolle, ebenso beim Verkauf von Streichhölzern, von Kakao und von Beförderungen auf dem Luftwege wie auch beim Verlegen (Abb. 30, 31, 32 und 33). Die Fähnchen und Fahnen wie auch die Wappen vermitteln zugleich ein Gefühl der Echtheit und Tradition (Abb. 34, 36 und 37). Die Medaillen, ob wirkliche oder nachgeahmte, sind gleichbedeutend mit Qualität geworden (Abb. 35 und 38). Bis zur Einführung der durchsichtigen Verpackungen kann man die appetitliche Darstellung des Produktes sehen, hauptsächlich im Bereich der Lebensmittel (Abb. 39, 40 und 41). Man könnte noch

30

31

32

33

30-33. The female form, in all its different aspects, frequently appears on labels, giving them an attraction which in most cases has nothing whatsoever to do with the product.

30-33. La femme, sous toutes ses formes et sous tous les angles apparaît fréquemment sur les étiquettes. Elle leur donne un attrait qui n'a, dans la plupart des cas, aucun rapport avec le produit.

30-33. Die Frau, in jeder Gestalt und unter allen Betrachtungswinkeln, erscheint oft auf den Etiketten. Sie verleiht ihnen eine Anziehungskraft, die meist nichts mit dem Produkt zu tun hat.

34

35

36

34-38. With the passage of time a number of different symbols, used all over the world and applied to all kinds of products, have come to be recognized as a mark of quality and authenticity. Thus labels frequently carry flags and banners, real or fake medals and coats of arms.

34-38. Un certain nombre d'éléments, largement utilisés dans le monde et pour tous les produits, sont devenus avec le temps des symboles de qualité et d'authenticité. C'est ainsi que se répandent sur les étiquettes les drapeaux et les oriflammes, les armoiries et les médailles, réelles ou factices.

34-38. Eine gewisse Anzahl von Elementen, die häufig in der Welt und bei allen Produkten Verwendung finden, sind mit der Zeit zu Symbolen der Qualität und der Echtheit geworden. So mehren sich auf den Etiketten die Fahnen und Fähnchen, die Wappen und Medaillen, wirkliche oder nachgeahmte.

37

38

SERIE RS 8000 · Nr. 8007 B · 12 x 9 CM

39

40

41

39-41. The label also represents the contents of the package in as favourable a light as possible. This is particularly true in the case of foodstuffs which need to be preserved in special non-transparent containers.

39-41. L'étiquette exprime également de façon aussi flatteuse que possible ce que contient l'emballage. Ceci est tout spécialement valable pour les produits alimentaires dont la conservation nécessite une enveloppe spéciale et non transparente.

39-41. Darüber hinaus stellt das Etikett den Inhalt der Verpackung so schmeichelhaft wie nur möglich dar. Dies gilt ganz besonders für Lebensmittel, deren Aufbewahrung eine spezielle undurchsichtige Umhüllung benötigt.

42

43

44

42-46. Like road signs, labels form an international language, often giving instructions and stating particular precautions to be taken.

42-46. Au même titre que les signaux routiers, langage international, l'étiquette peut être impérative et dicter des précautions particulières à prendre ou à observer.

42-46. Gleich den Straßenverkehrszeichen — eine internationale Sprache — kann auch das Etikett gebieterisch sein und bestimmte Maßregeln, die zu treffen oder zu berücksichtigen sind, vorschreiben.

45

46

12
M

Kanzleibriefumschläge
Enveloppes de
chancellerie
Buste di cancelleria

Gelb Bank   110 g
Banque jaune   110 g
Banca gialla   110 g

3 à 200 x 130 mm = 0
6 à 229 x 162 mm = C5
3 à 250 x 176 mm = B5

-.50

735.039

47

chirat

VINAIGRE DE TABLE
KARVA
TAFELESSIG   4,5°

1 Litre   Fr. 1.15

48

Vanaos
6
Lait bronzage rapide

L'ORÉAL

49

50

51

47-51. After passing through the stage of scientifically conditioning the consumer, the label is returning to its original function of providing objective information.
Isabelle Wittman's design for lubrication oil (fig. 50) combines objectivity with graphic expressiveness.

47-51. L'étiquette, après avoir dépassé le stade de conditionnement scientifique du consommateur, retrouve son rôle initial d'information objective.
Le projet d'Isabelle Wittman pout l'huile de vidange (fig. 50) ajoute à son objectivité un graphisme suggestif.

47-51. Nachdem das Etikett das Stadium der wissenschaftlichen Konditionierung des Verbrauchers überwunden hat, findet es seine ursprüngliche Rolle objektiver Information wieder.
Der Entwurf von Isabelle Wittman für das Reinigungsöl (Abb. 50) fügt seiner Objektivität eine suggestive grafische Darstellung hinzu.

resources and passed through a new intuitive phase, they will be compelled by the nature of things to return to supplying objective information.

The label is the first marketing area to show clear signs of this (figs. 47, 48, 49, 50 and 51).

Le consommateur conscient des moyens mis en œuvre pour le contraindre, commence à s'insurger contre cette main-mise sur sa liberté personnelle dans le choix et la quantité de ce qu'il veut consommer.

D'autre part, il faut en convenir, la publicité est à bout de souffle. Après avoir épuisé toutes ses ressources scientifiquement établies, passé par un nouveau stade intuitif, elle sera tout naturellement amenée à reprendre un rôle d'information objective.

L'étiquette est la première forme publicitaire à en donner des signes évidents (fig. 47, 48, 49, 50 et 51).

*NOTICE
Les dates figurant dans les légendes expriment la période d'utilisation des étiquettes.*

weitere wichtige Beispiele anführen; sie erscheinen von selbst auf den folgenden Seiten.

Wenn aber das Etikett, gleich in welcher Form, das Produkt identifiziert, so spielt es andererseits auch eine bedeutsame warnende Rolle, es schreibt gewisse Anordnungen vor: Lebensgefahr, dringend, äußerlicher Gebrauch, nicht vor Weihnachten öffnen, zerbrechlich, per Luftpost usw. (Abb. 42, 43, 44, 45 und 46).
Das Etikett geht dergestalt in eine visuelle internationale Sprache über, die mehr und mehr zur Fortentwicklung neigt.
Das Etikett spielt gegenwärtig eine wichtige Rolle im Zusammenhang mit dem Verkauf, der sehr eng mit der Verpackung verknüpft ist. Wie diese, beeinflußt es den Schritt, der den Kauf auslöst.
Aufgrund von Untersuchungen und Statistiken, die der Schaffung eines Etiketts vorausgehen, bestimmen die Fachleute sein Format, seine Farbe, seine Illustration, seine grafischen Proportionen, ohne jede Rücksicht auf die Ästhetik. Infolgedessen konditioniert es den Käufer auf wissenschaftliche Art, indem es ihm sehr oft mehr Eigenschaften verspricht als das Produkt wirklich besitzt. Der Verbraucher wird sich über die Mittel, mit denen er gelockt wird, bewußt und beginnt damit, sich zu sträuben gegen diesen Eingriff in seine persönliche Freiheit hinsichtlich der Auswahl und der Menge dessen, was er konsumieren will.

Weiterhin, man muß es gestehen, ist die Werbung erschöpft. Nachdem sie all ihre wissenschaftlich errichteten Hilfsmittel aufgebraucht und ein neues intuitives Stadium durchlaufen hat, wird sie ganz natürlich dahin kommen, wiederum eine objektive Informationsaufgabe zu erfüllen.

Das Etikett ist die erste Form der Werbung, die dafür offensichtliche Anzeichen liefert (Abb. 47, 48, 49, 50 und 51).

I. Typographical comparisons – Graphic and visual similarities

I. Confrontations typographiques – Analogies graphiques et optiques

I. Typographische Gegenüberstellungen – Grafische und optische Ähnlichkeiten

This chapter contains a brief survey of labels from different periods and countries. Starting from a straightforward written or printed wording, we pass via ornamentation, symbols, a central point of impact, traditional techniques and animals, ending with the introduction of the human figure.

Ce premier chapitre confronte, en raccourci, des étiquettes d'époques diverses et de pays différents. Partant du texte simple, dessiné ou typographique, nous aboutissons à l'introduction du personnage, en passant par l'ornement, le symbole, le point d'impact central, la technique traditionnelle et les animaux.

Dieses erste Kapitel stellt, in Kurzfassung, Etikette verschiedener Epochen und unterschiedlicher Länder einander gegenüber. Vom einfachen Text ausgehend, der entweder gezeichnet oder gesetzt ist, gelangen wir schließlich zur Einführung der Person, über das Ornament, das Symbol, den zentralen Schwerpunkt, die traditionelle Technik und die Tiere.

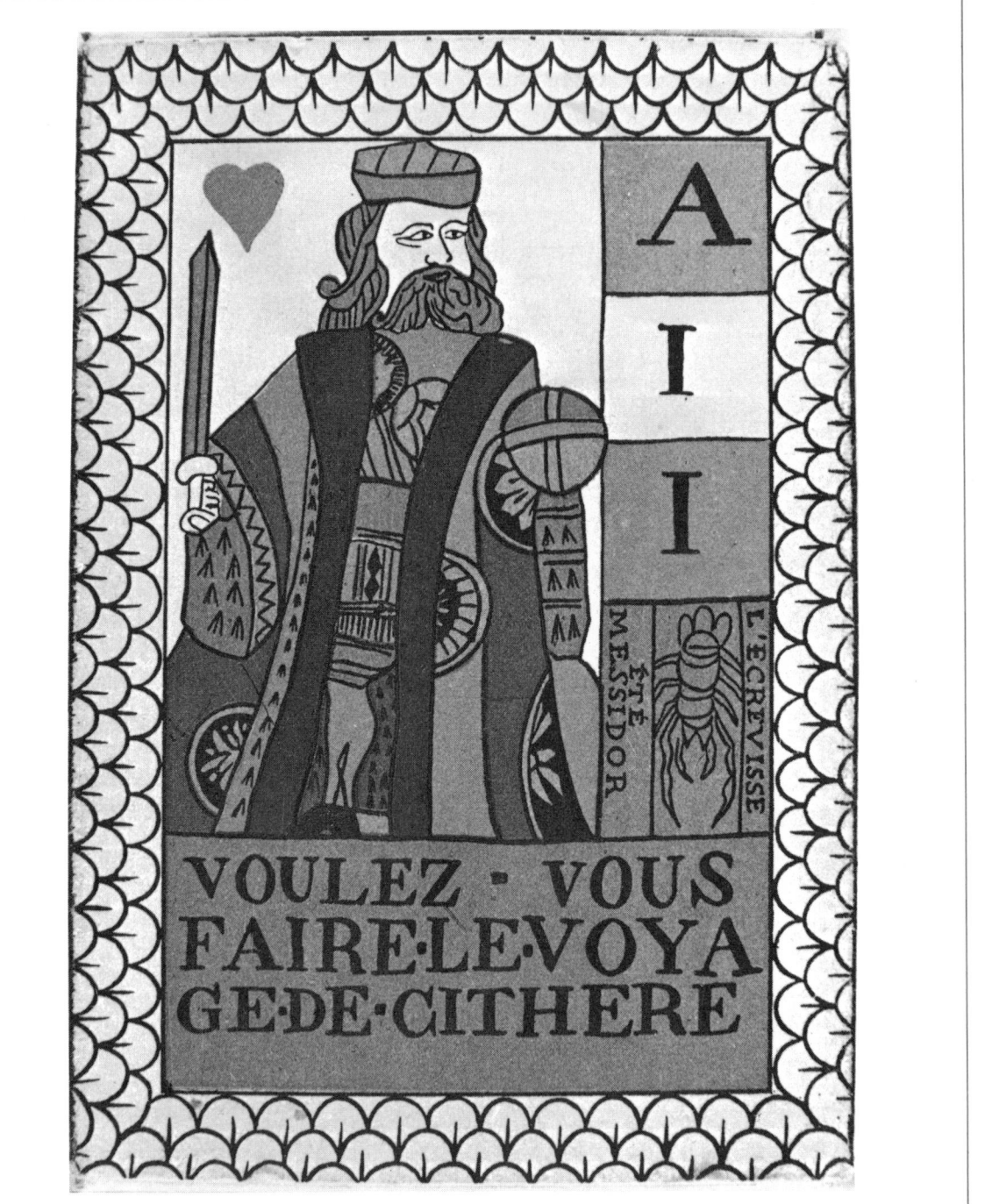

52

52. Matches. 2 $^{7}/_{8}$ × 4 $^{1}/_{8}$ in. Litho, 4 colours. France, 20th century.

52. Allumettes. 7,3 × 10,5 cm. Litho quatre coul. France, XXe siècle.

52. Streichhölzer. 7,3 × 10,5 cm. Lithographie, vier Farben. Frankreich, XX. Jahrhundert.

53

ORANGE

RAISIN.

54

Weisswein

55

53. Malaga wine. $3\,^{15}/_{16} \times 1\,^{3}/_{16}$ in. Litho, gold, on black paper. France, 19th century.
54. Syrups. $2\,^{1}/_{16} \times {}^{9}/_{16}$ in. Litho, monochrome. England 19th century.
55. Wine. $4\,^{1}/_{4} \times 1\,^{5}/_{8}$ in. Litho, monochrome. Germany, 19th century.
56. Cosmetic. $3\,^{1}/_{4} \times 2\,^{3}/_{8}$ in. Offset, monochrome. France, 1970.
57. Drugs. $1\,^{7}/_{8} \times {}^{1}/_{2}$ in. Litho, monochrome. England, 19th century.

53. Vin de Malaga. 10 × 3 cm. Litho or, papier noir. France, XIXᵉ siècle.
54. Sirop. 5,2 × 1,4 cm. Litho une coul. Angleterre, XIXᵉ siècle.
55. Vin. 10,7 × 4,1 cm. Litho une coul. Allemagne, XIXᵉ siècle.
56. Cosmétique. 8,3 × 6 cm. Offset une coul. France, 1970.
57. Droguerie. 4,8 × 1,2 cm. Litho une coul. Angleterre, XIXᵉ siècle.

53. Malaga-Wein. 10 × 3 cm. Lithographie, Gold, schwarzes Papier. Frankreich, XIX. Jahrhundert.
54. Sirup. 5,2 × 1,4 cm. Lithographie, eine Farbe. England, XIX. Jahrhundert.
55. Wein. 10,7 × 4,1 cm. Lithographie, eine Farbe. Deutschland, XIX. Jahrhundert.
56. Kosmetik. 8,3 × 6 cm. Offset, eine Farbe. Frankreich, 1970.
57. Drogerie. 4,8 × 1,2 cm. Lithographie, eine Farbe. England, XIX. Jahrhundert.

12 flacons

STRUCTURANT
PROFOND

Ineral

STRUKTURERNEUERNDE
LÖSUNG

L'ORÉAL

56

VOLATILE SALTS

SP.of MINDERERUS

57

SUPERIOR BLACK INK.

58

F.S.CLEAVER, MAKER, LONDON.

59

Rebhofweg 24
9500 Wil
Telefon 073 22 52 28

60

COGNAC VIEUX

61

FRERÈS DEMME

GENIÈVRE

THALMAZI-BERNE

62

58. Ink. 3 $^{1}/_{8}$ × 1 $^{1}/_{16}$ in. Letterpress, monochrome. England, 19th century.
59. Textile. 7 $^{1}/_{2}$ × 3 $^{15}/_{16}$ in. Litho, monochrome. England, 19th century.
60. Carpet. 3 $^{3}/_{16}$ × $^{15}/_{16}$ in. Offset, 2 colours. Design and printing, Bandfix AG, Zurich. Switzerland, 1971.
61. Brandy. 3 $^{3}/_{8}$ × 1 $^{7}/_{16}$ in. Litho, monochrome. France, 19th century.
62. Spirits. 4 $^{1}/_{8}$ × 2 $^{1}/_{8}$ in. Litho, gold, on black paper. Switzerland, 19th century.

58. *Encre. 8 × 2,7 cm. Typo une coul. Angleterre, XIXe siècle.*
59. *Textile. 19 × 10 cm. Litho une coul. Angleterre, XIXe siècle.*
60. *Tapis. 8,1 × 2,4 cm. Offset deux coul. Créat. imp. Bandfix A.G., Zurich. Suisse, 1971.*
61. *Cognac. 8,5 × 3,6 cm. Litho une coul. France, XIXe siècle.*
62. *Eau-de-vie. 10,5 × 5,4 cm. Litho or, papier noir. Suisse, XIXe siècle.*

58. Tinte. 8 × 2,7 cm. Buchdruck, eine Farbe. England, XIX. Jahrhundert.
59. Textilware. 19 × 10 cm. Lithographie, eine Farbe. England, XIX. Jahrhundert.
60. Teppich. 8,1 × 2,4 cm. Offset, zwei Farben. Urheber: Druckerei Bandfix A.G., Zürich. Schweiz, 1971.
61. Kognak. 8,5 × 3,6 cm. Lithographie, eine Farbe. Frankreich, XIX. Jahrhundert.
62. Branntwein. 10,5 × 5,4 cm. Lithographie, Gold, schwarzes Papier. Schweiz, XIX. Jahrhundert.

63

64

65

63. Sparkling wine. 3 $^3/_4$ × 1 $^7/_8$ in. Litho, gold. France, 1861.
64. Wine. 4 $^1/_2$ × 1 $^5/_8$ in. Litho, monochrome, on gold paper. France, 19th century.
65. Spirits. 4 $^7/_8$ × 2 $^{13}/_{16}$ in. Litho, gold. France, 19th century.
66. Luggage label. 4 $^{13}/_{16}$ × 2 $^3/_8$ in. Letterpress, monochrome. Pakistan, 20th century.
67. Cosmetic. 2$^3/_4$ 1$^{15}/_{16}$ in. Offset, 3 colours. France, 1970.

63. Vin mousseux. 9,6 × 4,8 cm. Litho or. France, 1861.
64. Vin. 11,3 × 4,2 cm. Litho une coul., papier or. France, XIXe siècle.
65. Eau-de-vie. 12,3 × 7,2 cm. Litho or. France, XIXe siècle.
66. Etiquette de bagage. 12,2 × 6 cm. Typo une coul. Pakistan, XXe siècle.
67. Cosmétique. 6,9 × 3,3 cm. Offset trois coul. France, 1970.

63. Schaumwein. 9,6 × 4,8 cm. Lithographie, Gold. Frankreich, 1861.
64. Wein. 11,3 × 4,2 cm. Lithographie, eine Farbe, Goldpapier. Frankreich, XIX. Jahrhundert.
65. Branntwein. 12,3 × 7,2 cm. Lithographie, Gold. Frankreich, XIX. Jahrhundert.
66. Gepäckschild. 12,2 × 6 cm. Buchdruck, eine Farbe, Pakistan, XX. Jahrhundert.
67. Kosmetik. 6,9 × 3,3 cm. Offset, drei Farben. Frankreich, 1970.

66

67

68

69

MUSCAT FRONTIGNAN

Charles Aubry.

70

71

28·92·40
Montreal

EASTERN

72

68. Paper. 6 $^{11}/_{16}$ × 5 $^{3}/_{4}$ in. Letterpress, monochrome, on grey paper. England, 1865.
69. Wine. 4 $^{15}/_{16}$ × 3 $^{5}/_{8}$ in. Offset, 4 colours and gold. Design and printing, Roth & Sauter SA, Lausanne/E. Bosshart. Switzerland, 20th century.
70. Wine. 2 $^{9}/_{16}$ × 1 $^{7}/_{8}$ in. Litho, gold. France, 19th century.
71. Children's game. 4 $^{3}/_{4}$ × 2 $^{3}/_{4}$ in. Silkscreen, 5 colours. Printing, P. Terbois, Geneva. Europe, 1969.
72. Airline. 1 $^{3}/_{4}$ × 2 $^{3}/_{8}$ in. Offset, monochrome. USA, 1969.

68. Papier. 17 × 14,5 cm. Typo une coul., papier gris. Angleterre, 1865.
69. Vin. 12,5 × 9,2 cm. Offset quatre coul. et or. Créat. imp. Roth & Sauter S.A., Lausanne/E. Bosshart. Suisse, XXᵉ siècle.
70. Vin. 6,5 × 4,8 cm. Litho or. France, XIXᵉ siècle.
71. Jeu pour enfants. 12 × 7 cm. Sérigraphie cinq coul. Imp. P. Terbois, Genève. Europe, 1969.
72. Compagnie aérienne. 4,4 × 6 cm. Offset une coul. U.S.A., 1969.

68. Papier. 17 × 14,5 cm. Buchdruck, eine Farbe, graues Papier. England, 1865.
69. Wein. 12,5 × 9,2 cm. Offset, vier Farben und Gold. Urheber: Druckerei Roth & Sauter S.A., Lausanne/E. Bosshart. Schweiz, XX. Jahrhundert.
70. Wein. 6,5 × 4,8 cm. Lithographie, Gold. Frankreich, XIX. Jahrhundert.
71. Kinderspiel. 12 × 7 cm. Siebdruck, fünf Farben. Druckerei P. Terbois, Genf. Europa, 1969.
72. Fluggesellschaft. 4,4 × 6 cm. Offset, eine Farbe. U.S.A., 1969.

73

74

75

73. Laxative. 1 13/16 × 1 3/8 in. Litho, monochrome. England, 19th century.
74. Address label. 6 1/16 × 3 1/2 in. Offset, 2 colours. Design, Lubain, Burns and Co. Inc., New York, USA, 1971.
75. Wine. 4 1/4 × 2 11/16 in. Litho, monochrome. France, 19th century.
76. Soap. 3 3/8 × 2 7/8 in. Litho, monochrome France, 19th century.
77. Pharmacist.   2 7/8 × 1 5/8 in.   Copper plate engraving, monochrome. England 18th century.

73. *Laxatif. 4,6 × 3,5 cm. Litho une coul. Angleterre, XIXe siècle.*
74. *Etiquette adresse. 15,4 × 8,8 cm. Offset deux coul. Créat. Lubalin, Burns & Co. Inc., New York. U.S.A., 1971.*
75. *Vin. 10,8 × 6,8 cm. Litho une coul. France, XIXe siècle.*
76. *Savon. 8,5 × 7,2 cm. Lithographie une coul. France XIXe siècle.*
77. *Pharmacie. 7,2 × 4,1 cm. Gravure sur cuivre une coul. Angleterre, XVIIIe siècle.*

73. Abführmittel. 4,6 × 3,5 cm. Lithographie, eine Farbe. England, XIX. Jahrhundert.
74. Adressenetikett. 15,4 × 8,8 cm. Offset, zwei Farben. Urheber: Lubalin, Burns & Co. Inc., New York. U.S.A., 1971.
75. Wein. 10,8 × 6,8 cm. Lithographie, eine Farbe. Frankreich, XIX. Jahrhundert.
76. Seife. 8,5 × 7,2 cm. Lithographie, eine Farbe. Frankreich, XIX. Jahrhundert.
77. Apotheke. 7,2 × 4,1 cm. Kupferstich, eine Farbe. England, XVIII. Jahrhundert.

76

77

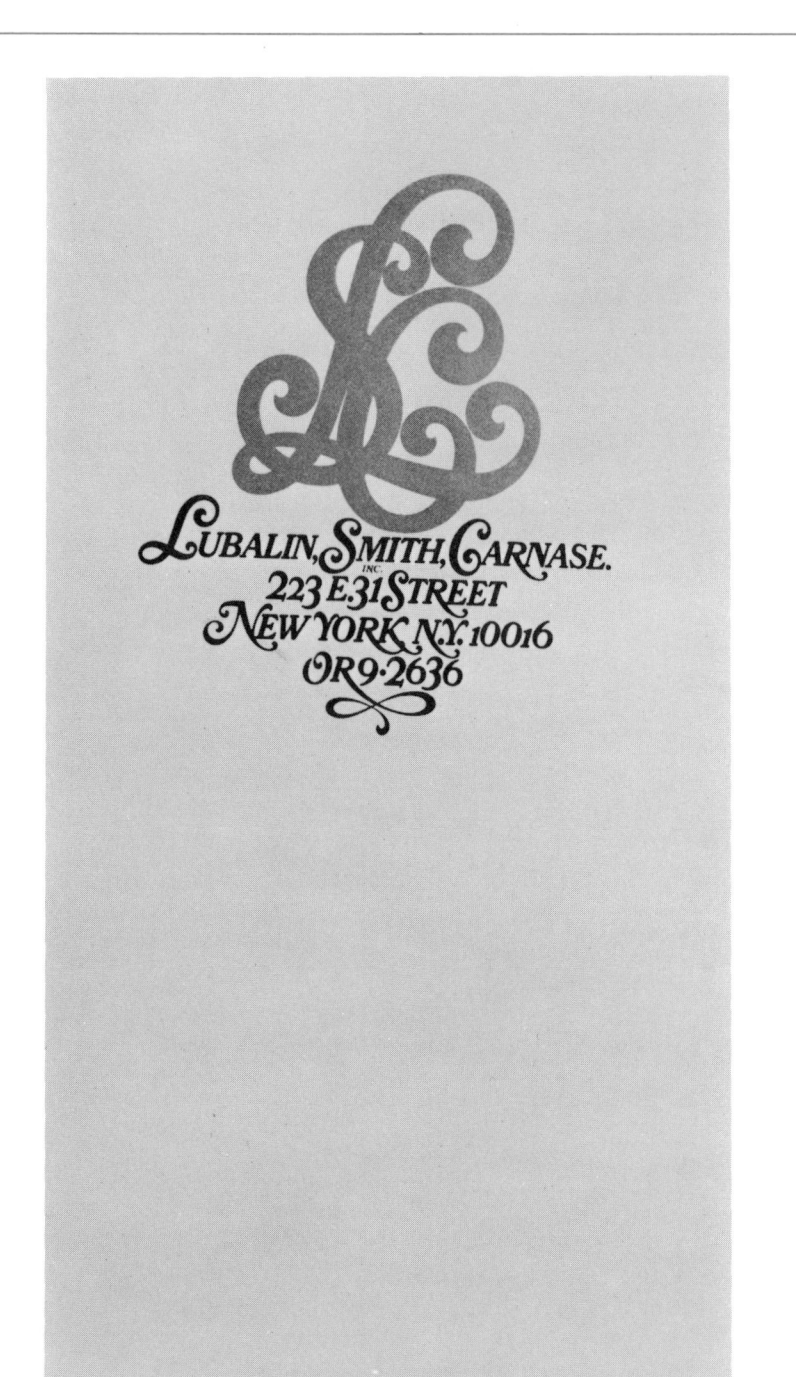

78. Address label. 3 $^5/_{16}$ × 6 $^1/_{16}$ in. Offset, 2 colours. Design, Lubalin, Smith, Carnase Inc., New York, USA, 1971.

78. Etiquette adresse. 8,3 × 15,4 cm. Offset deux coul. Créat. Lubalin, Smith, Carnase. Inc., New York. U.S.A., 1971.

78. Adressenetikett. 8,3 × 15,4 cm. Offset, zwei Farben. Urheber: Lubalin, Smith, Carnase. Inc., New York. U.S.A., 1971.

79

80

81

79. Pharmacist. 2 ¹/₄ × 1 ³/₁₆ in. Copper plate engraving, monochrome. England, 18th century.
80. Map. 3 ¹/₂ × 2 ³/₈ in. Litho, monochrome and gold. USA, 1912.
81. Wine. 4 ³/₁₆ × 2 ⁷/₁₆ in. Litho, monochrome. France, 19th century.
82. Wine. 4 ³/₄ × 3 ¹/₈ in. Offset, monochrome and embossed gold. Design and printing, Roth & Sauter SA, Lausanne/ E. Witzig. Switzerland, 1971.
83. Wine. 4 ⁵/₁₆ × 2 ⁹/₁₆ in. Litho, 2 colours. France, 19th century.

79. *Pharmacie. 5,7 × 3 cm. Gravure sur cuivre une coul. Angleterre, XVIIIᵉ siècle.*
80. *Carte géographique. 8,9 × 6 cm. Litho une coul. et or. U.S.A., 1912.*
81. *Vin. 10,6 × 6,2 cm. Litho une coul. France, XIXᵉ siècle.*
82. *Vin. 12 × 8 cm. Offset une coul. et or gaufré. Créat. imp. Roth & Sauter S.A., Lausanne/E. Witzig. Suisse, 1971.*
83. *Vin. 10,9 × 6,5 cm. Litho deux coul. France, XIXᵉ siècle.*

79. Apotheke. 5,7 × 3 cm. Kupferstich, eine Farbe. England, XVIII. Jahrhundert.
80. Landkarte. 8,9 × 6 cm. Lithographie, eine Farbe und Gold. U.S.A., 1912.
81. Wein. 10,6 × 6,2 cm. Lithographie, eine Farbe. Frankreich, XIX. Jahrhundert.
82. Wein. 12 × 8 cm. Offset, eine Farbe und Prägung in Gold. Urheber: Druckerei Roth & Sauter S.A., Lausanne/E. Witzig. Schweiz, 1971.
83. Wein. 10,9 × 6,5 cm. Lithographie, zwei Farben. Frankreich, XIX. Jahrhundert.

82

83

84

85

86

87

88

84. Wine. 4 $^1/_8$ × 2 $^7/_{16}$ in. Litho, monochrome, on blue paper. Printing, E. Bruaux, Epernay. France, 19th century.
85. Wine. 2 $^3/_4$ × $^7/_8$ in. Litho, monochrome, on silver paper. France, 19th century.
86. Teachers' convention. 1 $^{15}/_{16}$ × 1 in. Letterpress, monochrome. USA, 1941.
87. Cake. 9 $^7/_8$ × 2 $^3/_4$ in. Litho, monochrome and gold. England, 1890–1894.
88. Cosmetic. 2 $^9/_{16}$ × 1 in. Offset, 2 colours. France, 1971.

84. Vin. 10,4 × 6,2 cm. Litho une coul. papier bleu. Imp. E. Bruaux, Epernay. France, XIXe siècle.
85. Vin. 7 × 2,3 cm. Litho une coul. papier argent. France, XIXe siècle.
86. Forum d'enseignants. 5 × 2,5 cm. Typo une coul. U.S.A., 1941.
87. Cake. 25 × 7 cm. Litho une coul. et or. Angleterre, 1890-1894.
88. Cosmétique. 6,5 × 2,5 cm. Offset deux coul. France, 1971.

84. Wein. 10,4 × 6,2 cm. Lithographie, eine Farbe, blaues Papier. Druckerei E. Bruaux, Epernay. Frankreich, XIX. Jahrhundert.
85. Wein. 7 × 2,3 cm. Lithographie, eine Farbe, Silberpapier. Frankreich, XIX. Jahrhundert.
86. Dozentenforum. 5 × 2,5 cm. Buchdruck, eine Farbe. U.S.A., 1941.
87. Kuchen. 25 × 7 cm. Lithographie, eine Farbe und Gold. England, 1890–1894.
88. Kosmetik. 6,5 × 2,5 cm. Offset, zwei Farben. Frankreich, 1971.

89

91

89. Confectionery. 3 ¹/₈ × 1 ⁷/₈ in. Offset, monochrome. Greece, 1971.
90. Wine. 3 ¹/₂ × 5 ¹⁵/₁₆ in. Litho, 3 colours. Design, Laurent Marquart. Switzerland, 1964.
91. Library. 3 ¹/₈ × 2 ³/₄ in. Offset, monochrome. England, 1971.
92. Paint. 3 ⁷/₁₆ × 2 ³/₄ in. Litho and letterpress, monochrome. England, 19th century.
93. Visual communication. 2¹/₂ × 4⁷/₈ in. Letterpress, 2 colours. Design, Ecole des arts décoratifs, Geneva. Switzerland, 1970.

89. Confiserie. 8 × 4,8 cm. Offset une coul. Grèce, 1971.
90. Vin. 8,8 × 15,1 cm. Litho trois coul. Créat. Laurent Marquart. Suisse, 1964.
91. Bibliothèque. 8 × 7 cm. Offset une coul. Angleterre, 1971.
92. Peinture. 8,7 × 7 cm. Litho et typo une coul. Angleterre, XIXᵉ siècle.
93. Communication visuelle. 6,3 × 12,3 cm. Typo deux coul. Créat. Ecole des arts décoratifs, Genève. Suisse, 1970.

89. Konditorei. 8 × 4,8 cm. Offset, eine Farbe. Griechenland, 1971.
90. Wein. 8,8 × 15,1 cm. Lithographie, drei Farben. Urheber: Laurent Marquart. Schweiz, 1964.
91. Bibliothek. 8 × 7 cm. Offset, eine Farbe. England, 1971.
92. Ölfarbe. 8,7 × 7 cm. Lithographie und Buchdruck, eine Farbe. England, XIX. Jahrhundert.
93. Visuelle Kommunikation. 6,3 × 12,3 cm. Buchdruck, zwei Farben. Urheber: Ecole des arts décoratifs, Genf. Schweiz, 1970.

JONES'S
PATENT BRUNSWICK
VARNISH GREEN,
FOR
Painting Verandahs, Venetian Blinds, and all kinds of Fancy and Ornamental Garden Work, Flower Pots, &c. &c.

DIRECTIONS FOR USE.—To be used with a common Painting Brush, no preparation is required except well cleaning the articles before you paint them, if it gets too thick for use, thin it with a little Spirit of Turpentine by stirring it well with a stick.

Manufactory, ᵃᵗ Harland Court, Pimlico, London.

WHOLESALE AGENTS, JONES & EVANS, Bristol; EDWARDS, Liverpool; MANDER, WEAVER, & Co. Wolverhampton.

92

LA
COMMUNICATION
VISUELLE
EST
LE LANGAGE
DU
TEMPS
PRÉSENT

ELLE
SE MANIFESTE
PAR
L'IMAGE
SOUS TOUTES
SES
FORMES

COURS DE
COMMUNICATION
VISUELLE
ÉCOLE DES ARTS DÉCORATIFS / GENÈVE

93

94

95

96

97

98

94. Wine. 4 × 2 ⁵/₈ in. Litho, monochrome. Printing, E. Bruaux, Epernay. France, 19th century.
95. Mirrors and picture frames. 2 ³/₈ × 1 ³/₈ in. Litho, monochrome, on yellow paper. USA, 20th century.
96. Spirits. 3 ¹⁵/₁₆ × 2 ⁷/₁₆ in. Litho, 4 colours. Printing, Spengler, Lausanne. Switzerland, 20th century.
97. Matches. 2 ³/₁₆ × 1 ⁷/₁₆ in. Litho, 2 colours, on yellow paper. England, 20th century.
98. Wine. 3 ⁹/₁₆ × 1 ¹/₂ in. Litho, monochrome. Germany, 19th century.

94. Vin. 10,2 × 6,6 cm. Litho une coul. Imp. E. Bruaux, Epernay. France, XIXᵉ siècle.
95. Miroirs et encadrements. 6 × 3,5 cm. Litho une coul., papier jaune. U.S.A., XXᵉ siècle.
96. Eau-de-vie. 9,9 × 6,2 cm. Litho quatre coul. Imp. Spengler, Lausanne. Suisse, XXᵉ siècle.
97. Allumettes. 5,6 × 3,6 cm. Litho deux coul. papier jaune. Angleterre, XXᵉ siècle.
98. Vin. 9 × 3,8 cm. Litho une coul. Allemagne, XIXᵉ siècle.

94. Wein. 10,2 × 6,6 cm. Lithographie, eine Farbe. Druckerei E. Bruaux, Epernay. Frankreich, XIX. Jahrhundert.
95. Spiegel und Einrahmungen. 6 × 3,5 cm. Lithographie, eine Farbe, gelbes Papier. U.S.A., XX. Jahrhundert.
96. Branntwein. 9,9 × 6,2 cm. Lithographie, vier Farben. Druckerei Spengler, Lausanne. Schweiz, XX. Jahrhundert.
97. Streichhölzer. 5,6 × 3,6 cm. Lithographie, zwei Farben, gelbes Papier. England, XX. Jahrhundert.
98. Wein. 9 × 3,8 cm. Lithographie, eine Farbe. Deutschland, XIX. Jahrhundert.

99

100

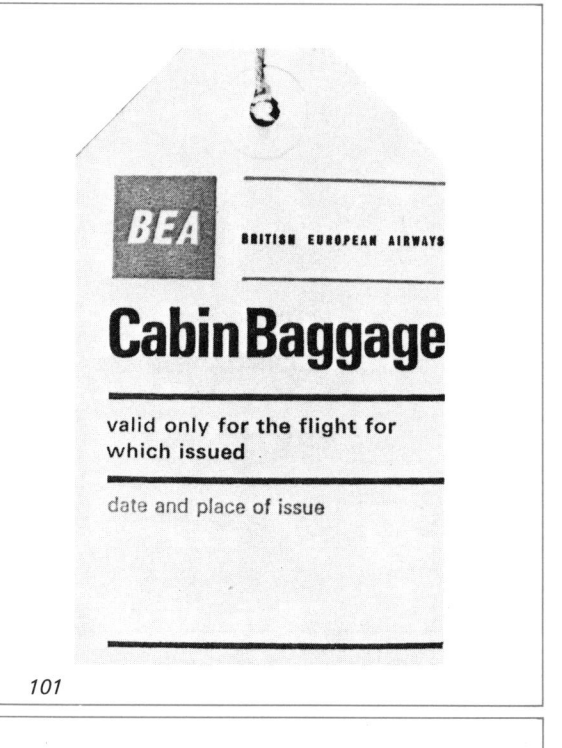

101

99. Ink and pencils. 6 $^1/_2$ × 8 $^5/_{16}$ in. Letter-press, monochrome. England, 1816.
100. Ink. 8 $^1/_2$ × 7 $^1/_4$ in. Litho, 2 colours. England, 1840–1850.
101. Airline. 2 $^1/_2$ × 4 $^1/_{16}$ in. Offset, 2 colours. England, 1969.
102. Cheese week. 2 $^1/_{16}$ × 2 $^3/_4$ in. Litho, 2 colours. USA, 20th century.
103. Textile. 2 $^1/_2$ × 4 $^1/_8$ in. Offset, monochrome and gold. USA, 1971.

99. Encre et crayons. 16,5 × 21 cm. Typo une coul. Angleterre, 1816.
100. Encre. 21,5 × 18,3 cm. Litho deux coul. Angleterre, 1840-1850.
101. Compagnie aérienne. 6,3 × 10,3 cm. Offset deux coul. Angleterre, 1969.
102. Semaine du fromage. 5,2 × 7 cm. Litho deux coul. U.S.A., XXe siècle.
103. Textile. 6,3 × 10,5 cm. Offset une coul. et or. U.S.A., 1971.

99. Tinte und Bleistifte. 16,5 × 21 cm. Buch-druck, eine Farbe. England, 1816.
100. Tinte. 21,5 × 18,3 cm. Lithographie, zwei Farben. England, 1840–1850.
101. Fluggesellschaft. 6,3 × 10,3 cm. Offset, zwei Farben. England, 1969.
102. Käsewoche. 5,2 × 7 cm. Lithographie, zwei Farben. U.S.A., XX. Jahrhundert.
103. Textilware. 6,3 × 10,5 cm. Offset, eine Farbe und Gold. U.S.A., 1971.

102

103

Clos de Chillon,

*Chillon, château-fée, vaisseau de pierre
et de rêve, forteresse de douceur,
rose d'automne contre le mur de la montagne
se devait d'avoir sa propre vigne, pour
communier vraiment avec l'esssentiel.
Levez votre verre, vignerons et amis du vin:
à la Patrie. A l'Amitié. A la durée!*

♣

104. Wine. 3 ¹/₈ × 3 ¹⁵/₁₆ in. Offset, 2 colours and gold. Design and printing, Roth & Sauter SA, Lausanne/R. Héritier. Switzerland, 1971.

104. Vin. 8 × 10 cm. Offset deux coul. et or. Créat. imp. Roth & Sauter S.A., Lausanne/ R. Héritier. Suisse, 1971.

104. Wein. 8 × 10 cm. Offset, zwei Farben und Gold. Urheber: Druckerei Roth & Sauter S.A., Lausanne/R. Héritier. Schweiz, 1971.

105

106

107

105. Wine. 3 ³/₁₆ × 3 ⁵/₈ in. Litho, monochrome and gold, on green paper. Switzerland, 19th century.
106. Liqueur. 3 ⁵/₈ × 2 ¹¹/₁₆ in. Litho, 2 colours. Switzerland, 19th century.
107. Biscuits. 7 ⁷/₁₆ × 5 ¹/₁₆ in. Litho, 3 colours and gold, on green paper. England,
19th century.
108. Liqueur. 4 ¹/₄ × 4 ¹/₄ in. Litho, monochrome. Switzerland, 19th century.
109. Liqueur. 3 ³/₄ × 2 in. Litho, 3 colours.
Switzerland, 19th century.

105. Vin. 8 × 9,1 cm. Litho une coul. et or,
papier vert. Suisse, XIXᵉ siècle.
106. Liqueur. 9,2 × 6,8 cm. Litho deux coul.
Suisse, XIXᵉ siècle.
107. Biscuits. 18,8 × 12,8 cm. Litho trois coul.
et or, papier vert. Angleterre, XIXᵉ siècle.
108. Liqueur. 10,8 × 10,7 cm. Litho une coul.
Suisse, XIXᵉ siècle.
109. Liqueur. 9,5 × 5 cm. Litho trois coul. Suisse,
XIXᵉ siècle.

105. Wein. 8 × 9,1 cm. Lithographie, eine Farbe
und Gold, grünes Papier. Schweiz, XIX.
Jahrhundert.
106. Likör. 9,2 × 6,8 cm. Lithographie, zwei
Farben. Schweiz, XIX. Jahrhundert.
107. Kekse. 18,8 × 12,8 cm. Lithographie, drei
Farben und Gold, grünes Papier. England,
XIX. Jahrhundert.
108. Likör. 10,8 × 10,7 cm. Lithographie, eine
Farbe. Schweiz, XIX. Jahrhundert.
109. Likör. 9,5 × 5 cm. Lithographie, drei Farben.
Schweiz, XIX. Jahrhundert.

108

109

110

111

112

113

114

110. Rice starch. $3\ ^{3}/_{16} \times 4\ ^{9}/_{16}$ in. Litho, monochrome. England, 19th century.
111. Absinthe. $3\ ^{3}/_{16} \times 3\ ^{15}/_{16}$ in. Litho, 4 colours. Design and printing, A. Gérin, Dijon. France, 19th century.
112. Cocoa essence. $7\ ^{5}/_{16} \times 3\ ^{5}/_{8}$ in. Litho, 7 colours. England, 1900.
113. Vermouth. $4\ ^{1}/_{8} \times 4\ ^{15}/_{16}$ in. Litho, 4 colours. Italy, 19th century.
114. Paper. $6\ ^{7}/_{16} \times 7\ ^{7}/_{8}$ in. Litho and letterpress, monochrome, on pink paper. England, 19th century.

110. Amidon de riz. 8 × 11,5 cm. Litho une coul. Angleterre, XIXᵉ siècle.
111. Absinthe. 8,1 × 10 cm. Litho quatre coul. Créat. imp. A. Gérin, Dijon. France, XIXᵉ siècle.
112. Essence de cacao. 18,5 × 9,2 cm. Litho sept coul. Angleterre, 1900.
113. Vermouth. 10,5 × 12,5 cm. Litho quatre coul. Italie, XIXᵉ siècle.
114. Papier. 16,3 × 20 cm. Litho et typo une coul., papier rose. Angleterre XIXᵉ siècle.

110. Reisstärke. 8 × 11,5 cm. Lithographie, eine Farbe. England, XIX. Jahrhundert.
111. Absinth. 8,1 × 10 cm. Lithographie, vier Farben. Urheber: Druckerei A. Gérin, Dijon. Frankreich, XIX. Jahrhundert.
112. Kakaoessenz. 18, 5 × 9,2 cm. Lithographie, sieben Farben. England, 1900.
113. Wermut. 10,5 × 12,5 cm. Lithographie, vier Farben. Italien, XIX. Jahrhundert.
114. Papier. 16,3 × 20 cm. Lithographie und Buchdruck, eine Farbe, rosa Papier. England, XIX. Jahrhundert.

115

116

117

118

119

115. Wine. 4 ³/₈ × 2 ⁹/₁₆ in. Litho, monochrome and silver. Printing, Chassetière, Marseilles. France, 19th century.
116. Wine. 4 ¹/₂ × 2 ⁵/₈ in. Litho, monochrome and gold. France, 19th century.
117. Wine. 4 ⁷/₈ × 2 ¹⁵/₁₆ in. Litho, monochrome. France, 19th century.
118. Wine. 4 ¹/₈ × 2 ³/₄ in. Litho, monochrome and gold. Printing, L. Landa, Chalon-sur-Saône. France, 19th century.
119. Tobacco. 5 ⁷/₁₆ × 3 in. Litho, 5 colours and gold. USA, 19th century.

115. Vin. 11 × 6,5 cm. Litho une coul. et argent. Imp. Chassetière, Marseille. France, XIXᵉ siècle.
116. Vin. 11,3 × 6,7 cm. Litho une coul. et or. France, XIXᵉ siècle.
117. Vin. 12,3 × 7,5 cm. Litho une coul. France, XIXᵉ siècle.
118. Vin. 10,5 × 7 cm. Litho une coul. et or. Imp. L. Landa, Chalon-sur-Saône. France, XIXᵉ siècle.
119. Tabac. 13,7 × 7,6 cm. Litho cinq coul. et or. U.S.A., XIXᵉ siècle.

115. Wein. 11 × 6,5 cm. Lithographie, eine Farbe und Silber. Druckerei Chassetière, Marseille. Frankreich, XIX. Jahrhundert.
116. Wein. 11,3 × 6,7 cm. Lithographie, eine Farbe und Gold. Frankreich, XIX. Jahrhundert.
117. Wein. 12,3 × 7,5 cm. Lithographie, eine Farbe. Frankreich, XIX. Jahrhundert.
118. Wein. 10,5 × 7 cm. Lithographie, eine Farbe und Gold. Druckerei L. Landa, Chalon-sur-Saône. Frankreich, XIX. Jahrhundert.
119. Tabak. 13,7 × 7,6 cm. Lithographie, fünf Farben und Gold. U.S.A., XIX. Jahrhundert.

120

122

123

124

120. Mustard. 6 5/16 × 5 11/16 in. Litho, 5 colours. England, 19th century.
121. Sewing machine. 2 11/16 × 4 7/16 in. Litho, 4 colours. USA, 19th century.
122. Soup. 12 3/8 × 4 3/8 in. Litho, 4 colours and gold. USA, 1936.
123. Spirits. 5 1/8 × 3 5/8 in. Litho, 4 colours. Switzerland, 1900.
124. Bank. 3 1/8 × 3 9/16 in. Offset, monochrome. Egypt, 1969.

120. Moutarde. 16 × 14,4 cm. Litho cinq coul. Angleterre, XIXe siècle.
121. Machine à coudre. 6,8 × 11,2 cm. Litho quatre coul. U.S.A., XIXe siècle.
122. Soupe. 31,3 × 11 cm. Litho quatre coul. et or. U.S.A., 1936.
123. Eau-de-vie. 13 × 9,2 cm. Litho quatre coul. Suisse, 1900.
124. Banque. 8 × 9 cm. Offset une coul. Egypte, 1969.

120. Senf. 16 × 14,4 cm. Lithographie, fünf Farben. England, XIX. Jahrhundert.
121. Nähmaschine. 6,8 × 11,2 cm. Lithographie, vier Farben. U.S.A., XIX. Jahrhundert.
122. Suppe. 31,3 × 11 cm. Lithographie, vier Farben und Gold. U.S.A., 1936.
123. Branntwein. 13 × 9,2 cm. Lithographie, vier Farben. Schweiz, 1900.
124. Bank. 8 × 9 cm. Offset, eine Farbe. Ägypten, 1969.

125

126

127

125. Pens. 4 $^9/_{16}$ × 2 $^9/_{16}$ in. Monochrome litho and embossing. England, 19th century.
126. Absinthe extract. 3 $^{15}/_{16}$ × 4 $^1/_2$ in. Litho, 4 colours. Design and printing, Romain & Parliart, Paris. France, 19th century.
127. Textile. 1 $^1/_2$ × 2 $^{15}/_{16}$ in. Litho, monochrome. USA, 19th century.
128. Wine. 4 $^3/_4$ × 3 $^{15}/_{16}$ in. Litho, monochrome and gold. Design, Gerstung. Germany, 1937.
129. Liqueur. 4 $^1/_{16}$ × 3 $^1/_4$ in. Litho, 4 colours. Design and printing, Lalande. France, 19th century.

125. Plumes à écrire. 11,5 × 6,5 cm. Litho une coul. avec gaufrage. Angleterre, XIXe siècle.
126. Extrait d'absinthe. 10 × 11,4 cm. Litho quatre coul. Créat. imp. Romain & Parliart, Paris. France, XIXe siècle.
127. Textile. 3,8 × 7,4 cm. Litho une coul. U.S.A., XIXe siècle.
128. Vin. 12 × 8,4 cm. Litho une coul. et or. Créat. Gerstung. Allemagne, 1937.
129. Liqueur. 10,3 × 8,2 cm. Litho quatre coul. Créat. imp. Lalande. France XIXe siècle.

125. Schreibfedern. 11,5 × 6,5 cm. Lithographie, eine Farbe, mit Blinddruck. England, XIX. Jahrhundert.
126. Absinthextrakt. 10 × 11,4 cm. Lithographie, vier Farben. Urheber: Druckerei Romain & Parliart, Paris. Frankreich, XIX. Jahrhundert.
127. Textilware. 3,8 × 7,4 cm. Lithographie, eine Farbe. U.S.A., XIX. Jahrhundert.
128. Wein. 12 × 8,4 cm. Lithographie, eine Farbe und Gold. Urheber: Gerstung. Deutschland, 1937.
129. Likör. 10,3 × 8,2 cm. Lithographie, vier Farben. Urheber: Druckerei Lalande. Frankreich, XIX. Jahrhundert.

128

129

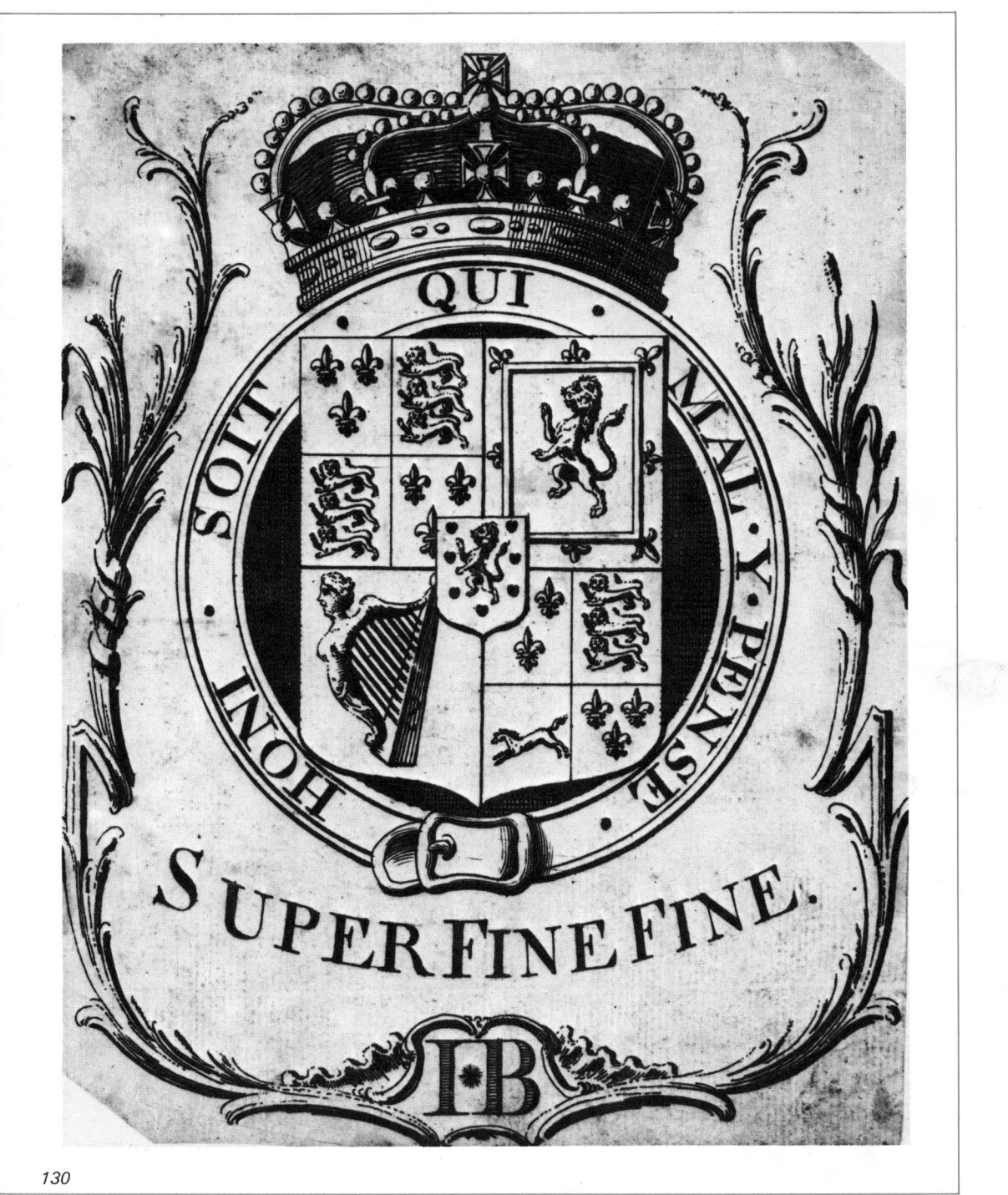

130. Paper.   4 $^{15}/_{16}$ × 6 $^1/_8$ in.   Copper plate engraving, monochrome.   England, 18th century.

130. Papier. 12,5 × 15,5 cm. Gravure sur cuivre une coul. Angleterre, XVIIIe siècle.

130. Papier. 12,5 × 15,5 cm. Kupferstich, eine Farbe. England, XVIII. Jahrhundert.

131

132

133

134

135

131. Vermouth.   4 $^1/_2$ × 2 $^{15}/_{16}$ in.   Litho, 4 colours. Italy, 19th century.
132. Wine.   3 $^1/_{16}$ × 5 $^3/_{16}$ in.   Letterpress, 4 colours. England, mid-20th century.
133. Matches. 2 $^3/_{16}$ × 1 $^7/_{16}$ in. Litho, 2 colours. Japan, 19th century.
134. Wine.   5 $^5/_{16}$ × 3 $^3/_4$ in. Offset, 3 colours and gold. Design and printing, Roth & Sauter SA, Lausanne/E. Bosshart. Greece, 1969.
135. Soap. 6 $^{11}/_{16}$ × 3 $^7/_{16}$ in. Litho, 2 colours and gold. France, 1900.

131. *Vermouth. 11,4 × 7,5 cm. Litho quatre coul. Italie, XIXe siècle.*
132. *Vin. 7,7 × 13 cm. Typo quatre coul. Angleterre, milieu du XXe siècle.*
133. *Allumettes. 5,5 × 3,6 cm. Litho deux coul. Japon, XIXe siècle.*
134. *Vin. 13,5 × 9,5 cm. Offset trois coul. et or. Créat. imp. Roth & Sauter S.A., Lausanne/ E. Bosshart. Grèce, 1969.*
135. *Savon. 17 × 8,7 cm. Litho deux coul. et or. France, 1900.*

131. Wermut. 11,4 × 7,5 cm. Lithographie, vier Farben. Italien, XIX. Jahrhundert.
132. Wein. 7,7 × 13 cm. Buchdruck, vier Farben. England, Mitte des XX. Jahrhunderts.
133. Streichhölzer. 5,5 × 3,6 cm. Lithographie, zwei Farben. Japan, XIX. Jahrhundert.
134. Wein. 13,5 × 9,5 cm. Offset, drei Farben und Gold. Urheber: Roth & Sauter S.A., Lausanne/E. Bosshart. Griechenland, 1969.
135. Seife. 17 × 8,7 cm. Lithographie, zwei Farben und Gold. Frankreich, 1900.

136

137

138

139

140

136. Airline. 2 5/8 × 3 3/8 in. Offset, 2 colours. USA, 1971.
137. Textile. 4 7/8 × 5 3/4. Litho, gold, on black paper. India, 20th century.
138. Wine. 3 9/16 × 4 3/4 in. Offset, 3 colours. Design and printing, Roth & Sauter SA, Lausanne/Gilioli. Switzerland, 1971.
139. Wine. 3 9/16 × 4 3/4 in. Offset, 3 colours and embossed gold. Design and printing, Roth & Sauter SA, Lausanne/R. Héritier. Switzerland, 1971.
140. Wine. 4 3/8 × 3 9/16 in. Offset, 2 colours and gold. Design and printing, Roth & Sauter SA, Lausanne/E. Witzig. Switzerland, 1971.

136. Compagnie aérienne. 6,6 × 8,5 cm. Offset deux coul. U.S.A., 1971.
137. Textile. 12,4 × 14,5 cm. Litho or, papier noir. Inde, XXe siècle.
138. Vin. 9 × 12 cm. Offset trois coul. Créat. imp. Roth & Sauter S.A., Lausanne/ Gilioli. Suisse, 1971.
139. Vin. 9 × 12 cm. Offset trois coul. et or gaufré. Créat. imp. Roth & Sauter S.A., Lausanne/R. Héritier. Suisse, 1971.
140. Vin. 11 × 9 cm. Offset deux coul. et or. Créat. imp. Roth et Sauter S.A., Lausanne/ E. Witzig. Suisse, 1971.

136. Fluggesellschaft. 6,6 × 8,5 cm. Offset, zwei Farben. U.S.A., 1971.
137. Textilware. 12,4 × 14,5 cm. Lithographie, Gold, schwarzes Papier. Indien, XX. Jahrhundert.
138. Wein. 9 × 12 cm. Offset, drei Farben. Urheber: Druckerei Roth & Sauter S.A., Lausanne/Gilioli. Schweiz, 1971.
139. Wein. 9 × 12 cm. Offset, drei Farben und Prägung in Gold. Urheber: Druckerei Roth & Sauter S.A., Lausanne/R. Héritier. Schweiz, 1971.

140. Wein. 11 × 9 cm. Offset, zwei Farben und Gold. Urheber: Druckerei Roth und Sauter S.A., Lausanne/E. Witzig. Schweiz, 1971.

141. Wine. 4 $^3/_8$ × 4 $^3/_4$ in. Offset, 3 colours and gold. Greece, 1969.
142. Clothing. 5 $^1/_2$ × 3 $^3/_8$ in. Litho, 5 colours and gold. USA, 1876.
143. Club. 5 $^1/_8$ × 3 $^3/_{16}$ in. Silk-screen, 3 colours. International, 20th century.
144. Matches. 2 $^3/_{16}$ × 1 $^7/_{16}$ in. Litho, 2 colours. Japan, 19th century.
145a) Advertising agency. 4 $^3/_{16}$ × 1 $^3/_8$ in. Offset, 3 colours. Design, C. Julien. Switzerland, 1961.
145b) Toilet paper. 9 $^1/_{16}$ × 11 $^9/_{16}$ in. Litho, monochrome, on yellow paper. England, 1900.

141. Vin. 11 × 12 cm. Offset trois coul. et or. Grèce, 1969.
142. Vêtements. 14 × 8,5 cm. Litho cinq coul. et or. U.S.A., 1876.
143. Club. 13 × 15,7 cm. Sérigraphie trois coul. International, XXᵉ siècle.
144. Allumettes. 5,5 × 3,6 cm. Litho deux coul. Japon, XIXᵉ siècle.
145a) Agence de publicité. 12,2 × 3,5 cm. Offset trois coul. Créat. C. Julien. Suisse, 1961.
145b) Papier hygiénique. 23 × 29,4 cm. Litho une coul. papier jaune. Angleterre, 1900.

141. Wein. 11 × 12 cm. Offset, drei Farben und Gold. Griechenland, 1969.
142. Kleider. 14 × 8,5 cm. Lithographie, fünf Farben und Gold. U.S.A., 1876.
143. Klub. 13 × 15,7 cm. Siebdruck, drei Farben. International, XX. Jahrhundert.
144. Streichhölzer. 5,5 × 3,6 cm. Lithographie, zwei Farben. Japan, XIX. Jahrhundert.
145a) Werbeagentur. 12,2 × 3,5 cm. Offset, drei Farben. Urheber: C. Julien. Schweiz, 1961.
145b) Toilettenpapier. 23 × 29,4 cm. Lithographie, eine Farbe, gelbes Papier. England, 1900.

141

142

143

144

145a

145b

146

147

148

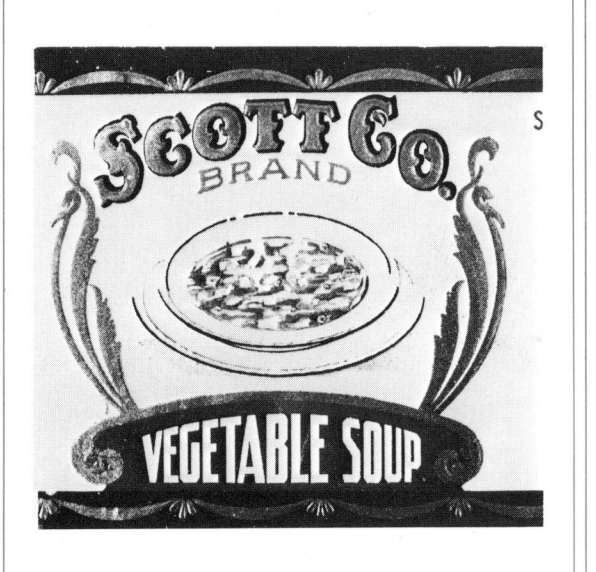

149

150

146. Committee of vigilance. 3 $1/4$ × 3 $1/4$ in. Wood engraving and letterpress, monochrome. USA, 19th century.
147. Food. 3 $15/16$ × 3 $15/16$ in. Litho, 5 colours. England, 19th century.
148. Soap. 3 $3/4$ × 3 $3/4$ in. Litho, monochrome. France, 19th century.
149. Soup. 12 $3/8$ × 4 $3/8$ in. Litho, 4 colours and gold. USA, 1936.
150. Scales. 3 $1/8$ × 5 $1/2$ in. Wood engraving and letterpress, monochrome. USA, 19th century.

146. Comité de vigilance. 8,2 × 8,2 cm. Gravure sur bois et typo une coul. U.S.A., XIXe siècle.
147. Alimentation. 10 × 10 cm. Litho cinq coul. Angleterre, XIXe siècle.
148. Savon. 9,5 × 9,5 cm. Litho une coul. France, XIXe siècle.
149. Soupe. 31,3 × 11 cm. Litho quatre coul. et or. U.S.A., 1936.
150. Balances. 8 × 13,9 cm. Gravure sur bois et typo une coul. U.S.A., XIXe siècle.

146. Wachdienst. 8,2 × 8,2 cm. Holzschnitt und Buchdruck, eine Farbe. U.S.A., XIX. Jahrhundert.
147. Lebensmittel. 10 × 10 cm. Lithographie, fünf Farben. England, XIX. Jahrhundert.
148. Seife. 9,5 × 9,5 cm. Lithographie, eine Farbe. Frankreich, XIX. Jahrhundert.
149. Suppe. 31,3 × 11 cm. Lithographie, vier Farben und Gold. U.S.A., 1936.
150. Waagen. 8 × 13,9 cm. Holzschnitt und Buchdruck, eine Farbe. U.S.A., XIX. Jahrhundert.

151

152

153

151. Matches. 5 $^7/_{16}$ × 2 $^{15}/_{16}$ in. Wood engraving, 2 colours. England, 1880.
152. Fish. 6 $^{11}/_{16}$ × 3 $^{15}/_{16}$ in. Litho, 4 colours. England, 1880.
153. Matches. 11 $^1/_4$ × 6 $^{11}/_{16}$ in. Offset, 2 colours, on yellow paper. Sweden, 20th century.
154. Rum. 3 $^{15}/_{16}$ × 4 $^9/_{16}$ in. Offset, 4 colours and gold. Design and printing, Roth & Sauter SA, Lausanne/C. Kuhn. Switzerland, 1965.
155. Wine. 3 $^9/_{16}$ × 6 $^5/_{16}$ in. Litho, monochrome and gold. Germany, 1936–1937.

151. Allumettes. 13,7 × 7,5 cm. Gravure sur bois deux coul. papier jaune. Angleterre, 1880.
152. Poisson. 17 × 10 cm. Litho quatre coul. Angleterre, 1880.
153. Allumettes. 28,5 × 16,9 cm. Offset deux coul., papier jaune. Suède, XXe siècle.
154. Rhum. 10 × 11,5 cm. Offset quatre coul. et or. Créat. imp. Roth & Sauter S.A., Lausanne/C. Kuhn. Suisse, 1965.
155. Vin. 9 × 16 cm. Litho une coul. et or. Allemagne, 1936-1937.

151. Streichhölzer. 13,7 × 7,5 cm. Holzschnitt, zwei Farben. England, 1880.
152. Fisch. 17 × 10 cm. Lithographie, vier Farben. England, 1880.
153. Streichhölzer. 28,5 × 16,9 cm. Offset, zwei Farben, gelbes Papier. Schweden, XX. Jahrhundert.
154. Rum. 10 × 11,5 cm. Offset, vier Farben und Gold. Urheber: Druckerei Roth & Sauter S.A., Lausanne/C. Kuhn. Schweiz, 1965.
155. Wein. 9 × 16 cm. Lithographie, eine Farbe und Gold. Deutschland, 1936–1937.

154

155

156

156. Liqueur. 3 ³/₁₆ × 4 ¹/₄ in. Litho, 4 colours. France, 19th century.

156. Liqueur. 8,1 × 10,7 cm. Litho quatre coul. France, XIXᵉ siècle.

156. Likör. 8,1 × 10,7 cm. Lithographie, vier Farben. Frankreich, XIX. Jahrhundert.

157

158

159

157. Textile. 3 $^9/_{16}$ × 4 $^9/_{16}$ in. Litho, 7 colours. India, 19th century.
158. Lawn mower. 5 $^{15}/_{16}$ × 6 $^{11}/_{16}$ in. Litho, 5 colours. USA, 19th century.
159. Eau de Cologne. 1 $^{11}/_{16}$ × 3 $^{11}/_{16}$ in. Litho, 3 colours. Engraving by Silverlook. England, 19th century.
160. Cotton. 4 $^9/_{16}$ × 2 $^{15}/_{16}$ in. Litho, 8 colours. Printing, Trautmann, Bailey & Blampey, New York. USA, 19th century.
161. Wines and cigars. 5 $^1/_2$ × 2 $^7/_8$ in. Litho, 4 colours. USA, 19th century.

157. Textile. 9 × 11,5 cm. Litho sept coul. Inde, XIXe siècle.
158. Tondeuse à gazon. 15 × 17 cm. Litho cinq coul. U.S.A., XIXe siècle.
159. Eau de Cologne. 4,3 × 9,4 cm. Litho trois coul. Silverlook sculp. Angleterre, XIXe siècle.
160. Coton. 11,6 × 7,4 cm. Litho huit coul. Imp. Trautmann, Bailey & Blampey, New York. U.S.A., XIXe siècle.
161. Vins et cigares. 14 × 7,3 cm. Litho quatre coul. U.S.A., XIXe siècle.

157. Textilware. 9 × 11,5 cm. Lithographie, sieben Farben. Indien, XIX. Jahrhundert.
158. Rasenmäher. 15 × 17 cm. Lithographie, fünf Farben. U.S.A., XIX. Jahrhundert.
159. Kölnisch Wasser. 4,3 × 9,4 cm. Lithographie, drei Farben. Gestochen von Silverlook. England, XIX. Jahrhundert.
160. Baumwolle. 11,6 × 7,4 cm. Lithographie, acht Farben. Druckerei Trautmann, Bailey & Blampey, New York. U.S.A., XIX. Jahrhundert.
161. Weine und Zigarren. 14 × 7,3 cm. Lithographie, vier Farben. U.S.A., XIX. Jahrhundert.

160

161

162

163

164

165

166

162. Matches. 2 ³/₈ × 2 ¹/₂ in. Litho, 5 colours. Japan, 1968.
163. Textile. 4 ⁷/₈ × 6 ⁷/₁₆ in. Litho, 7 colours. India, 20th century.
164. Fruit. 9 ¹/₁₆ × 9 ¹/₁₆ in. Litho, 6 colours. Printing, Woodward & Tiernan, St. Louis. USA, 20th century.
165. Soap. 3 ³/₄ × 3 ⁵/₈ in. Litho, monochrome. France, 19th century.
166. Cotton. 1 ¹³/₁₆ × 3 ¹/₈ in. Litho, 7 colours and gold. USA, 19th century.

162. Allumettes. 6 × 6,3 cm. Litho cinq coul. Japon, 1968.
163. Textile. 12,4 × 16,3 cm. Litho sept coul. Inde, XXᵉ siècle.
164. Fruits. 23 × 23 cm. Litho six coul. Imp. Woodward & Tiernan, St. Louis. U.S.A., XXᵉ siècle.
165. Savon. 9,5 × 9,2 cm. Litho une coul. France, XIXᵉ siècle.
166. Coton. 4,6 × 8 cm. Litho sept coul. et or. U.S.A., XIXᵉ siècle.

162. Streichhölzer. 6 × 6,3 cm. Lithographie, fünf Farben. Japan, 1968.
163. Textilware. 12,4 × 16,3 cm. Lithographie, sieben Farben. Indien, XX. Jahrhundert.
164. Früchte. 23 × 23 cm. Lithographie, sechs Farben. Druckerei Woodward & Tiernan, St. Louis. U.S.A., XX. Jahrhundert.
165. Seife. 9,5 × 9,2 cm. Lithographie, eine Farbe. Frankreich, XIX. Jahrhundert.
166. Baumwolle. 4,6 × 8 cm. Lithographie, sieben Farben und Gold. U.S.A., XIX. Jahrhundert.

167

168

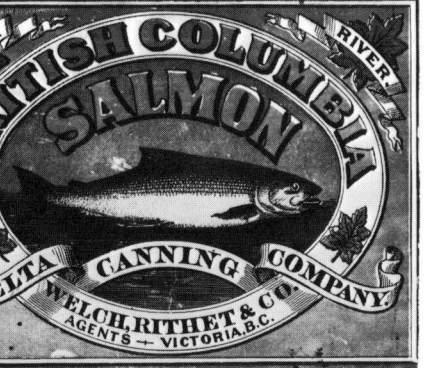

169

167. Fish. 2 $^{15}/_{16}$ × 4 $^1/_4$ in. Litho, 6 colours. Norway, 20th century.
168. Fish. 5 $^3/_4$ × 4 $^1/_4$ in. Litho, 4 colours. England, 1880.
169. Soap. 5 × 3 $^1/_{16}$ in. Litho, 5 colours. Printing, Bufford, Boston. USA, 19th century.
170. Wine. 3 $^1/_8$ × 4 $^3/_4$ in. Offset, 4 colours and gold. Design and printing, Roth & Sauter SA, Lausanne. Switzerland, 1970.
171. Mustard. 7 $^7/_8$ × 3 $^1/_8$ in. Offset, 2 colours. Design and printing, Roth & Sauter SA, Lausanne. Switzerland, 1971.

167. Poisson. 7,5 × 10,7 cm. Litho six coul. Norvège, XXe siècle.
168. Poisson. 14,5 × 10,7 cm. Litho quatre coul. Angleterre, 1880.
169. Savon. 12,7 × 7,8 cm. Litho cinq coul. Imp. Bufford, Boston. U.S.A., XIXe siècle.
170. Vin. 8 × 12 cm. Offset quatre coul. et or. Créat. imp. Roth & Sauter S.A., Lausanne. Suisse, 1970.
171. Moutarde. 20 × 8 cm. Offset deux coul. Créat. imp. Roth & Sauter S.A., Lausanne. Suisse, 1971.

167. Fisch. 7,5 × 10,7 cm. Lithographie, sechs Farben. Norwegen, XX. Jahrhundert.
168. Fisch. 14,5 × 10,7 cm. Lithographie, vier Farben. England, 1880.
169. Seife. 12,7 × 7,8 cm. Lithographie, fünf Farben. Druckerei Bufford, Boston. U.S.A., XIX. Jahrhundert.
170. Wein. 8 × 12 cm. Offset, vier Farben und Gold. Urheber: Druckerei Roth & Sauter S.A., Lausanne. Schweiz, 1970.
171. Senf. 20 × 8 cm. Offset, zwei Farben. Urheber: Druckerei Roth & Sauter S.A., Lausanne. Schweiz, 1971.

170

171

172

173

174

175

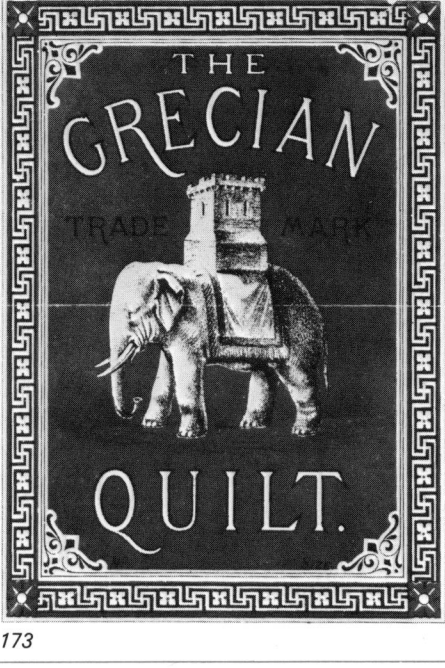

176

172. Textile. 6 $^7/_8$ × 9 $^1/_{16}$ in. Litho, 8 colours. India, 20th century.
173. Eiderdown. 4 $^3/_8$ × 5 $^3/_4$ in. Litho, monochrome and gold. England, 20th century.
174. Textile. 4 $^{15}/_{16}$ × 4 $^{15}/_{16}$ in. Litho, gold. India, 20th century.
175. Corned beef. 6 $^{11}/_{16}$ × 4 $^1/_4$ in. Litho, 4 colours. England, 1900.
176. Meat. 5 $^5/_{16}$ × 3 $^1/_4$ in. Litho, 2 colours and gold. Printing, Donaldson Brothers, New York. USA, 19th century.

172. Textile. 17,5 × 23 cm. Litho huit coul. Inde, XXe siècle.
173. Edredon. 11 × 14,5 cm. Litho une coul. et or. Angleterre, XXe siècle.
174. Textile. 12,5 × 12,5 cm. Litho or. Inde, XXe siècle.
175. Corned Beef. 17 × 10,8 cm. Litho quatre coul. Angleterre, 1900.
176. Viande. 13,4 × 8,2 cm. Litho deux coul. et or. Imp. Donaldson Brothers, New York. U.S.A., XIXe siècle.

172. Textilware. 17,5 × 23 cm. Lithographie, acht Farben. Indien, XX. Jahrhundert.
173. Federbett. 11 × 14,5 cm. Lithographie, eine Farbe und Gold. England, XX. Jahrhundert.
174. Textilware. 12,5 × 12,5 cm. Lithographie, Gold. Indien, XX. Jahrhundert.
175. Corned Beef. 17 × 10,8 cm. Lithographie, vier Farben. England, 1900.
176. Fleisch. 13,4 × 8,2 cm. Lithographie, zwei Farben und Gold. Druckerei Donaldson Brothers, New York. U.S.A., XIX. Jahrhundert.

177

178

179

180

181

177. Hatter. 3 × 1 7/16 in. Wood engraving, monochrome. France, 15th century.
178. Wine. 3 9/16 × 4 3/4 in. Offset, 4 colours. Design and printing, Roth & Sauter, SA, Lausanne/R. Héritier & E. Bosshard. Switzerland, 1971.
179. Wine. 3 9/16 × 4 3/4 in. Offset, 2 colours and gold. Design and printing, Roth & Sauter, SA, Lausanne/R. Héritier. Switzerland, 1971.
180. Hatter. 3 3/16 × 3 3/16 in. Wood engraving, monochrome. France, 15th century.
181. Matches. 2 1/2 × 2 7/16 in. Litho, 5 colours. Japan, 1967.

177. Chapelier. 7,5 × 3,7 cm. Gravure sur bois une coul. France, XVe siècle.
178. Vin. 9 × 12 cm. Offset quatre coul. Créat. imp. Roth & Sauter S.A., Lausanne/ R. Héritier & E. Bosshart. Suisse, 1971.
179. Vin. 9 × 12 cm. Offset deux coul. et or. Créat. imp. Roth & Sauter S.A., Lausanne/ R. Héritier. Suisse, 1971.
180. Chapelier. 8 × 8 cm. Gravure sur bois une coul. France, XVe siècle.
181. Allumettes. 6,3 × 6,1 cm. Litho cinq coul. Japon, 1967.

177. Huthändler. 7,5 × 3,7 cm. Holzschnitt, eine Farbe. Frankreich, XV. Jahrhundert.
178. Wein. 9 × 12 cm. Offset, vier Farben. Urheber: Roth & Sauter S.A., Lausanne/ R. Héritier & E. Bosshart. Schweiz, 1971.
179. Wein. 9 × 12 cm. Offset, zwei Farben und Gold. Urheber: Druckerei Roth & Sauter S.A., Lausanne/R. Héritier. Schweiz, 1971.
180. Huthändler. 8 × 8 cm. Holzschnitt, eine Farbe. Frankreich, XV. Jahrhundert.
181. Streichhölzer. 6,3 × 6,1 cm. Lithographie, fünf Farben. Japan, 1967.

188

189

190

191

192

188. Starch. 3 1/4 × 5 1/8 in. Wood engraving, monochrome. USA, 19th century.
189. Haberdashery. 8 3/16 × 7 3/4 in. Litho, 7 colours. China, 19th century.
190. Textile. 6 7/8 × 9 1/16 in. Litho, 8 colours. India, 20th century.
191. Liqueur. 4 7/16 × 3 13/16 in. Litho, 5 colours. Printing, Chassetière, Marseilles. France, 19th century.
192. Skirt. 3 3/8 × 4 7/8 in. Litho, monochrome. Printing, Taylor & Smith, Philadelphia. USA, 1870.

188. Amidon. 8,2 × 13 cm. Gravure sur bois une coul. U.S.A., XIXe siècle.
189. Mercerie. 20,8 × 19,6 cm. Litho sept coul. Chine, XIXe siècle.
190. Textile. 17,5 × 23 cm. Litho huit coul. Inde, XXe siècle.
191. Liqueur. 11,2 × 9,7 cm. Litho cinq coul. Chassetière, Marseille. France, XIXe siècle.
192. Jupes. 8,5 × 12,3 cm. Litho une coul. Imp. Taylor & Smith, Philadelphie. U.S.A., 1870.

188. Stärke. 8,2 × 13 cm. Holzschnitt, eine Farbe. U.S.A., XIX. Jahrhundert.
189. Kurzwarengeschäft. 20,8 × 19,6 cm. Lithographie, sieben Farben. China, XIX. Jahrhundert.
190. Textilware. 17,5 × 23 cm. Lithographie, acht Farben. Indien, XX. Jahrhundert.
191. Likör. 11,2 × 9,7 cm. Lithographie, fünf Farben. Chassetière, Marseille. Frankreich, XIX. Jahrhundert.
192. Röcke. 8,5 × 12,3 cm. Lithographie, eine Farbe. Druckerei Taylor & Smith, Philadelphia. U.S.A., 1870.

193

194

195

193. Lawn mower.   5 $^{15}/_{16}$ × 6 $^{3}/_{4}$ in.   Litho, 5 colours.   USA, 19th century.
194. Textile.   6 $^{15}/_{16}$ × 9 $^{1}/_{16}$ in.   Litho, 8 colours.   India, 20th century.
195. Matches.   2 $^{1}/_{2}$ × 3 $^{15}/_{16}$ in.   Litho, 4 colours.   Japan, 19th century.
196. Reels of cotton.   2 $^{15}/_{16}$ × 4 $^{9}/_{16}$ in.   Litho, 8 colours.   Design and printing, Trautmann, Bailey & Blampey, New York.   USA, 19th century.
197. Chocolate dragees.   10 $^{1}/_{2}$ × 7 $^{1}/_{2}$ in.   Litho, 7 colours.   Printing, Barclay and Fry Ltd., London.   England, 19th century.

193. Tondeuse à gazon. 15 × 17 cm. Litho cinq coul. U.S.A., XIXe siècle.
194. Textile 17,5 × 23 cm. Litho huit coul. Inde, XXe siècle.
195. Allumettes. 6,3 × 10 cm. Litho quatre coul. Japon, XIXe siècle.
196. Bobines de coton. 7,4 × 11,6 cm. Litho huit coul. Créat. imp. Trautmann, Bailey & Blampey, New York. U.S.A., XIXe siècle.
197. Dragées au chocolat. 26,5 × 19 cm. Litho sept coul. Imp. Barclay & Fry Ltd., Londres. Angleterre, XIXe siècle.

193. Rasenmäher. 15 × 17 cm. Lithographie, fünf Farben. U.S.A., XIX. Jahrhundert.
194. Textilware. 17,5 × 23 cm. Lithographie, acht Farben. Indien, XX. Jahrhundert.
195. Streichhölzer. 6,3 × 10 cm. Lithographie, vier Farben. Japan, XIX. Jahrhundert.
196. Baumwollspulen. 7,4 × 11,6 cm. Lithographie, acht Farben. Urheber: Druckerei Trautmann, Bailey & Blampey, New York. U.S.A., XIX. Jahrhundert.
197. Schokoladendragees. 26,5 × 19 cm. Lithographie, sieben Farben. Urheber: Drukkerei Barclay & Fry Ltd., London. England, XIX. Jahrhundert.

196

197

198

199

200

201

202

198. Matches. 1 $^{7}/_{16}$ × 2 $^{15}/_{16}$ in. Litho, 4 colours. Japan, 19th century.
199. Textile. 2 $^{3}/_{4}$ × 3 $^{13}/_{16}$ in. Litho, 6 colours. India, 20th century.
200. Starch. 2 $^{15}/_{16}$ × 5 $^{1}/_{2}$ in. Litho, 5 colours. USA, 19th century.
201. Liqueur. 4 $^{1}/_{2}$ × 2 $^{7}/_{8}$ in. Litho, 4 colours. Design and printing, Spengler & Co., Lausanne. Switzerland, 19th century.
202. Matches. 1 $^{7}/_{16}$ × 2 $^{3}/_{16}$ in. Litho, 3 colours. Japan, 19th century.

198. Allumettes. 3,6 × 5,8 cm. Litho quatre coul. Japon, XIXᵉ siècle.
199. Textile. 7 × 9,7 cm. Litho six coul. Inde, XXᵉ siècle.
200. Amidon. 7,4 × 14 cm. Litho cinq coul. U.S.A., XIXᵉ siècle.
201. Liqueur. 11,4 × 7,2 cm. Litho quatre coul. Créat. imp. Spengler & Co., Lausanne. Suisse, XIXᵉ siècle.
202. Allumettes. 3,6 × 5,6 cm. Litho trois coul. Japon, XIXᵉ siècle.

198. Streichhölzer. 3,6 × 5,8 cm. Lithographie, vier Farben. Japan, XIX. Jahrhundert.
199. Textilware. 7 × 9,7 cm. Lithographie, sechs Farben. Indien, XX. Jahrhundert.
200. Stärke. 7,4 × 14 cm. Lithographie, fünf Farben. U.S.A., XIX. Jahrhundert.
201. Likör. 11,4 × 7,2 cm. Lithographie, vier Farben. Urheber: Druckerei Spengler und Co., Lausanne. Schweiz, XIX. Jahrhundert.
202. Streichhölzer. 3,6 × 5,6 cm. Lithographie, drei Farben. Japan, XIX. Jahrhundert.

203

204

205

203. Liqueur. 3 ³/₁₆ × 4 ³/₈ in. Litho, 4 colours. France, 19th century.
204. Cotton. 5 ³/₄ × 6 ¹/₂ in. Litho, 7 colours. China, 19th century.
205. Textile. 4 ³/₈ × 5 ³/₄ in. Litho, 7 colours. Greece, 20th century.
206. Clothing. 5 ¹/₂ × 3 ³/₈ in. Litho, 5 colours and gold. USA, 1876.
207. Shoes. 5 × 3 ¹/₁₆ in. Litho, 4 colours. USA, 19th century.

203. Liqueur. 8,1 × 11 cm. Litho quatre coul. France, XIXᵉ siècle.
204. Coton. 14,5 × 16,5 cm. Litho sept coul. Chine, XIXᵉ siècle.
205. Textile. 11 × 14,5 cm. Litho sept coul. Grèce, XXᵉ siècle.
206. Vêtements. 14 × 8,5 cm. Litho cinq coul. et or. U.S.A., 1876.
207. Chaussures. 12,6 × 7,8 cm. Litho quatre coul. U.S.A., XIXᵉ siècle.

203. Likör. 8,1 × 11 cm. Lithographie, vier Farben. Frankreich, XIX. Jahrhundert.
204. Baumwolle. 14,5 × 16,5 cm. Lithographie, sieben Farben. China, XIX. Jahrhundert.
205. Textilware. 11 × 14,5 cm. Lithographie, sieben Farben. Griechenland, XX. Jahrhundert.
206. Kleider. 14 × 8,5 cm. Lithographie, fünf Farben und Gold. U.S.A., 1876.
207. Schuhe. 12,6 × 7,8 cm. Lithographie, vier Farben. U.S.A., XIX. Jahrhundert.

206

207

208

208. Cigarettes. 7 1/8 × 3 7/16 in. Litho, monochrome, on brown paper. Peru, 19th century.

208. *Cigarillos. 18 × 8,7 cm. Litho une coul., papier brun. Pérou, XIXe siècle.*

208. Zigarillos. 18 × 8,7 cm. Lithographie, eine Farbe, braunes Papier. Peru, XIX. Jahrhundert.

209

210

211

209. Ex-libris. 3 $^1/_{16}$ × 4 $^3/_4$ in. Litho, 5 colours and gold. USA, 1879.
210. Laundry-blue. 3 $^{13}/_{16}$ × 6 $^1/_{16}$ in. Litho, 4 colours. Printing, Courbe et Robelin, Dôle. France, 19th century.
211. Skirts. 3 $^3/_8$ × 4 $^7/_{16}$ in. Litho, monochrome, hand-coloured. USA, 19th century.
212. Liqueur. 3 $^1/_2$ × 4 $^{11}/_{16}$ in. Litho, 6 colours. France, 19th century.
213. Soap. 3 $^5/_{16}$ × 5 $^5/_{16}$ in. Litho, 5 colours. USA, 1875.

209. Ex-libris. 7,7 × 12 cm. Litho cinq coul. et or. U.S.A., 1879.
210. Bleu pour lessive. 9,7 × 15,3 cm. Litho quatre coul. Imp. Courbe et Robelin, Dôle. France, XIXe siècle.
211. Jupes. 8,5 × 11,2 cm. Litho une coul. coloriée à la main. U.S.A., XIXe siècle.
212. Liqueur. 8,8 × 11,8 cm. Litho six coul. France, XIXe siècle.
213. Savon. 8,3 × 13,5 cm. Litho cinq coul. U.S.A., 1875.

209. Exlibris. 7,7 × 12 cm. Lithographie, fünf Farben und Gold. U.S.A., 1879.
210. Waschblau. 9,7 × 15,3 cm. Lithographie, vier Farben. Druckerei Courbe und Robelin, Dôle. Frankreich, XIX. Jahrhundert.
211. Röcke. 8,5 × 11,2 cm. Lithographie, eine Farbe, handkoloriert. U.S.A., XIX. Jahrhundert.
212. Likör. 8,8 × 11,8 cm. Lithographie, sechs Farben. Frankreich, XIX. Jahrhundert.
213. Seife. 8,3 × 13,5 cm. Lithographie, fünf Farben. U.S.A., 1875.

212

213

214. Haberdashery. 8 $^3/_{16}$ × 7 $^3/_4$ in. Litho, 7 colours. China, 19th century.

214. *Mercerie. 20,8 × 19,6 cm. Litho sept coul. Chine, XIXe siècle.*

214. Kurzwarengeschäft. 20,8 × 19,6 cm. Lithographie, sieben Farben. China, XIX. Jahrhundert.

215

216

217

215. Wallpaper. 6 $^7/_8$ × 5 $^{15}/_{16}$ in. Copper plate engraving, monochrome. England, 1765.
216. Haberdashery. 7 $^1/_{16}$ × 8 $^7/_{16}$ in. Litho, 7 colours. China, 19th century.
217. Textile. 6 $^3/_8$ × 8 in. Litho, 7 colours. India, 20th century.
218. Auctioneer. 5 $^{15}/_{16}$ × 7 $^1/_8$ in. Litho, monochrome. England, 1805–1839.
219. Undertaker. 8$^1/_8$ × 5$^5/_{16}$ in. Litho, monochrome. England, 1781.

215. *Papiers peints. 17,5 × 15 cm. Gravure sur cuivre une coul. Angleterre, 1765.*
216. *Mercerie. 18,8 × 21,4 cm. Litho sept coul. Chine, XIXe siècle.*
217. *Textile. 16,2 × 20,3 cm. Litho sept coul. Inde, XXe siècle.*
218. *Commissaire-priseur. 15 × 18 cm. Litho une coul. Angleterre, 1805-1839.*
219. *Pompes funèbres. 20,5 × 13,5 cm. Litho une coul. Angleterre, 1781.*

215. Tapeten. 17,5 × 15 cm. Kupferstich, eine Farbe. England, 1765.
216. Kurzwarengeschäft. 18,8 × 21,4 cm. Lithographie, sieben Farben. China, XIX. Jahrhundert.
217. Textilware. 16,2 × 20,3 cm. Lithographie, sieben Farben. Indien, XX. Jahrhundert.
218. Versteigerer. 15 × 18 cm. Lithographie, eine Farbe. England, 1805–1839.
219. Bestattungsinstitut. 20,5 × 13,5 cm. Lithographie, eine Farbe. England, 1781.

218

219

II. The concept of the label in a company context – Evolution – World markets

II. Conceptions de l'étiquette au sein d'une Compagnie – Evolution – Marchés mondiaux

II. Auffassung des Etiketts in einer Handelsgesellschaft – Entwicklung – Weltmärkte

The examples in this chapter have been freely chosen to illustrate: uniformity of graphic design throughout a series of labels; the evolution of a label over a period of time; the range of labels used by one company; comparisons of labels for the same product made by different companies; the modification of a label design for different world markets. Also included are examples of research in label design and labels in the context of packaging.

Nous avons choisi librement les exemples qui figurent dans ce deuxième chapitre, afin de donner un aperçu de: l'unité graphique et les normes fixées pour un ensemble d'étiquettes, l'évolution d'une étiquette dans le temps, l'ensemble des étiquettes utilisées par une Compagnie, la comparaison d'étiquettes pour un produit similaire mais de marques différentes, l'adaptation d'une étiquette sur les marchés mondiaux. Nous avons ajouté des étiquettes au stade de la recherche et l'étiquette prise dans le contexte de l'emballage.

Wir haben die in diesem zweiten Kapitel angeführten Beispiele frei gewählt, um Einblick in folgendes zu gewähren: in die grafische Einheit und die für eine Gruppe von Etiketten festgelegten Normen, in die Entwicklung eines Etiketts im Verlauf der Zeit, in die Gesamtheit der von einer Handelsgesellschaft verwendeten Etikette, in den Vergleich von Etiketten desselben, jedoch von unterschiedlichen Markenfirmen erzeugten Produktes, in die Anpassung eines Etiketts an die Weltmärkte. Wir haben im Forschungsstadium befindliche Etikette hinzugefügt, ebenso wie das im Zusammenhang mit der Verpackung verstandene Etikett.

220

221

222

223

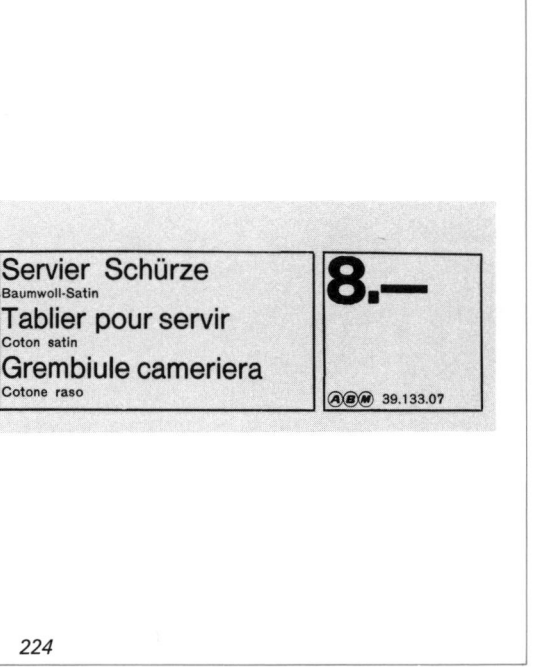

224

220. Specification for labels used by ABM (Au Bon Marché). 6 $1/_4$ × 11 $11/_{16}$ in. Letterpress, 2 colours. Design, E. & U. Hiestand, Zurich. Switzerland, 1971.
221. Trousers, ABM. 3 $3/_4$ × 2 $15/_{16}$ in. Letterpress, monochrome. Design, E. & U. Hiestand, Zurich. Switzerland, 1971.
222. Textile, ABM. 1 $5/_{16}$ × 2 $15/_{16}$ in. Letterpress, monochrome. Design, E. & U. Hiestand, Zurich. Switzerland, 1971.
223. Pyjamas, ABM. 2 $5/_8$ × 2 $15/_{16}$ in. Letterpress, monochrome. Design, E. & U. Hiestand, Zurich. Switzerland, 1971.
224. Apron, ABM. 3 $13/_{16}$ × 1 $5/_8$ in. Letterpress, monochrome. Design, E. & U. Hiestand, Zurich. Switzerland, 1971.

220. Enoncé du principe des étiquettes ABM (Au Bon Marché). 15,8 × 29,7 cm. Typo deux coul. Créat. E. & U. Hiestand, Zurich. Suisse, 1971.
221. Pantalons, ABM. 9,6 × 7,4 cm. Typo une coul. Créat. E. & U. Hiestand, Zurich. Suisse, 1971.
222. Textile, ABM. 3,4 × 7,4 cm. Typo une coul. Créat. E. & U. Hiestand, Zurich. Suisse, 1971.
223. Pyjamas, ABM. 6,7 × 7,4 cm. Typo une coul. Créat. E. & U. Hiestand, Zurich. Suisse, 1971.
224. Tabliers, ABM. 9,7 × 4,2 cm. Typo une coul. Créat. E. & U. Hiestand, Zurich. Suisse, 1971.

222. Textilware, ABM. 3,4 × 7,4 cm. Buchdruck, eine Farbe. Urheber: E. & U. Hiestand, Zürich. Schweiz, 1971.
223. Pyjamas, ABM. 6,7 × 7,4 cm. Buchdruck, eine Farbe. Urheber: E. & U. Hiestand, Zürich. Schweiz, 1971.
224. Schürzen, ABM. 9,7 × 4,2 cm. Buchdruck, eine Farbe. Urheber: E. & U. Hiestand, Zürich. Schweiz, 1971.

220. Erläuterung des Prinzips der ABM-Etiketts (Au Bon Marché: zum guten Markt). 15,8 × 29,7 cm. Buchdruck, zwei Farben. Urheber: E. & U. Hiestand, Zürich. Schweiz, 1971.
221. Hosen, ABM. 9,6 × 7,4 cm. Buchdruck, eine Farbe. Urheber: E. & U. Hiestand, Zürich. Schweiz, 1971.

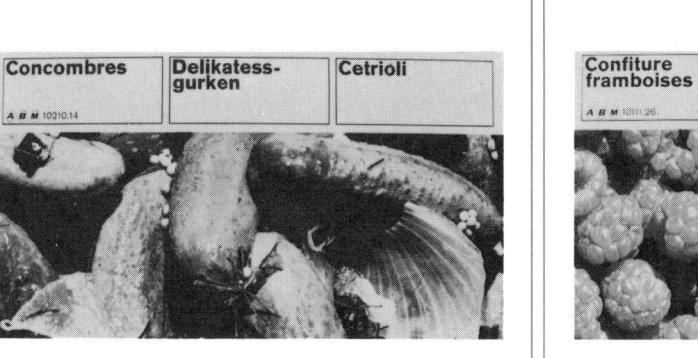

Confiture oranges amères	Konfitüre Orangen bitter	Confettura arance amare

A B M 10111.27

225

Concombres	Delikatess-gurken	Cetrioli

A B M 10210.14

226

Confiture framboises	Konfitüre Himbeer	Confettura lamponi

A B M 10111.26

227

225. Marmalade, ABM. 5 $^1/_8$ × 2 $^{13}/_{16}$ in. Offset, 4 colours. Design, E. & U. Hiestand, Zurich. Switzerland, 1963.
226. Gherkins, ABM. 5 $^1/_8$ × 2 $^{13}/_{16}$ in. Offset, 4 colours. Design, E. & U. Hiestand, Zurich. Switzerland, 1963.
227. Jam, ABM. 5 $^1/_8$ × 2 $^{13}/_{16}$ in. Offset, 4 colours. Design, E. & U. Hiestand, Zurich. Switzerland, 1963.
228. Honey, ABM. 9 $^5/_{16}$ × 3 $^1/_8$ in. Letter-press, 2 colours. Design, E. & U. Hiestand, Zurich. Switzerland, 1963.
229. Deodorant, ABM. 6 $^{11}/_{16}$ × 5 $^3/_{16}$ in. Offset, 2 colours. Design, E. & U. Hiestand, Zurich. Switzerland, 1966.

225. Confiture, ABM. 13 × 7,2 cm. Offset quatre coul. Créat. E. & U. Hiestand, Zurich. Suisse, 1963.
226. Cornichons, ABM. Offset quatre coul. Créat. E. & U. Hiestand, Zurich. Suisse, 1963.
227. Confiture, ABM. 13 × 7,2 cm. Offset quatre coul. Créat. E. & U. Hiestand, Zurich. Suisse, 1963.
228. Miel, ABM. 23,6 × 8 cm. Typo deux coul. Créat. E. & U. Hiestand, Zurich. Suisse, 1963.
229. Désodorisant, ABM. 17 × 13,1 cm. Offset deux coul. Créat. E. & U. Hiestand, Zurich. Suisse, 1966.

225. Marmelade, ABM. 13 × 7,2 cm. Offset, vier Farben. Urheber: E. & U. Hiestand, Zürich. Schweiz, 1963.
226. Delikatessgurken, ABM. Offset, vier Farben. Urheber: E. & U. Hiestand, Zürich. Schweiz, 1963.
227. Marmelade, ABM. 13 × 7,2 cm. Offset, vier Farben. Urheber: E. & U. Hiestand, Zürich. Schweiz, 1963.

Miel étranger	··· Echter ausländischer Bienenhonig	Miele straniero

228

228. Honig, ABM. 23,6 × 8 cm. Buchdruck, zwei Farben. Urheber: E. & U. Hiestand, Zürich. Schweiz, 1963.
229. Luftreiniger, ABM. 17 × 13,1 cm. Offset, zwei Farben. Urheber: E. & U. Hiestand, Zürich. Schweiz, 1966.

2.–	Luftreiniger Spray	Désodorisant	*A ## 70023.5*	Purificatore dell'aria

229

230

231

232

233

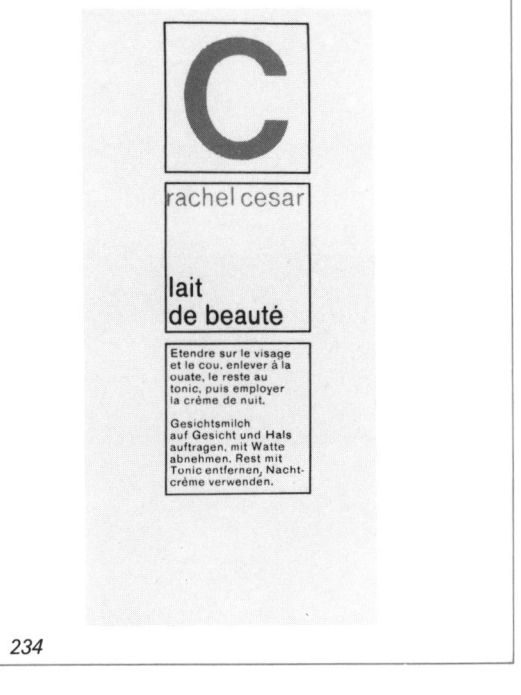

234

230. After-shave lotion, ABM. $1^5/_{16} \times 3^1/_2$ in. Offset, monochrome and gold. Design, E. & U. Hiestand, Zurich. Switzerland, 1966.

231. Face cream, ABM. $2^1/_4 \times 4^1/_{16}$ in. Offset, monochrome and gold. Design, E. & U. Hiestand, Zurich. Switzerland, 1966.

232. Skin tonic, ABM. $2^3/_8 \times 4^3/_4$ in. Offset, monochrome and gold. Design, E. & U. Hiestand, Zurich. Switzerland, 1966.

233. Hair spray, ABM. $7^1/_8 \times 3^5/_{16}$ in. Offset, monochrome and gold. Design, E. & U. Hiestand, Zurich. Switzerland, 1966.

234. Cleansing milk, ABM. $2^3/_8 \times 4^3/_4$ in. Offset, monochrome and gold. Design, E. & U. Hiestand, Zurich. Switzerland, 1966.

230. Lotion à raser, ABM. 3,3 × 8,9 cm. Offset une coul. et or. Créat. E. & U. Hiestand, Zurich. Suisse, 1966.

231. Crème de jour, ABM. 5,8 × 10,3 cm. Offset une coul. et or. Créat. E. & U. Hiestand, Zurich. Suisse, 1966.

232. Tonic, ABM. 6 × 12 cm. Offset une coul. et or. Créat. E. & U. Hiestand, Zurich. Suisse, 1966.

233. Fixatif, ABM. 18 × 8,3 cm. Offset une coul. et or. Créat. E. & U. Hiestand, Zurich. Suisse, 1966.

234. Lait de beauté, ABM. 6 × 12 cm. Offset une coul. et or. Créat. E. & U. Hiestand, Zurich. Suisse, 1966.

232. Tonikum, ABM. 6 × 12 cm. Offset, eine Farbe und Gold. Urheber: E. & U. Hiestand, Zürich. Schweiz, 1966.

233. Haarspray, ABM. 18 × 8,3 cm. Offset, eine Farbe und Gold. Urheber: E. & U. Hiestand, Zürich. Schweiz, 1966.

234. Gesichtsmilch, ABM. 6 × 12 cm. Offset, eine Farbe und Gold. Urheber: E. & U. Hiestand, Zürich. Schweiz, 1966.

230. Rasierwasser, ABM. 3,3 × 8,9 cm. Offset, eine Farbe und Gold. Urheber: E. & U. Hiestand, Zürich. Schweiz, 1966.

231. Tagescreme, ABM. 5,8 × 10,3 cm. Offset, eine Farbe und Gold. Urheber: E. & U. Hiestand, Zürich. Schweiz, 1966.

235

236

237

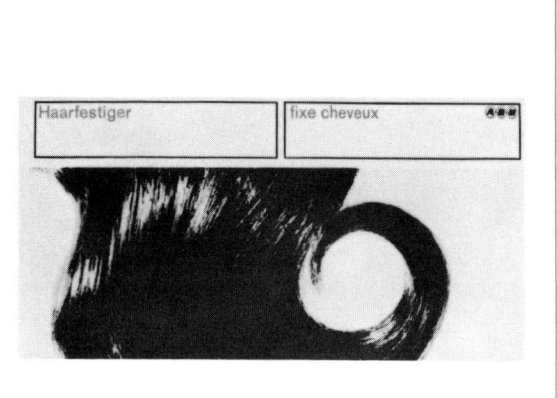

238

239

235. Knitting wool, ABM. 7 $^{7}/_{16}$ × 2 $^{15}/_{16}$ in. Offset, monochrome and gold. Design, E. & U. Hiestand, Zurich. Switzerland, 1971.
236. Paint, ABM. 8 $^{11}/_{16}$ × 5 $^{3}/_{4}$ in. Offset, 4 colours. Design, E. & U. Hiestand, Zurich. Switzerland, 1964.
237. Foot spray, ABM. 6 $^{11}/_{16}$ × 4 in. Offset, 2 colours. Design, E. & U. Hiestand, Zurich. Switzerland, 1964.
238. Hair lacquer, ABM. 5 $^{1}/_{2}$ × 2 $^{3}/_{4}$ in. Offset, 2 colours. Design, E. & U. Hiestand, Zurich. Switzerland, 1967.
239. Sun-tan oil, ABM. 7 $^{1}/_{2}$ × 4 in. Offset, 3 colours. Design, E. & U. Hiestand, Zurich. Switzerland, 1964.

235. Laine, ABM. 18,8 × 7,5 cm. Offset une coul. et or. Créat. E. & U. Hiestand, Zurich. Suisse, 1971.
236. Peinture, ABM. 22 × 14,5 cm. Offset quatre coul. Créat. E. & U. Hiestand, Zurich. Suisse, 1964.
237. Spray pour les pieds, ABM. 17 × 10,2 cm. Offset deux coul. Créat. E. & U. Hiestand, Zurich. Suisse, 1964.
238. Fixatif, ABM. 14 × 7 cm. Offset deux coul. Créat. E. & U. Hiestand, Zurich. Suisse, 1967.
239. Huile antisolaire, ABM. 19 × 10,2 cm. Offset trois coul. Créat. E. & U. Hiestand, Zurich. Suisse, 1964.

235. Wolle, ABM. 18,8 × 7,5 cm. Offset, eine Farbe und Gold. Urheber: E. & U. Hiestand, Zürich. Schweiz, 1971.
236. Lackfarbe, ABM. 22 × 14,5 cm. Offset, vier Farben. Urheber: E. & U. Hiestand, Zürich. Schweiz, 1964.
237. Fuss-Spray, ABM. 17 × 10,2 cm. Offset, zwei Farben. Urheber: E. & U. Hiestand, Zürich. Schweiz, 1964.

238. Haarfestiger, ABM. 14 × 7 cm. Offset, zwei Farben. Urheber: E. & U. Hiestand, Zürich. Schweiz, 1967.
239. Sonnenschutzöl, ABM. 19 × 10,2 cm. Offset, drei Farben. Urheber: E. & U. Hiestand, Zürich. Schweiz, 1964.

240. Labels designed for a range of car-maintenance products, ABM. Design, E. & U. Hiestand, Zurich. Switzerland, 1970.

240. *Etiquettes conçues pour un ensemble de produits d'entretien pour voitures, ABM. Créat. E. & U. Hiestand, Zurich. Suisse, 1970.*

240. Etikette, die für eine Serie von Autopflege-mitteln konzipiert wurden, ABM. Urheber: E. & U. Hiestand, Zürich. Schweiz, 1970.

241

242

243

241. Beer. 3 ³/₄ × 2 ¹¹/₁₆ in. Offset, 2 colours and silver, on gold paper. Greece, 1967.
242. Beer. 2 ¹⁵/₁₆ × 3 ³/₄ in. Offset, monochrome, on gold paper. Greece, 1964.
243. Beer. 3 ¹/₄ × 1 ⁷/₈ in. Offset, 2 colours, on silver paper. Greece, 1967.
244. Beer. 3 ³/₄ × 2 ⁵/₈ in. Offset, 2 colours, on gold paper. Greece, 1967.
245. Beer. 2 ¹⁵/₁₆ × 3 ¹/₄ in. Offset, 2 colours and silver, on gold paper. Greece, 1967.

241. Bière. 9,5 × 6,8 cm. Offset deux coul. et argent, papier or. Grèce, 1967.
242. Bière. 7,5 × 9,5 cm. Offset une coul., papier or. Grèce, 1964.
243. Bière. 8,2 × 4,8 cm. Offset deux coul., papier argent. Grèce, 1967.
244. Bière. 9,6 × 6,7 cm. Offset deux coul., papier or. Grèce, 1967.
245. Bière. 7,5 × 8,2 cm. Offset deux coul. et argent, papier or. Grèce, 1967.

241. Bier. 9,5 × 6,8 cm. Offset, zwei Farben und Silber, Goldpapier. Griechenland, 1967.
242. Bier. 7,5 × 9,5 cm. Offset, eine Farbe, Goldpapier. Griechenland, 1964.
243. Bier. 8,2 × 4,8 cm. Offset, zwei Farben, Silberpapier. Griechenland, 1967.
244. Bier. 9,6 × 6,7 cm. Offset, zwei Farben, Goldpapier. Griechenland, 1967.
245. Bier. 7,5 × 8,2 cm. Offset, zwei Farben und Silber, Goldpapier. Griechenland, 1967.

244

245

246

247

248

249

250

246. Cocoa. 3 $^3/_4$ × 5 $^1/_{16}$ in. Offset, 5 colours. Switzerland, 1971.
247. Cocoa. 4 $^3/_4$ × 7 $^1/_8$ in. Offset, 4 colours. Switzerland, 1971.
248. Cocoa. 3 $^3/_4$ × 5 $^{11}/_{16}$ in. Offset, 4 colours. Switzerland, 1971.
249. Cocoa. 4 $^3/_8$ × 6 $^{11}/_{16}$ in. Offset, 4 colours. Switzerland, 1971.
250. Cocoa. 4 $^1/_8$ × 5 $^7/_{16}$ in. Offset, 3 colours. Switzerland, 1971.

246. Cacao. 9,5 × 12,8 cm. Offset cinq coul. Suisse, 1971.
247. Cacao. 12 × 18 cm. Offset quatre coul. Suisse, 1971.
248. Cacao. 9,6 × 14,4 cm. Offset quatre coul. Suisse, 1971.
249. Cacao. 11 × 17 cm. Offset quatre coul. Suisse, 1971.
250. Cacao. 10,5 × 13,8 cm. Offset trois coul. Suisse, 1971.

246. Kakao. 9,5 × 12,8 cm. Offset, fünf Farben. Schweiz, 1971.
247. Kakao. 12 × 18 cm. Offset, vier Farben. Schweiz, 1971.
248. Kakao. 9,6 × 14,4 cm. Offset, vier Farben. Schweiz, 1971.
249. Kakao. 11 × 17 cm. Offset, vier Farben. Schweiz, 1971.
250. Kakao. 10,5 × 13,8 cm. Offset, drei Farben. Schweiz, 1971.

251

252

253

251–255. Lozenges for the throat and other purposes.   2 $^7/_{16}$ × 1 $^5/_8$ in.   Litho, monochrome.   England, early 19th. century.

251-255. Droguerie, pastilles diverses, pour le bain, la gorge, etc. 6,2 × 4,4 cm. Litho une coul. Angleterre, début XIXe siècle.

251–255. Drogerie, verschiedenartige Tabletten, für das Bad, den Hals usw. 6,2 × 4,2 cm. Lithographie, eine Farbe. England, Anfang des XIX. Jahrhunderts.

254

255

256

257

258

259

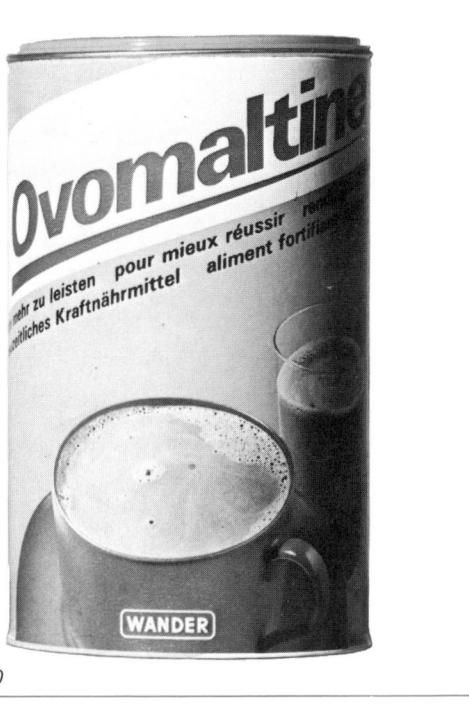

260

Graphic evolution of a label for an energy drink.   Switzerland.

256. 1904–1912
257. 1913–1951
258. 1952–1965
259. 1965–1970
260. 1970

Evolution graphique d'une étiquette pour un produit fortifiant. Suisse.

256. 1904-1912
257. 1913-1951
258. 1952–1965
259. 1965-1970
260. 1970

Grafische Entwicklung eines Etiketts für ein Stärkungsmittel. Schweiz.

256. 1904–1912.
257. 1913–1951.
258. 1952–1965.
259. 1965–1970.
260. 1970

261

262

263

264

265

261. Airline. 2 $^3/_8$ × 5 $^1/_2$ in. Letterpress, 2 colours. Switzerland, 1971.
262. Airline. 2$^3/_4$ × 4 $^3/_8$ in. Offset, 4 colours. Switzerland, 1958.
263. Airline. 3 $^7/_8$ × 3 $^5/_8$ in. Letterpress, monochrome. Switzerland, 1971.
264. Airline. a) 6 $^1/_2$ × 1 $^1/_4$ in. Offset, 2 colours. Switzerland, 1971. b) 8$^{15}/_{16}$ × 1 $^3/_{16}$ in. Offset, monochrome. Switzerland, 1971.
265. Airline, cigar. 2 $^9/_{16}$ × 1 in. Litho, monochrome and embossed gold. Switzerland, 1965.

261. Compagnie aérienne. 6 × 14 cm. Typo deux coul. Suisse, 1971.
262. Compagnie aérienne. 7 × 11 cm. Offset quatre coul. Suisse, 1958.
263. Compagnie aérienne. 9,8 × 9,2 cm. Typo une coul. Suisse, 1971.
264. Compagnie aérienne. a) 16,5 × 3,2 cm. Offset deux coul. Suisse, 1971. b) 21 × 3,1 cm. Offset une coul. Suisse, 1971.
265. Compagnie aérienne, cigare. 6,5 × 2,6 cm. Litho une coul. et or gaufré. Suisse, 1965.

261. Fluggesellschaft. 6 × 14 cm. Buchdruck, zwei Farben. Schweiz, 1971.
262. Fluggesellschaft. 7 × 11 cm. Offset, vier Farben. Schweiz, 1958.
263. Fluggesellschaft. 9,8 × 9,2 cm. Buchdruck, eine Farbe. Schweiz, 1971.
264. Fluggesellschaft. a) 16,5 × 3,2 cm. Offset, zwei Farben. Schweiz, 1971. b) 21 × 3,1 cm. Offset, eine Farbe. Schweiz, 1971.
265. Fluggesellschaft, Zigarre. 6,5 × 2,6 cm. Lithographie, eine Farbe und Prägung in Gold. Schweiz, 1965.

266

267

268

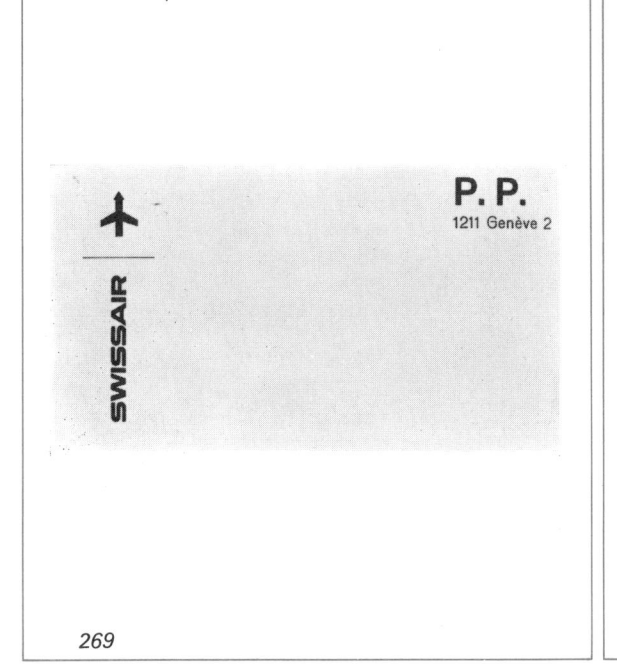

269

270

266. Airline. 3 $^3/_8$ in. diameter. Offset, mono-chrome. Switzerland, 1971.
267. Airline. 2 $^3/_4$ × 4 $^3/_8$ in. Offset, 4 col-ours. Switzerland, 1958.
268. Airline. 3 $^3/_8$ in. diameter. Offset, mono-chrome. Switzerland, 1971.
269. Airline. 5 $^1/_8$ × 2 $^3/_4$ in. Letterpress, monochrome. Switzerland, 1971.
270. Airline. 6 × 2 $^{11}/_{16}$ in. Letterpress, 2 col-ours. Switzerland, 1971.

266. *Compagnie aérienne. Diam. 8,5 cm. Offset une coul. Suisse, 1971.*
267. *Compagnie aérienne. 7 × 11 cm. Offset quatre coul. Suisse, 1958.*
268. *Compagnie aérienne. Diam. 8,5 cm. Offset une coul. Suisse, 1971.*
269. *Compagnie aérienne. 13 × 7 cm. Typo une coul. Suisse, 1971.*
270. *Compagnie aérienne. 15,2 × 6,8 cm. Typo deux coul. Suisse, 1971.*

266. Fluggesellschaft. Durchmesser 8,5 cm. Offset, eine Farbe. Schweiz, 1971.
267. Fluggesellschaft. 7 × 11 cm. Offset, vier Farben. Schweiz, 1958.
268. Fluggesellschaft. Durchmesser 8,5 cm. Offset, eine Farbe. Schweiz, 1971.
269. Fluggesellschaft. 13 × 7 cm. Buchdruck, eine Farbe. Schweiz, 1971.
270. Fluggesellschaft. 15,2 × 6,8 cm. Buch-druck, zwei Farben. Schweiz, 1971.

271. Instant coffee. 3 $^9/_{16}$ × 2 $^7/_{16}$ in. Offset, 2 colours and gold. Switzerland, 1953.
272. Instant coffee. 4 $^9/_{16}$ × 2 $^3/_4$ in. Offset, 2 colours and embossed gold. Sweden, 1961.
273. Instant coffee. 4 $^{11}/_{16}$ × 2 $^3/_4$ in. Offset, 4 colours. Australia, 1970–1971.
274. Instant coffee. 4 $^3/_4$ × 2 $^3/_{16}$ in. Offset, 2 colours, on silver paper. Mexico, 1960.
275. Instant coffee. 4$^3/_4$ × 2 $^{11}/_{16}$ in. Offset, 2 colours and gold. Canada, 1961.

271. Café en poudre. 9 × 6,2 cm. Offset deux coul. et or. Suisse, 1953.
272. Café en poudre. 11,5 × 7 cm. Offset deux coul. et or gaufré. Suède, 1961.
273. Café en poudre. 11,8 × 7 cm. Offset quatre coul. Australie, 1970-1971.
274. Café en poudre. 12 × 5,6 cm. Offset deux coul., papier argent. Mexique, 1960.
275. Café en poudre. 12 × 6,8 cm. Offset deux coul. et or. Canada, 1961.

271. Pulverkaffee. 9 × 6,2 cm. Offset, zwei Farben und Gold. Schweiz, 1953.
272. Pulverkaffee. 11,5 × 7 cm. Offset, zwei Farben und Prägung in Gold. Schweden, 1961.
273. Pulverkaffee. 11,8 × 7 cm. Offset, vier Farben. Australien, 1970–1971.
274. Pulverkaffee. 12 × 5,6 cm. Offset, zwei Farben, Silberpapier. Mexiko, 1960.
275. Pulverkaffee. 12 × 6,8 cm. Offset, zwei Farben und Gold. Kanada, 1961.

276

277

278

279

280

276. Instant coffee.   4 $^3/_4$ × 2 $^{11}/_{16}$ in.   Offset, 2 colours and gold.   USA, 1960.
277. Instant coffee.   4 $^3/_4$ × 2 $^{11}/_{16}$ in.   Offset, 4 colours and gold.   USA, 1961.
278. Instant coffee.   4 $^3/_4$ × 2 $^{13}/_{16}$ in.   Offset, 3 colours and gold.   New Zealand, 1960.
279. Instant coffee.   4$^3/_4$ × 2 $^{13}/_{16}$ in.   Offset, 4 colours and gold.   New Zealand, 1961.
280. Instant coffee.   3 $^3/_8$ × 2 $^3/_8$ in.   Offset, 3 colours and gold.   France, 1961.

276. Café en poudre. 12 × 6,8 cm. Offset deux coul. et or. U.S.A., 1960.
277. Café en poudre. 12 × 6,8 cm. Offset quatre coul. et or. U.S.A., 1961.
278. Café en poudre. 12 × 7,2 cm. Offset trois coul. et or. Nouvelle-Zélande, 1960.
279. Café en poudre. 12 × 7,2 cm. Offset quatre coul. et or. Nouvelle-Zélande, 1961.
280. Café en poudre. 8,6 × 6 cm. Offset trois coul. et or. France, 1961.

276. Pulverkaffee. 12 × 6,8 cm. Offset, zwei Farben und Gold. U.S.A., 1960.
277. Pulverkaffee. 12 × 6,8 cm. Offset, vier Farben und Gold. U.S.A., 1961.
278. Pulverkaffee. 12 × 7,2 cm. Offset, drei Farben und Gold. Neuseeland, 1960.
279. Pulverkaffee. 12 × 7,2 cm. Offset, vier Farben und Gold. Neuseeland, 1961.
280. Pulverkaffee. 8,6 × 6 cm. Offset, drei Farben und Gold. Frankreich, 1961.

281

282

283

281. Instant coffee. 4 ³/₄ × 3 ⁵/₁₆ in. Offset, 3 colours and gold. Australia, 1960.
282. Instant coffee. 4 ¹³/₁₆ × 3 ¹/₄ in. Offset, 4 colours and gold. Australia, 1961.
283. Instant coffee. 3 ³/₈ × 2 ³/₈ in. Offset, 4 colours and gold. Denmark, 1961.
284. Instant coffee. 2 ⁵/₈ × 3 ⁵/₁₆ in. Offset, 3 colours and gold. Export, 1961.
285. Instant coffee. 2 ³/₄ × 3 ³/₈ in. Offset, 3 colours and gold. Austria, 1961.

281. *Café en poudre. 12 × 8,3 cm. Offset trois coul. et or. Australie, 1960.*
282. *Café en poudre. 12,2 × 8,2 cm. Offset quatre coul. et or. Australie, 1961.*
283. *Café en poudre. 8,5 × 6,1 cm. Offset quatre coul. et or. Danemark, 1961.*
284. *Café en poudre. 6,7 × 8,4 cm. Offset trois coul. et or. Exportation, 1961.*
285. *Café en poudre. 6,9 × 8,5 cm. Offset trois coul. et or. Autriche, 1961.*

281. Pulverkaffee. 12 × 8,3 cm. Offset, drei Farben und Gold. Australien, 1960.
282. Pulverkaffee. 12,2 × 8,2 cm. Offset, vier Farben und Gold. Australien, 1961.
283. Pulverkaffee. 8,5 × 6,1 cm. Offset, vier Farben und Gold. Dänemark, 1961.
284. Pulverkaffee. 6,7 × 8,4 cm. Offset, drei Farben und Gold. Export, 1961.
285. Pulverkaffee. 6,9 × 8,5 cm. Offset, drei Farben und Gold. Österreich, 1961.

284

285

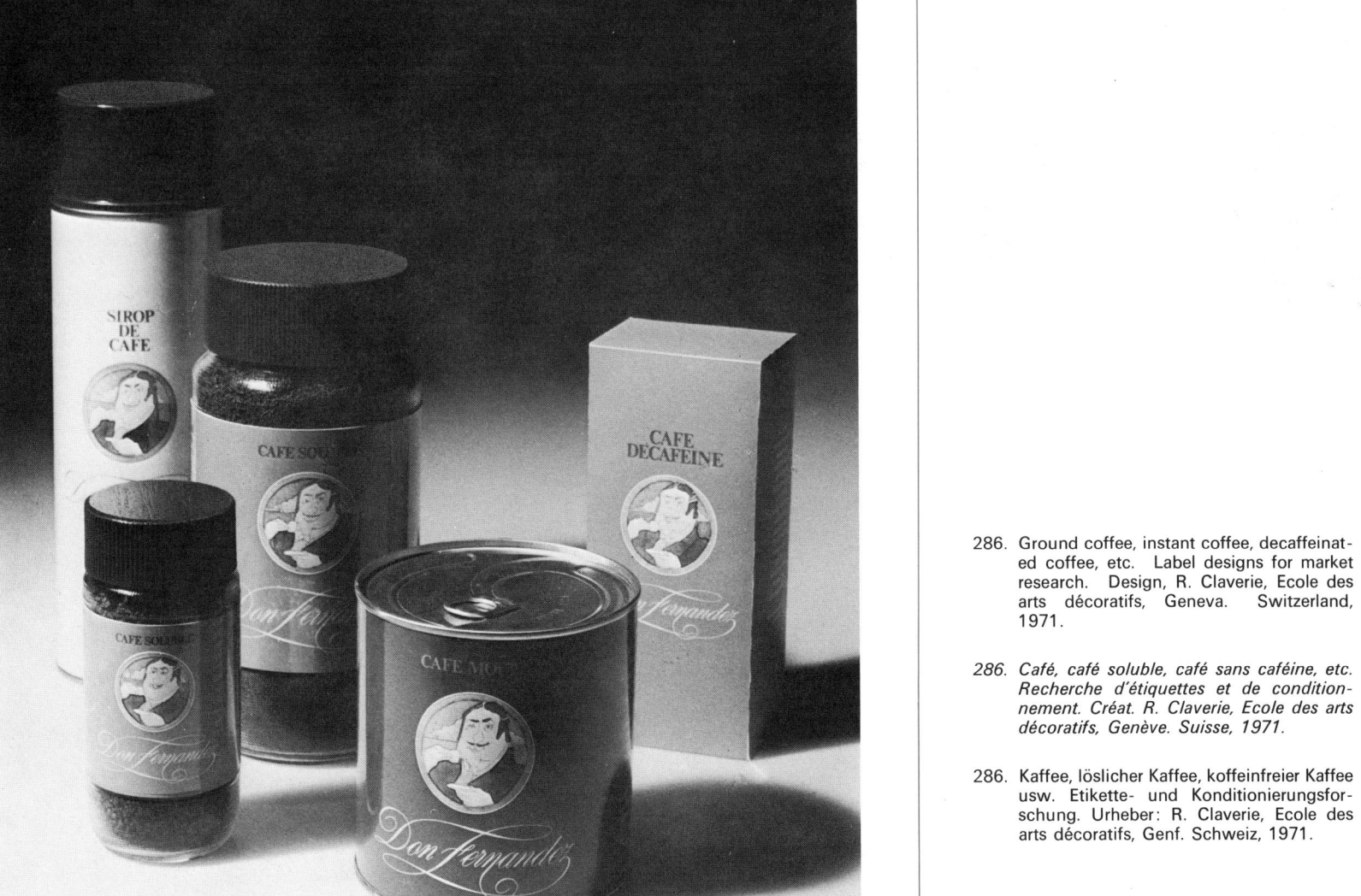

286. Ground coffee, instant coffee, decaffeinated coffee, etc. Label designs for market research. Design, R. Claverie, Ecole des arts décoratifs, Geneva. Switzerland, 1971.

286. *Café, café soluble, café sans caféine, etc. Recherche d'étiquettes et de conditionnement. Créat. R. Claverie, Ecole des arts décoratifs, Genève. Suisse, 1971.*

286. Kaffee, löslicher Kaffee, koffeinfreier Kaffee usw. Etikette- und Konditionierungsforschung. Urheber: R. Claverie, Ecole des arts décoratifs, Genf. Schweiz, 1971.

287

288

289

287. Razor blades.   2 $^5/_8$ × 1 $^3/_8$ in.   Offset,
3 colours.   United Kingdom, 1971.
288. Razor blades.   2 $^5/_8$ × 1 $^3/_8$ in.   Offset,
3 colours.   France, 1971.
289. Razor blades.   2 $^5/_8$ × 1 $^3/_8$ in.   Offset,
3 colours and silver.   Germany, 1971.
290. Razor blades.   2 $^5/_8$ × 1 $^3/_8$ in.   Offset,
3 colours.   Italy, 1971.
291. Razor blades.   2 $^5/_8$ × 1 $^3/_8$ in.   Offset,
3 colours.   International, 1971.

287. *Lames de rasoir. 6,6 × 3,5 cm. Offset trois*
coul. Royaume-Uni, 1971.
288. *Lames de rasoirs. 6,6 × 3,5 cm. Offset trois*
coul. France, 1971.
289. *Lames de rasoir. 6,6 × 3,5 cm. Offset trois*
coul. et argent. Allemagne, 1971.
290. *Lames de rasoir. 6,6 × 3,5 cm. Offset trois*
coul. Italie, 1971.
291. *Lames de rasoir. 6,6 × 3,5 cm. Offset trois*
coul. International, 1971.

287. Rasierklingen. 6,6 × 3,5 cm. Offset, drei
Farben. Vereinigtes Königreich, 1971.
288. Rasierklingen. 6,6 × 3,5 cm. Offset, drei
Farben. Frankreich, 1971.
289. Rasierklingen. 6,6 × 3,5 cm. Offset, drei
Farben und Silber. Deutschland, 1971.
290. Rasierklingen. 6,6 × 3,5 cm. Offset, drei
Farben. Italien, 1971.
291. Rasierklingen. 6,6 × 3,5 cm. Offset, drei
Farben. International, 1971.

290

291

292

293

294

295

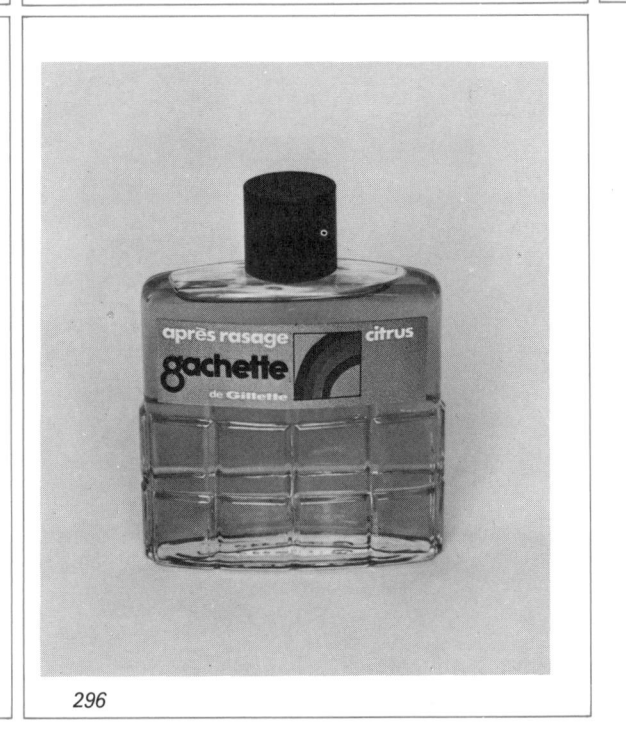

296

292–296. Project for an after-shave product, to be launched in spring 1972. Design, Agence L. Gaget, Annecy. France, 1971.

292-296. Etude pour un produit après rasage, lancement printemps 1972. Créat. Agence L. Gaget, Annecy. France, 1971.

292–296. Studie für ein After-Shave-Mittel, Lancierung Frühjahr 1972. Urheber: Agentur L. Gaget, Annecy. Frankreich, 1971.

297

298

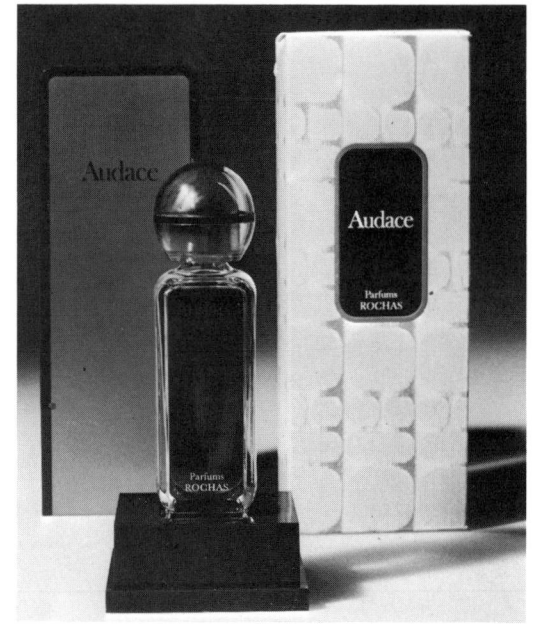

299

297–299. Perfume, toilet water, aerosol deodorant. Metal label with relief impression
(297), printing on plastic (298), printing
on embossed silver paper (299). France,
1971.

*297-299. Parfum, eau de toilette, spray. Eti-
quette métal avec relief (297), impression
sur matière plastique (298), impression
sur papier argent gaufré (299). France,
1971.*

297–299. Parfüm, Gesichtswasser, Spray. Me-
talletikett mit Prägung (297), Druck auf
Kunststoff (298), Druck auf Silberpapier
mit Prägung (299). Frankreich, 1971.

297

299

III. Round and oval labels – Ornamented labels

III. Etiquettes rondes et ovales – Etiquettes ornementées

III. Runde und ovale Etikette – Verzierte Etikette

This third chapter contains examples of round and oval labels whose design is regulated by their shape, and additionally, examples of ornamented labels from different periods.

Ce troisième chapitre groupe les étiquettes rondes et ovales régies par une conception de composition qui leur est propre. Nous l'avons complété par les étiquettes ornementées au gré des époques.

Dieses dritte Kapitel faßt die runden und die ovalen Etikette zusammen, die einer eigenen Kompositionsauffassung unterworfen sind. Wir haben es durch zeitgemäß verzierte Etikette ergänzt.

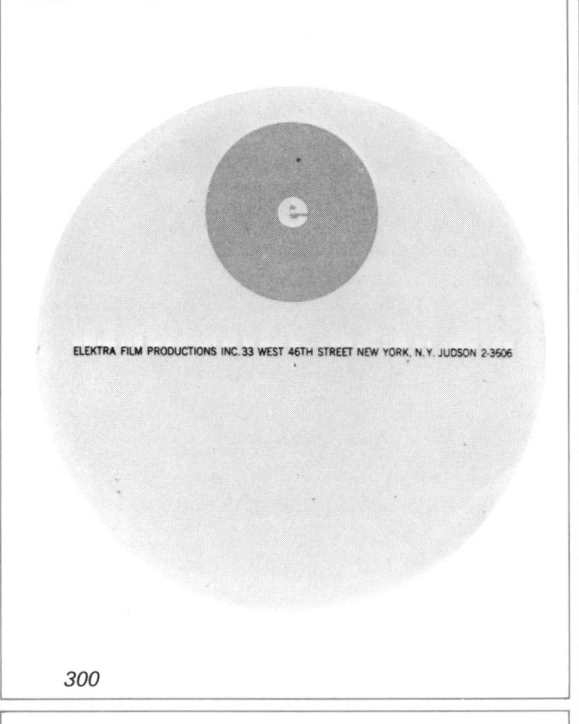

ELEKTRA FILM PRODUCTIONS INC. 33 WEST 46TH STREET NEW YORK, N.Y. JUDSON 2-3506

300

301

302

303

GILBERT MUIR
Nº 19, BRUNSWICK ROAD
TOP OF ISLINGTON.
FINE OLD WHISKEY
AND
Nº 8, LODGE LANE.
LIVERPOOL.

304

300. Film company. 2 7/8 in. diameter. Offset, 2 colours. Design, Push Pin Studios Inc. Milton Glaser, New York. USA, 1971.
301. Beer. 5 in. diameter. Litho, monochrome. England, 1860–1870.
302. Address label. 4 1/8 in. diameter. Offset, 3 colours. Design, Push Pin Studios Inc/ Milton Glaser, New York. USA, 1971.
303. Brandy. 2 3/8 × 2 13/16 in. Litho, 2 colours. England, 19th century.
304. Whisky. 2 1/2 in. diameter. Litho, monochrome. England, 19th century.

300. *Production de films. Diam. 7,3 cm. Offset deux coul. Créat. Push Pin Studios Inc./ Milton Glaser, New York. U.S.A., 1971.*
301. *Bière. Diam. 12,7 cm. Litho une coul. Angleterre, 1860-1870.*
302. *Etiquette adresse. Diam. 10,5 cm. Offset trois coul. Créat. Push Pin Studios Inc./ Milton Glaser, New York. U.S.A., 1971.*
303. *Brandy. 6 × 7,2 cm. Litho deux coul. Angleterre, XIXᵉ siècle.*
304. *Whisky. Diam. 6,3 cm. Litho une coul. Angleterre, XIXᵉ siècle.*

300. Filmproduktion. Durchmesser 7,3 cm. Offset, zwei Farben. Urheber: Push Pin Studios Inc./Milton Glaser, New York. U.S.A., 1971.
301. Bier. Durchmesser 12,7 cm. Lithographie, eine Farbe. England, 1860–1870.
302. Adressenetikett. Durchmesser 10,5 cm. Offset, drei Farben. Urheber: Push Pin Studios Inc./Milton Glaser, New York. U.S.A., 1971.
303. Brandy. 6 × 7,2 cm. Lithographie, zwei Farben. England, XIX. Jahrhundert.
304. Whisky. Durchmesser 6,3 cm. Lithographie, eine Farbe. England, XIX. Jahrhundert.

305

306

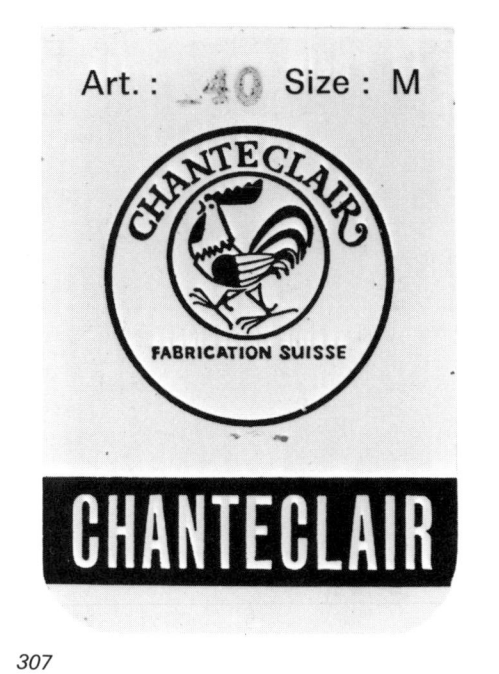

307

305. Oranges. 3 ¹/₄ in. diameter. Rubber plate rotary, 4 colours and gold. Italy, 1970.
306. Tourism. 2 ³/₄ × 2 ³/₄ in. Offset, 3 colours. Switzerland, 1971.
307. Textile. 1 ³/₄ × 2 ³/₈ in. Offset, 2 colours. Switzerland, 1969.
308. Biscuits. 3 ⁹/₁₆ × 3 ¹/₄ in. Rubber plate rotary, 2 colours. England, 20th century.
309. Mustard. 2 ⁹/₁₆ in. diameter. Litho, monochrome. England, 19th century.

305. Oranges. Diam. 8,2 cm. Rotative caoutchouc. quatre coul. et or. Italie, 1970.
306. Tourisme. 7 × 7 cm. Offset trois coul. Suisse, 1971.
307. Textile. 4,4 × 6 cm. Offset deux coul. Suisse, 1969.
308. Biscuits. 9 × 8,2 cm. Rotative caoutchouc deux coul. Angleterre, XXᵉ siècle.
309. Moutarde. Diam. 6,5 cm. Litho une coul. Angleterre, XIXᵉ siècle.

305. Apfelsinen. Durchmesser 8,2 cm. Rotationsmaschine, Gummi, vier Farben und Gold. Italien, 1970.
306. Tourismus. 7 × 7 cm. Offset, drei Farben. Schweiz, 1971.
307. Textilware. 4,4 × 6 cm. Offset, zwei Farben. Schweiz, 1969.
308. Zwieback. 9 × 8,2 cm. Rotationsmaschine, Gummi, zwei Farben. England, XX. Jahrhundert.
309. Senf. Durchmesser 6,5 cm. Lithographie, eine Farbe. England, XIX. Jahrhundert.

308

309

310

311

312

313

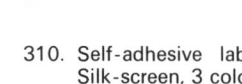

314

310. Self-adhesive label. 3 $5/8$ × 3 $15/16$ in. Silk-screen, 3 colours. International, 1971.
311. Skis. 3 $15/16$ in. diameter. Silk-screen, monochrome. Austria, 1971.
312. Sailing boat. 3 $15/16$ in. diameter. Silk-screen, 3 colours. Printing, P. Terbois, Geneva. International, 1970.
313. Motoring club. 2 $5/8$ × 2 $13/16$ in. Silk-screen, 5 colours. Switzerland, 1970.
314. Beer. 2 $1/8$ × 3 $1/8$ in. Litho, monochrome. England, 19th century.

310. Etiquette autocollante. 9,2 × 10 cm. Sérigraphie trois coul. International, 1971.
311. Skis. Diam. 10 cm. Sérigraphie une coul. Autriche, 1971.
312. Voilier. Diam. 10 cm. Sérigraphie trois coul. Imp. P. Terbois, Genève. International, 1970.
313. Club automobile. 6,6 × 7,2 cm. Sérigraphie cinq coul. Suisse, 1970.
314. Bière. 6,4 × 8 cm. Litho une coul. Angleterre, XIXᵉ siècle.

310. Selbstklebendes Etikett. 9,2 × 10 cm. Siebdruck, drei Farben. International, 1971.
311. Schier. Durchmesser 10 cm. Siebdruck, eine Farbe. Österreich, 1971.
312. Segelschiff. Durchmesser 10 cm. Siebdruck, drei Farben. Druckerei P. Terbois, Genf. International, 1970.
313. Automobilklub. 6,6 × 7,2 cm. Siebdruck, fünf Farben. Schweiz, 1970.
314. Bier. 6,4 × 8 cm. Lithographie, eine Farbe. England, XIX. Jahrhundert.

315

316a

316b

317

315. Matches. 8 $^{13}/_{16}$ × 6 $^{3}/_{8}$ in. Wood engraving, 3 colours. England, 1880.
316a) Cigars. 2 $^{5}/_{8}$ × 1 $^{3}/_{8}$ in. Offset, 4 colours and embossed gold. USA, 1970.
316b) Cigars. 5 $^{13}/_{16}$ × 2 $^{15}/_{16}$ in. Litho, 5 colours and embossed gold. Europe, 1965.
317. Punch. 2 $^{3}/_{4}$ × 2 $^{3}/_{16}$ in. Litho, monochrome. Printing, Holloway & Son, Bristol. England, 1880.
318. Haberdashery. 4 $^{15}/_{16}$ × 7 in. Copper plate engraving, monochrome. England, 1774.
319. Pins. 3 $^{15}/_{16}$ × 6 $^{5}/_{16}$ in. Wood engraving, monochrome. England, 1756.

315. Allumettes. 22,4 × 16,2 cm. Gravure sur bois trois coul. Angleterre, 1880.
316a) Cigares. 6,7 × 3,5 cm. Offset quatre coul. et or gaufré. U.S.A., 1970.
316b) Cigares. 14,7 × 7,5 cm. Litho cinq coul. et or gaufré. Europe, 1965.
317. Punch. 7 × 5,6 cm. Litho une coul. Imp. Holloway & Son, Bristol. Angleterre, 1880.
318. Mercerie. 12,5 × 17,7 cm. Gravure sur cuivre une coul. Angleterre, 1774.
319. Aiguilles. 10 × 16 cm. Gravure sur bois une coul. Angleterre, 1756.

315. Streichhölzer. 22,4 × 16,2 cm. Holzschnitt, drei Farben. England, 1880.
316a) Zigarren. 6,7 × 3,5 cm. Offset, vier Farben und Prägung in Gold. U.S.A., 1970.
316b) Zigarren. 14,7 × 7,5 cm. Lithographie, fünf Farben und Prägung in Gold. Europa, 1965.
317. Punsch. 7 × 5,6 cm. Lithographie, eine Farbe. Druckerei Holloway & Son, Bristol. England, 1880.
318. Kurzwarengeschäft. 12,5 × 17,7 cm. Kupferstich, eine Farbe. England, 1774.
319. Nadeln. 10 × 16 cm. Holzschnitt, eine Farbe. England, 1756.

318

319

320

321

322

323

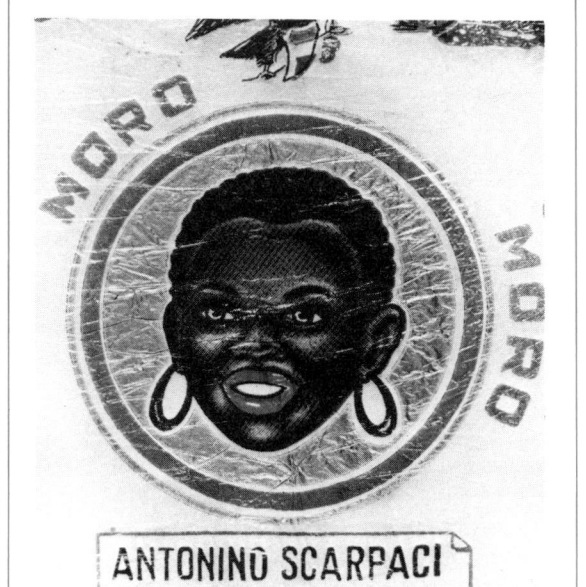

324

320. Ski fasteners. 1 $^9/_{16}$ in. diameter. Silk-screen, 2 colours. France, 1971.
321. Orange drink. 3$^{15}/_{16}$ × 3$^9/_{16}$ in. Letter-press, 4 colours. Design, A. Stankowski, Stuttgart. Germany, 1971.
322. Cigars. 2 $^9/_{16}$ × 2 $^7/_{16}$ in. Offset, 4 colours and gold. USA, 20th century.
323. Self-adhesive label. 5 $^1/_2$ in. diameter. Silk-screen, 4 colours. France, 1971.
324. Oranges. 3 $^9/_{16}$ in. diameter. Rubber plate rotary, 4 colours and gold. Italy, 1969.

320. *Fixations de skis. Diam. 4 cm. Sérigraphie deux coul. France, 1971.*
321. *Limonade. 10 × 9 cm. Typo quatre coul. Créat. A. Stankowski, Stuttgart. Allemagne, 1971.*
322. *Cigares. 6,5 × 6,2 cm. Offset quatre coul. et or. U.S.A., XXe siècle.*
323. *Etiquette autocollante. Diam. 14 cm. Sérigraphie quatre coul. France, 1971.*
324. *Oranges. Diam. 9 cm. Rotative caoutchouc quatre coul. et or. Italie, 1969.*

320. Schibindung. Durchmesser 4 cm. Siebdruck, zwei Farben. Frankreich, 1971.
321. Limonade. 10 × 9 cm. Buchdruck, vier Farben. Urheber: A. Stankowski, Stuttgart. Deutschland, 1971.
322. Zigarren. 6,5 × 6,2 cm. Offset, vier Farben und Gold. U.S.A., XX. Jahrhundert.
323. Selbstklebendes Etikett. Durchmesser 14 cm. Siebdruck, vier Farben. Frankreich, 1971.
324. Apfelsinen. Durchmesser 9 cm. Rotationsmaschine, Gummi, vier Farben und Gold. Italien, 1969.

325

326

327

325. Mineral water. 2 ^{3}/$_{16}$ × 2 ^{13}/$_{16}$ in. Litho,
2 colours. England, 1880.

326. Disinfectant. 1 ^{9}/$_{16}$ in. diameter. Litho,
monochrome, on green paper. England,
1887.

327. Beer. 2 ^{7}/$_8$ × 3 ^{5}/$_8$ in. Litho, monochrome,
on yellow paper. Switzerland, 19th cen-
tury.

328. Hotel. 4 ^{3}/$_4$ × 3 ^{1}/$_4$ in. Litho, monochrome. Belgium, 19th century.

329. Mineral water. 2 ^{1}/$_{16}$ in. diameter. Litho,
monochrome. France, 1880.

325. Eau minérale. 5,6 × 7,2 cm. Litho deux
coul. Angleterre, 1880.

326. Désinfectant. Diam. 4 cm. Litho une coul.,
papier vert. Angleterre, 1887.

327. Bière. 7,3 × 9,2 cm. Litho une coul., papier
jaune. Suisse, XIXe siècle.

328. Hôtel. 12,1 × 8,2 cm. Litho une coul.
Belgique, XIXe siècle.

329. Eau minérale. Diam. 5,3 cm. Litho une coul.
France, 1880.

328

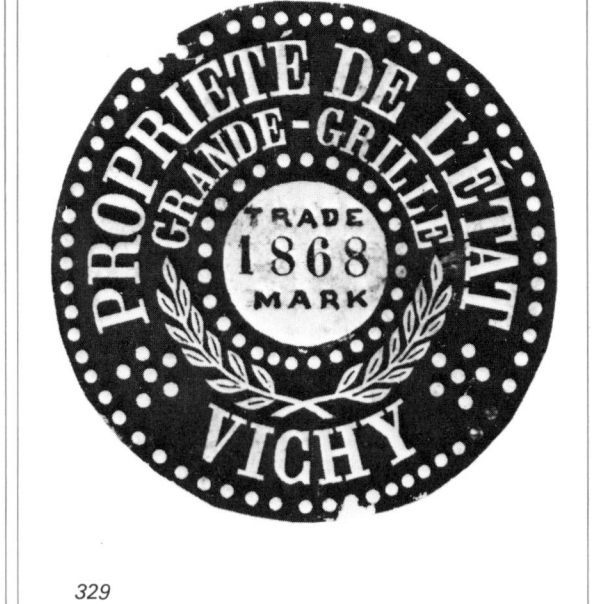

329

325. Mineralwasser. 5,6 × 7,2 cm. Lithographie,
zwei Farben. England, 1880.

326. Desinfektionsmittel. Durchmesser 4 cm.
Lithographie, eine Farbe, grünes Papier.
England, 1887.

327. Bier. 7,3 × 9,2 cm. Lithographie, eine
Farbe, gelbes Papier. Schweiz, XIX. Jahrhundert.

328. Hotel. 12,1 × 8,2 cm. Lithographie, eine
Farbe. Belgien, XIX. Jahrhundert.

329. Mineralwasser. Durchmesser 5,3 cm. Lithographie, eine Farbe. Frankreich, 1880.

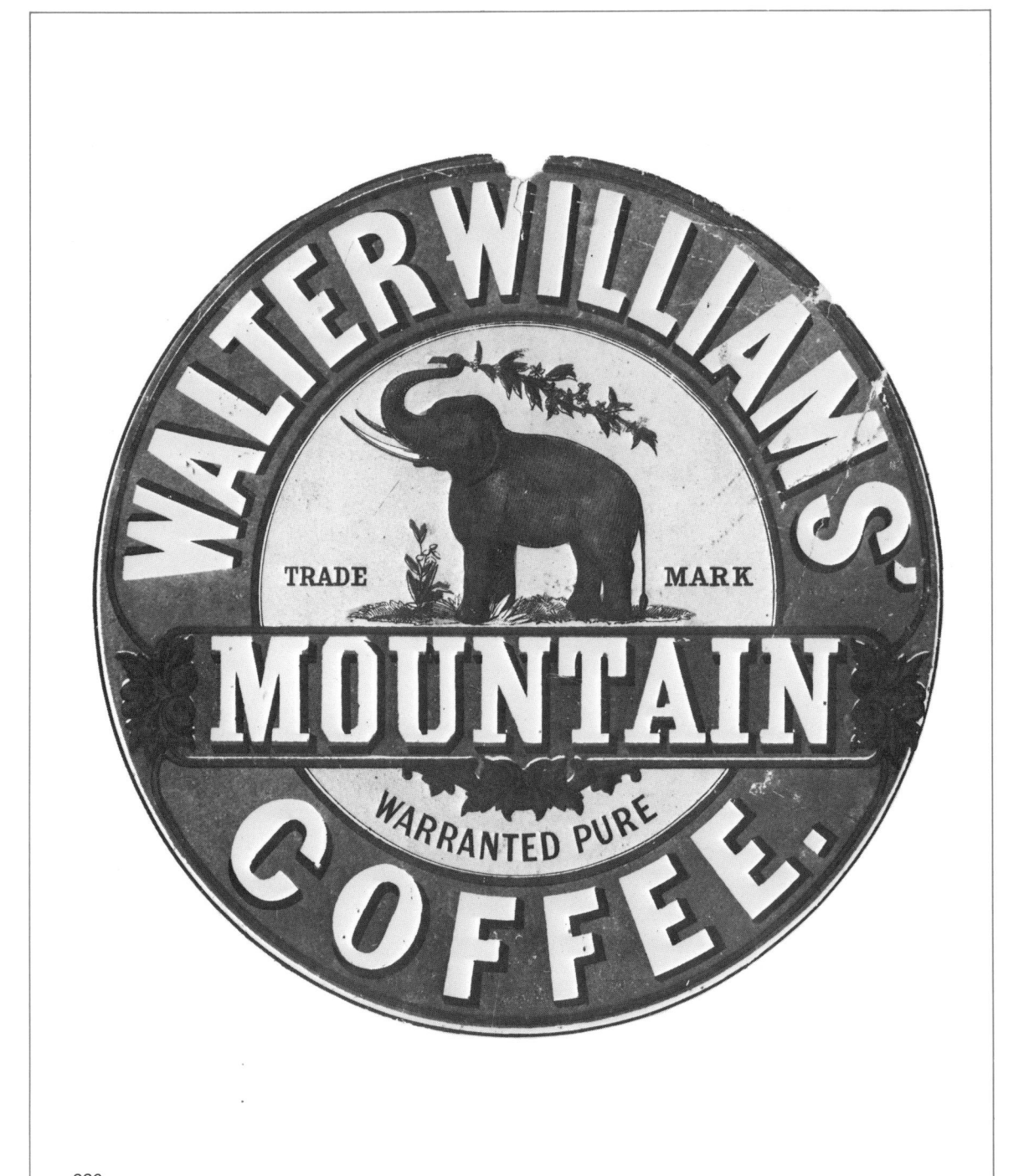

330

330. Coffee. 7 5/16 in. diameter. Litho, 5 colours. England, 1880.

330. Café. Diam. 18,5 cm. Litho cinq coul. Angleterre, 1880.

330. Kaffee. Durchmesser 18,5 cm. Lithographie, fünf Farben. England, 1880.

331

332

333

331. Fish. 4¹/₁₆ × 4¹/₁₆ in. Litho, 4 colours. England, 1880.
332. Self-adhesive label. 6¹⁵/₁₆ × 4⁹/₁₆ in. Silk-screen, 2 colours. Printing, Treuder AG, Zurich. Europe, 1971.
333. Bank. 1⁹/₁₆ × 2¹/₈ in. Litho, 3 colours. Algeria, late 19th century.
334. Scented pastilles. 2⁷/₁₆ × 1⁵/₈ in. Litho, monochrome. England, early 19th century.
335. Textile. 2⁵/₈ in. diameter. Offset, 2 colours. Design, A. Stankowski, Stuttgart. Germany, 1971.

331. Poisson. 10,3 × 10,3 cm. Litho quatre coul. Angleterre, 1880.
332. Etiquette autocollante. 17,6 × 11,6 cm. Sérigraphie deux coul. Imp. Treuder A.G., Zurich. Europe, 1971.
333. Banque. 4 × 5,4 cm. Litho trois coul. Algérie, fin du XIXᵉ siècle.
334. Pastilles parfumées. 6,2 × 4,2 cm. Litho une coul. Angleterre, début du XIXᵉ siècle.
335. Textile. Diam. 6,6 cm. Offset deux coul. Créat. A. Stankowski, Stuttgart. Allemagne, 1971.

334

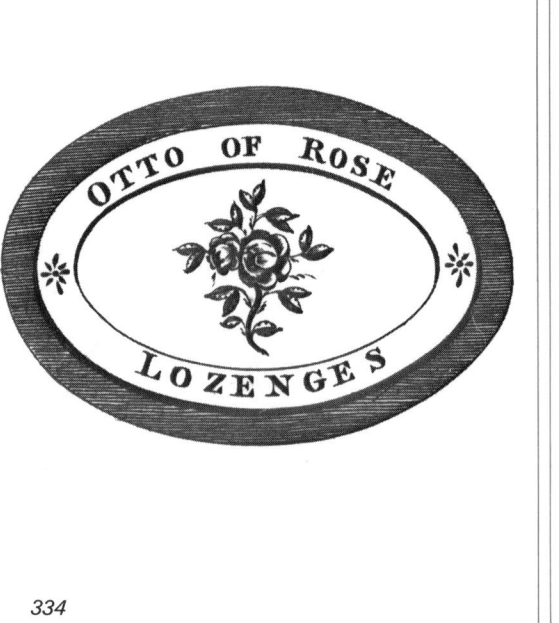

335

331. Fisch. 10,3 × 10,3 cm. Lithographie, vier Farben. England, 1880.
332. Selbstklebendes Etikett. 17,6 × 11,6 cm. Siebdruck, zwei Farben. Druckerei Treuder A.G., Zürich. Europa, 1971.
333. Bank. 4 × 5,4 cm. Lithographie, drei Farben. Algerien, Ende des XIX. Jahrhunderts.
334. Wohlduftende Pastillen. 6,2 × 4,2 cm. Lithographie, eine Farbe. England, Anfang des XIX. Jahrhunderts.
335. Textilware. Durchmesser 6,6 cm. Offset, zwei Farben. Urheber: A. Stankowski, Stuttgart. Deutschland, 1971.

356

357

358

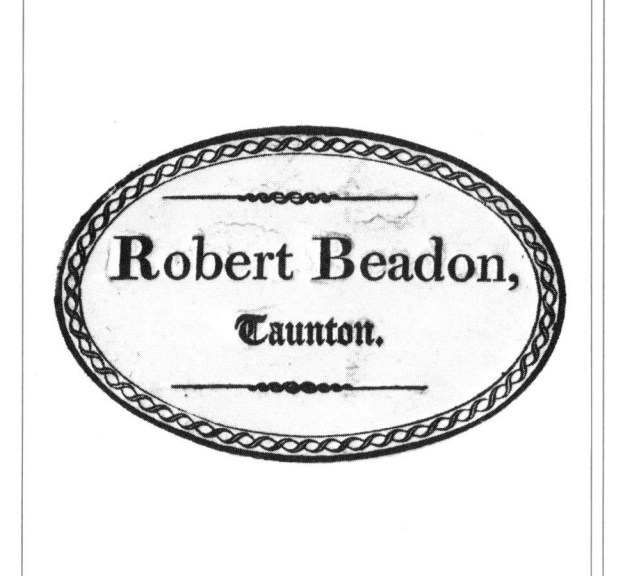

359

360

356. Colouring. 1 15/16 in. diameter. Original design for engraving, France, 19th century.
357. Spirits. 4 1/8 × 5 in. Litho, 5 colours. Switzerland, 1900.
358. Cleansing cream. 2 9/16 in. diameter. Offset, 3 colours. England, early 20th century.
359. Address label. 3 1/4 × 2 1/16 in. Letterpress, monochrome. England, 19th century.
360. Boot polish. 1 15/16 in. diameter. Litho, monochrome. England, 19th century.

356. Couleur. Diam. 4,9 cm. Dessin original de préparation pour la gravure. France, XIXe siècle.
357. Eau-de-vie. 10,4 × 12,6 cm. Litho cinq coul. Suisse, 1900.
358. Démaquillant. Diam. 6,5 cm. Offset trois coul. Angleterre, début du XXe siècle.
359. Etiquette adresse. 8,2 × 5,2 cm. Typo une coul. Angleterre, XIXe siècle.
360. Cirage. Diam. 5 cm. Litho une coul. Angleterre, XIXe siècle.

356. Farbe. Durchmesser 4,9 cm. Originalzeichnung als Gravierungsvorlage. Frankreich, XIX. Jahrhundert.
357. Branntwein. 10,4 × 12,6 cm. Lithographie, fünf Farben. Schweiz, 1900.
358. Abschminkemittel. Durchmesser 6,5 cm. Offset, drei Farben. England, Beginn des XX. Jahrhunderts.
359. Adressenetikett. 8,2 × 5,2 cm. Buchdruck, eine Farbe. England, XIX. Jahrhundert.
360. Schuhcreme. Durchmesser 5 cm. Lithographie, eine Farbe. England, XIX. Jahrhundert.

361

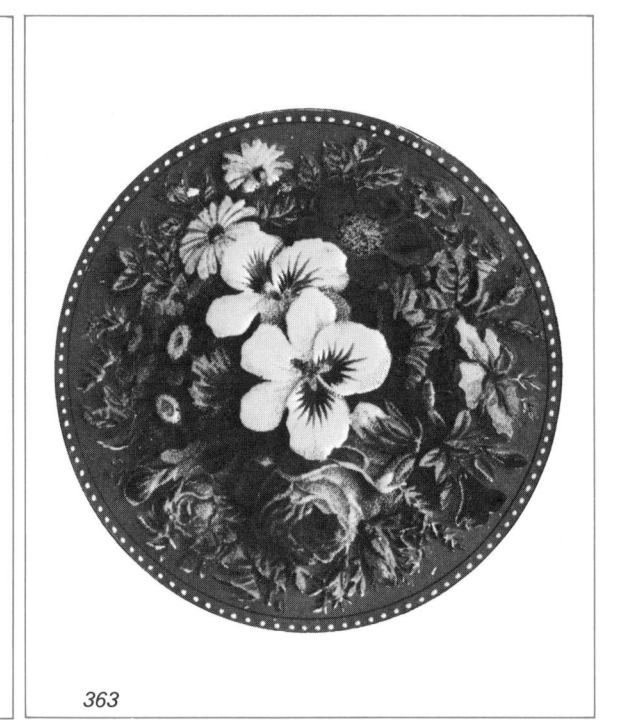

362

363

361. Setting lotion. 1 $^9/_{16}$ in. diameter. Litho, monochrome and embossed gold. France, late 19th century.
362. Cold cream. 2 $^5/_{16}$ in. diameter. Litho, monochrome. England, late 19th century.
363. Sweets. 3 $^1/_8$ in. diameter. Litho, 7 colours and gold. USA, 19th century.
364. Cold cream. 2 $^1/_{16}$ in. diameter. Litho, 2 colours and gold. England, 19th century.
365. Castor oil. 1 $^7/_8$ in. diameter. Copper plate engraving, monochrome. England, 19th century.

361. Fixateur pour les cheveux. Diam. 4 cm. Litho une coul. et or gaufré. France, fin du XIXe siècle.
362. Crème. Diam. 5,9 cm. Litho une coul. Angleterre, fin du XIXe siècle.
363. Bonbons. Diam. 8 cm. Litho sept coul. et or. U.S.A., XIXe siècle.
364. Crème. Diam. 5,3 cm. Litho deux coul. et or. Angleterre, XIXe siècle.
365. Huile de castor. diam. 4,8 cm. Gravure sur cuivre une coul. Angleterre, XIXe siècle.

361. Haarfestiger. Durchmesser 4 cm. Lithographie, eine Farbe und Prägung in Gold. Frankreich, Ende des XIX. Jahrhunderts.
362. Creme. Durchmesser 5,9 cm. Lithographie, eine Farbe. England, Ende des XIX. Jahrhunderts.
363. Bonbons. Durchmesser 8 cm. Lithographie, sieben Farben und Gold. U.S.A., XIX. Jahrhundert.
364. Creme. Durchmesser 5,3 cm. Lithographie, zwei Farben und Gold. England, XIX. Jahrhundert.
365. Biberöl. Durchmesser 4,8 cm. Kupferstich, eine Farbe. England, XIX. Jahrhundert.

364

365

366. Crystallized fruit. 6 $^7/_8$ in. diameter. Litho, black with hand colouring. England, late 19th century.

366. *Bonbons aux fruits. Diam. 17,5 cm. Litho noire coloriée à la main. Angleterre, fin du XIXe siècle.*

366. Früchtebonbons. Durchmesser 17,5 cm. Lithographie, schwarz, handkoloriert. England, Ende des XIX. Jahrhunderts.

366

367

369

367. Linen Drapery. 5 $^5/_8$ × 7 $^1/_4$ in. Copper plate engraving, monochrome. England, 1791.
368. Marital advice bureau. 1 $^5/_{16}$ × 1 $^1/_2$ in. Offset, monochrome. Design, T. Vellve, Barcelona. Spain, 1968.
369. Hosiery. 4 $^{11}/_{16}$ × 6 $^1/_8$ in. Copper plate engraving, monochrome. England, 18th century.
370. Hotel. 4 $^3/_4$ × 3 $^3/_4$ in. Copper plate engraving. 'H. Mutlow fecit.' England, 19th century.
371. Cigarette papers. 1 $^9/_{16}$ × 2 $^3/_4$ in. Litho, monochrome. Italy, early 20th century.

367. Commerce de nouveautés. 14,3 × 18,4 cm. Gravure sur cuivre une coul. Angleterre, 1791.
368. Institut d'orientation matrimoniale. 3,3 × 3,8 cm. Offset une coul. Créat. T. Vellve, Barcelone. Espagne, 1968.
369. Bonneterie. 11,8 × 15,6 cm. Gravure sur cuivre une coul. Angleterre, XVIIIe siècle.
370. Hôtel. 12 × 9,5 cm. Gravure sur cuivre. H. Mutlow fecit. Angleterre, XIXe siècle.
371. Papier à cigarettes. 4 × 7 cm. Litho une coul. Italie, début du XXe siècle.

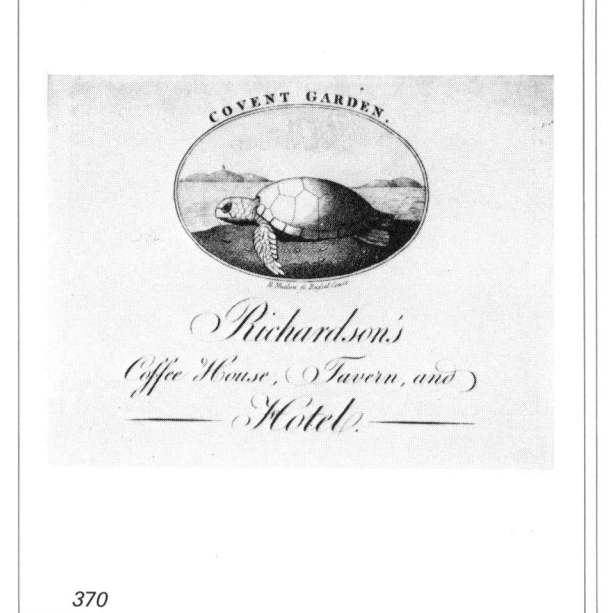

370

371

367. Neuheitenhandel. 14,3 × 18,4 cm. Kupferstich, eine Farbe. England, 1791.
368. Eheberatungsinstitut. 3,3 × 3,8 cm. Offset, eine Farbe. Urheber: T. Vellve, Barcelona. Spanien, 1968.
369. Strumpfwarenhandel. 11,8 × 15,6 cm. Kupferstich, eine Farbe. England, XVIII. Jahrhundert.
370. Hotel. 12 × 9,5 cm. Kupferstich. H. Mutlow fecit. England, XIX. Jahrhundert.
371. Zigarettenpapier. 4 × 7 cm. Lithographie, eine Farbe. Italien, Beginn des XX. Jahrhunderts.

372

373

374

375

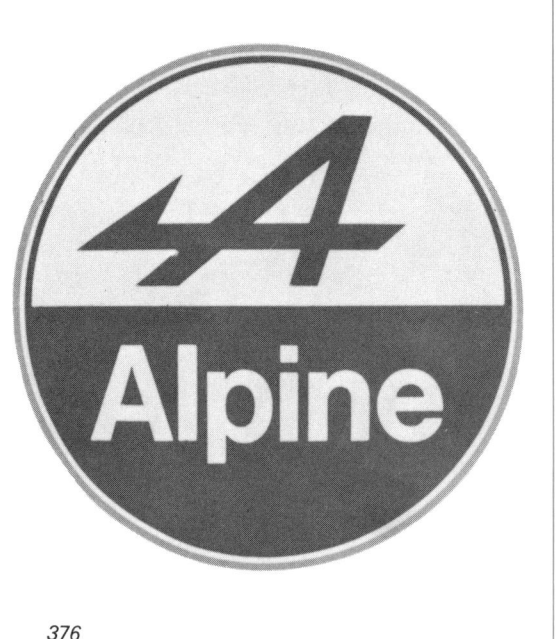

376

372. Soap. 2 $^{11}/_{16}$ × 3 $^{3}/_{4}$ in. Litho, 7 colours. France, 1900.
373. Graphic arts. 1 $^{1}/_{4}$ in. diameter. Offset, monochrome. Design, T. Vellve, Barcelona. Spain, 1969.
374. Tomatoes. 3 $^{15}/_{16}$ in. diameter. Litho, 2 colours. Printing, Mason & Sons, Batavia, New York. USA, early 20th century.
375. Cigars. 2 $^{9}/_{16}$ × 1 $^{13}/_{16}$ in. Litho, 2 colours and gold. Denmark, 20th century.
376. Motor car. 3 $^{13}/_{16}$ in. diameter. Silkscreen, 3 colours. Printing, P. Terbois, Geneva. Europe, 1971.

372. Savon. 6,8 × 9,5 cm. Litho sept coul. France, 1900.
373. Arts graphiques. Diam. 3,2 cm. Offset une coul. Créat. T. Vellve, Barcelone. Espagne, 1969.
374. Tomates. Diam. 10 cm. Litho deux coul. Imp. Mason & Sons, Batavia, New York. U.S.A., début du XXᵉ siècle.
375. Cigares. 6,5 × 4,6 cm. Litho deux coul. et or. Danemark, XXᵉ siècle.
376. Voiture. Diam. 9,7 cm. Sérigraphie trois coul. Imp. P. Terbois, Genève. Europe, 1971.

372. Seife. 6,8 × 9,5 cm. Lithographie, sieben Farben. Frankreich, 1900.
373. Grafik-Design. Durchmesser 3,2 cm. Offset, eine Farbe. Urheber: T. Vellve, Barcelona. Spanien, 1969.
374. Tomaten. Durchmesser 10 cm. Lithographie, zwei Farben. Druckerei Mason & Sons, Batavia, New York. U.S.A., Beginn des XX. Jahrhunderts.
375. Zigarren. 6,5 × 4,6 cm. Lithographie, zwei Farben und Gold. Dänemark, XX. Jahrhundert.
376. Wagen. Durchmesser 9,7 cm. Siebdruck, drei Farben. Druckerei P. Terbois, Genf. Europa, 1971.

377

378

379

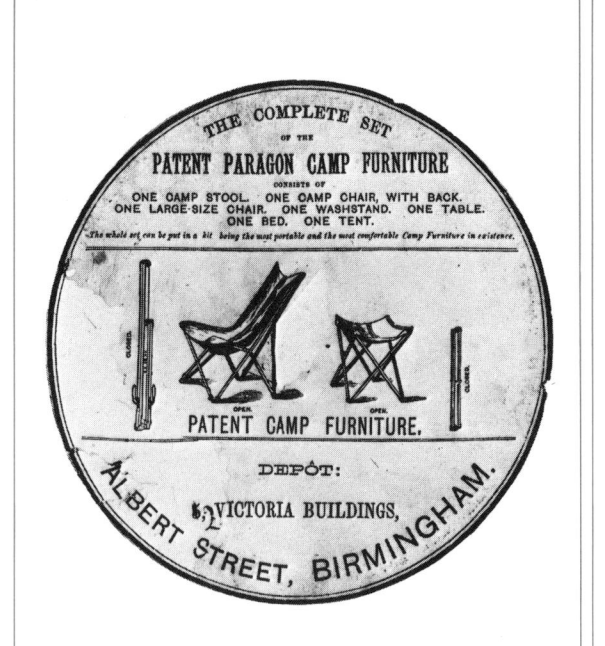

380

381

377. Chemical products.   3 × 1 ³/₈ in.   Silk-screen, monochrome.   Printing, P. Terbois, Geneva.   International, 1970.
378. Tourism.   6 ¹¹/₁₆ × 4 ⁹/₁₆ in.   Silk-screen, 3 colours.   Printing, Treuder AG, Zurich. Switzerland, 1971.
379. Energy food.   8 ⁷/₈ × 5 ¹⁵/₁₆ in.   Litho, 3 colours.   England, 19th century.
380. Camp furniture.   6 ⁹/₁₆ in. diameter.   Litho, monochrome.   England, 19th century.
381. Jewellers.   3 ¹¹/₁₆ × 2 ¹/₂ in.   Copper plate engraving, monochrome.   England, 1790–1793.

377. Produits chimiques.   7,6 × 3,5 cm.   Sérigraphie une coul.   Imp. P. Terbois, Genève. International, 1970.
378. Tourisme.   17 × 11,5 cm.   Sérigraphie trois coul.   Imp. Treuder A.G., Zurich.   Suisse, 1971.
379. Fortifiant.   22,5 × 15 cm.   Litho trois coul. Angleterre, XIXᵉ siècle.
380. Meubles de camping.   Diam. 16,6 cm. Litho une coul.   Angleterre, XIXᵉ siècle.
381. Bijouterie-joaillerie.   9,3 × 6,3 cm.   Gravure sur cuivre une coul.   Angleterre, 1790-1793.

377. Chemische Erzeugnisse.   7,6 × 3,5 cm.   Siebdruck, eine Farbe.   Druckerei P. Terbois, Genf.   International, 1970.
378. Tourismus.   17 × 11,5 cm.   Siebdruck, drei Farben.   Druckerei Treuder A.G., Zürich. Schweiz, 1971.
379. Stärkungsmittel.   22,5 × 15 cm.   Lithographie, drei Farben.   England, XIX. Jahrhundert.
380. Campingmöbel.   Durchmesser 16,6 cm. Lithographie, eine Farbe.   England, XIX. Jahrhundert.

381. Schmuck- und Juwelhändler.   9,3 × 6,3 cm. Kupferstich, eine Farbe.   England, 1790–1793.

382

383

384

385

386

382. Tonic drink. 2 ³/₄ in. diameter. Litho, 3 colours. England, 1900.
383. Wine. 5 × 3 ⁷/₁₆ in. Litho, gold, on black paper. Switzerland, 19th century.
384. Oranges. 2 ⁹/₁₆ in. diameter. Rubber plate rotary, monochrome and gold. Spain, 1969.
385. Public meeting. 1 ⁷/₈ in. diameter. Litho, monochrome. USA, 1907.
386. Hotel. 5 ¹³/₁₆ × 4 ⁹/₁₆ in. Litho, 4 colours. Printing, Bonniers. Sweden, 1900.

382. *Boisson tonique. Diam. 7 cm. Litho trois coul. Angleterre, 1900.*
383. *Vin. 12,7 × 8,7 cm. Litho or, papier noir. Suisse, XIXe siècle.*
384. *Oranges. Diam. 6,5 cm. Rotative caoutchouc une coul. et or. Espagne, 1969.*
385. *Meeting. Diam. 4,7 cm. Litho une coul. U.S.A., 1907.*
386. *Hôtel. 14,8 × 11,5 cm. Litho quatre coul. Imp. Bonniers. Suède, 1900.*

382. Stärkungsgetränk. Durchmesser 7 cm. Lithographie, drei Farben. England, 1900.
383. Wein. 12,7 × 8,7 cm. Lithographie, Gold, schwarzes Papier. Schweiz, XIX. Jahrhundert.
384. Apfelsinen. Durchmesser 6,5 cm. Rotationsmaschine, Gummi, eine Farbe und Gold. Spanien, 1969.
385. Versammlung. Durchmesser 4,7 cm. Lithographie, eine Farbe. U.S.A., 1907.
386. Hotel. 14,8 × 11,5 cm. Lithographie, vier Farben. Druckerei Bonniers. Schweden, 1900.

387

388

389

390

391

387. Ex-libris. 2 ¹/₂ × 2 ¹/₂ in. Letterpress, monochrome. England, 1900.
388. Cognac. 4 ³/₄ × 4 ¹⁵/₁₆ in. Litho, 6 colours. Printing, Pichot, Paris. France, 1930.
389. Emery powder. 3 ⁹/₁₆ × 4 ¹/₂ in. Litho, monochrome and gold. England, early 20th century.
390. Alpaca. 5 ¹⁵/₁₆ × 8 ⁵/₁₆ in. Litho, monochrome embossed. England, late 19th century.
391. Laundry-blue. 4 ³/₈ × 7 in. Litho, monochrome and gold. England, late 19th century.

387. Ex-libris. 6,3 × 6,3 cm. Typo une coul. Angleterre, 1900.
388. Cognac. 12 × 12,5 cm. Litho six coul. Imp. Pichot, Paris. France, 1930.
389. Poudre d'émeri. 9 × 11,4 cm. Litho une coul. et or. Angleterre, début du XXᵉ siècle.
390. Alpaca. 15 × 21 cm. Litho une coul. gaufrée. Angleterre, fin du XIXᵉ siècle.
391. Bleu pour lessive. 11 × 17,7 cm. Litho une coul. et or. Angleterre, fin du XIXᵉ siècle.

387. Exlibris. 6,3 × 6,3 cm. Buchdruck, eine Farbe. England, 1900.
388. Kognak. 12 × 12,5 cm. Lithographie, sechs Farben. Druckerei Pichot, Paris. Frankreich, 1930.
389. Poliersand. 9 × 11,4 cm. Lithographie, eine Farbe und Gold. England, Beginn des XX. Jahrhunderts.
390. Alpaka. 15 × 21 cm. Lithographie, eine Farbe, Prägung. England, Ende des XIX. Jahrhunderts.
391. Waschblau. 11 × 17,7 cm. Lithographie, eine Farbe und Gold. England, Ende des XIX. Jahrhunderts.

392

393

394

395

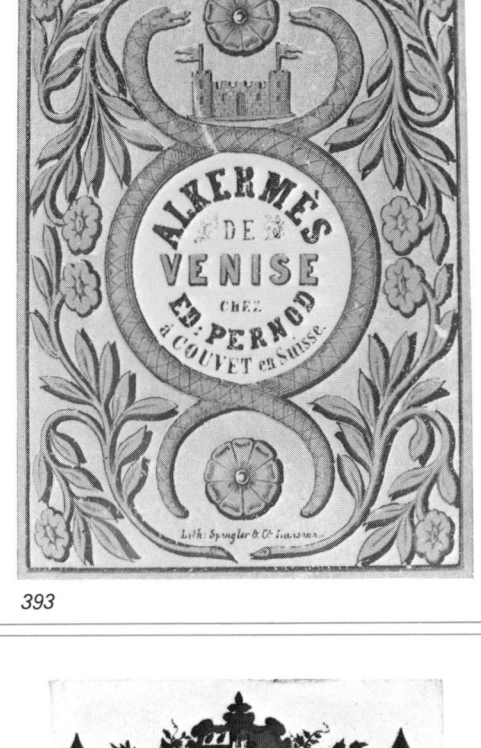

396

392. Vermouth. 4 $^1/_4$ × 5 $^7/_{16}$ in. Litho, 3 colours and gold. Switzerland-Italy, 1965.
393. Liqueur. 2 $^{15}/_{16}$ × 3 $^7/_8$ in. Litho, 3 colours. Printing, Spengler & Co., Lausanne. Switzerland, 19th century.
394. Ex-libris. 1 $^5/_8$ × 2 $^9/_{16}$ in. Letterpress, monochrome. England, 1900.
395. Paper. 7 $^7/_{16}$ × 10 $^7/_{16}$ in. Litho, 2 colours. England, 20th century.
396. Gingerwine. 3 $^5/_{16}$ × 5 in. Litho, 2 colours and gold. Printing, Le Blond & Co., London. England, 19th century.

392. Vermouth. 10,8 × 13,8 cm. Litho trois coul. et or. Suisse-Italie, 1965.
393. Liqueur. 7,4 × 9,8 cm. Litho trois coul. Imp. Spengler & Cie, Lausanne. Suisse, XIXe siècle.
394. Ex-libris. 4,2 × 6,5 cm. Typo une coul. Angleterre, 1900.
395. Papier. 18,8 × 26,4 cm. Litho deux coul. Angleterre, XXe siècle.
396. Vin au gingembre. 8,3 × 12,6 cm. Litho deux coul. et or. Imp. Le Blond & Co., Londres. Angleterre, XIXe siècle.

392. Wermut. 10,8 × 13,8 cm. Lithographie, drei Farben und Gold. Schweiz-Italien, 1965.
393. Likör. 7,4 × 9,8 cm. Lithographie, drei Farben. Druckerei Spengler & Co., Lausanne. Schweiz, XIX. Jahrhundert.
394. Exlibris. 4,2 × 6,5 cm. Buchdruck, eine Farbe. England, 1900.
395. Papier. 18,8 × 26,4 cm. Lithographie, zwei Farben. England, XX. Jahrhundert.
396. Ingwerwein. 8,3 × 12,6 cm. Lithographie, zwei Farben und Gold. Druckerei Le Blond & Co., London. England, XIX. Jahrhundert.

397

398

399

400

401

397. Robes. 4 $^{11}/_{16}$ × 6 $^5/_{16}$ in.   Copper plate engraving, monochrome.   England, 18th century.
398. Textile. 2 $^{15}/_{16}$ × 3 $^3/_4$ in.   Copper plate engraving, monochrome.   England, 19th century.
399. Shoes. 6 $^{11}/_{16}$ × 7 $^9/_{16}$ in.   Copper plate engraving, monochrome.   England, 1758.
400. Rosewater. 1 $^{11}/_{16}$ × 2 $^3/_8$ in.   Litho, monochrome.   England, 19th century.
401. Optician. 4 $^9/_{16}$ × 6 $^1/_2$ in.   Copper plate engraving, monochrome.   England, 18th century.

397. Robes. 11,8 × 16 cm. Gravure sur cuivre une coul. Angleterre, XVIIIe siècle.
398. Textile. 7,5 × 9,5 cm. Gravure sur cuivre une coul. Angleterre, XIXe siècle.
399. Chaussures. 17 × 19,2 cm. Gravure sur cuivre une coul. Angleterre, 1758.
400. Eau de rose. 4,3 × 6 cm. Litho une coul. Angleterre, XIXe siècle.
401. Opticien. 11,5 × 16,5 cm. Gravure sur cuivre une coul. Angleterre, XVIIIe siècle.

397. Kleider. 11,8 × 16 cm. Kupferstich, eine Farbe. England, XVIII. Jahrhundert.
398. Textilware. 7,5 × 9,5 cm. Kupferstich, eine Farbe. England, XIX. Jahrhundert.
399. Schuhe. 17 × 19,2 cm. Kupferstich, eine Farbe. England, 1758.
400. Rosenwasser. 4,3 × 6 cm. Lithographie, eine Farbe. England, XIX. Jahrhundert.
401. Optiker. 11,5 × 16,5 cm. Kupferstich, eine Farbe. England, XVIII. Jahrhundert.

402

403

404

405

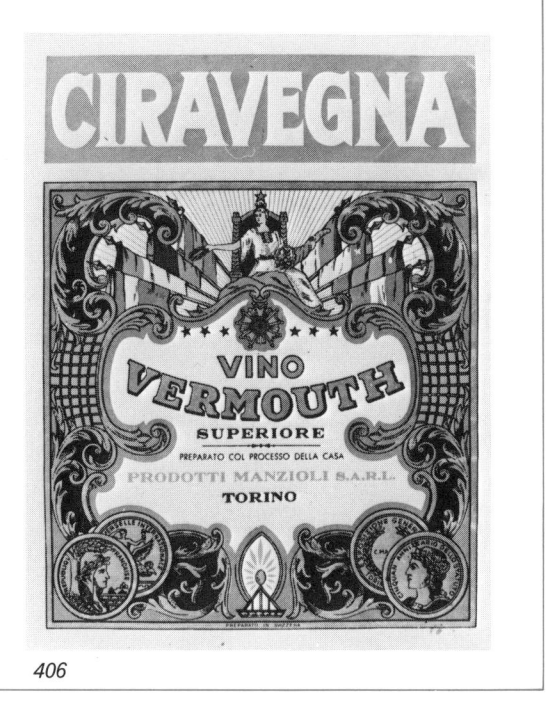

406

402. Tea. 7 ³/₁₆ × 11 ¹/₄ in. Litho, mono-chrome, on grey paper. Belgium, early 19th century.
403. China and glassware. 5 ¹/₂ × 6 ⁷/₈ in. Copper plate engraving, monochrome. England, 18th century.
404. Polishing powder. 3 ⁹/₁₆ × 4 ¹/₂ in. Litho, monochrome and gold. England, 1930–1940.
405. Bird cages. 5 ¹/₈ × 7 ¹/₈ in. Copper plate engraving, monochrome. England, 18th century.
406. Vermouth. 4 ¹/₂ × 5 ¹³/₁₆ in. Offset, 4 colours and gold. Italy, 1970.

402. *Thé. 18,2 × 28,5 cm. Litho une coul., papier gris. Belgique, début du XIXe siècle.*
403. *Porcelaine et verrerie. 14 × 17,5 cm. Gravure sur cuivre une coul. Angleterre, XVIIIe siècle.*
404. *Poudre à polir. 9 × 11,4 cm. Litho une coul. et or. Angleterre, 1930-1940.*
405. *Cages à oiseaux. 13 × 18 cm. Gravure sur cuivre une coul. Angleterre, XVIIIe siècle.*
406. *Vermouth. 11,4 × 14,8 cm. Offset quatre coul. et or. Italie, 1970.*

402. Tee. 18,2 × 28,5 cm. Lithographie, eine Farbe, graues Papier. Belgien, Beginn des XIX. Jahrhunderts.
403. Porzellangeschirr und Glaswaren. 14 × 17,5 cm. Kupferstich, eine Farbe. England, XVIII. Jahrhundert.
404. Poliersand. 9 × 11,4 cm. Lithographie, eine Farbe und Gold. England, 1930–1940.
405. Vogelkäfige. 13 × 18 cm. Kupferstich, eine Farbe. England, XVIII. Jahrhundert.
406. Wermut. 11,4 × 14,8 cm. Offset, vier Farben und Gold. Italien, 1970.

407

408

409

407. Cigarette papers. 2 $^{15}/_{16}$ × 1 $^9/_{16}$ in. Litho, monochrome. France, early 20th century.
408. Sherry. 4 $^1/_{16}$ × 3 $^1/_8$ in. Litho, monochrome. England, 20th century.
409. Salad oil. 2 $^3/_8$ × 1 $^9/_{16}$ in. Litho, monochrome. England, 19th century.
410. Wine. 4 $^1/_8$ × 3 $^5/_8$ in. Litho, 4 colours. Design, Gerstung. Germany, 1936–1937.
411. Self-adhesive label. 5 $^7/_8$ × 4 $^1/_8$ in. Offset, 2 colours. Design, Publistar. France, 1971.

407. Papier à cigarettes. 7,5 × 4 cm. Litho une coul. France, début du XXe siècle.
408. Sherry. 10,3 × 7,9 cm. Litho une coul. Angleterre, XXe siècle.
409. Huile pour salade. 6 × 4 cm. Litho une coul. Angleterre, XIXe siècle.
410. Vin. 10,4 × 9,2 cm. Litho quatre coul. Créat. Gerstung. Allemagne, 1936-1937.
411. Etiquette autocollante. 14,9 × 10,5 cm. Offset deux coul. Créat. Publistar. France, 1971.

407. Zigarettenpapier. 7,5 × 4 cm. Lithographie, eine Farbe. Frankreich, Beginn des XX. Jahrhunderts.
408. Sherry. 10,3 × 7,9 cm. Lithographie, eine Farbe. England, XX. Jahrhundert.
409. Salatöl. 6 × 4 cm. Lithographie, eine Farbe. England, XIX. Jahrhundert.
410. Wein. 10,4 × 9,2 cm. Lithographie, vier Farben. Urheber: Gerstung. Deutschland, 1936–1937.
411. Selbstklebendes Etikett. 14,9 × 10,5 cm. Offset, zwei Farben. Urheber: Publistar. Frankreich, 1971.

410

411

412

413

414

415

416

412. Wine. 4 $^{13}/_{16}$ × 3 $^{1}/_{16}$ in. Litho, monochrome and gold. Printing, Zimmerman, Mainz. Greece, 19th century.
413. Jeans. 4 $^{1}/_{8}$ × 3 $^{11}/_{16}$ in. Offset, 2 colours and gold. USA, 1968.
414. Liqueur. 4 $^{1}/_{4}$ × 2 $^{5}/_{8}$ in. Litho, 5 colours. Switzerland, 19th century.
415. Goan arrack. 4 $^{1}/_{8}$ × 2 $^{9}/_{16}$ in. Litho, gold. Germany, 19th century.
416. Liqueur. 3 $^{7}/_{8}$ × 2 $^{1}/_{2}$ in. Litho, 4 colours. Switzerland, 19th century.

412. *Vin. 12,2 × 7,7 cm. Litho une coul. et or. Imp. Zimmerman, Mayence. Grèce, XIXe siècle.*
413. *Pantalons. 10,4 × 9,4 cm. Offset deux coul. et or. U.S.A., 1968.*
414. *Liqueur. 10,8 × 6,6 cm. Litho cinq coul. Suisse, XIXe siècle.*
415. *Arac de Goa. 10,4 × 6,5 cm. Litho or. Allemagne, XIXe siècle.*
416. *Liqueur. 9,8 × 6,3 cm. Litho quatre coul. Suisse, XIXe siècle.*

412. Wein. 12,2 × 7,7 cm. Lithographie, eine Farbe und Gold. Druckerei Zimmerman, Mainz. Griechenland, XIX. Jahrhundert.
413. Hosen. 10,4 × 9,4 cm. Offset, zwei Farben und Gold. U.S.A., 1968.
414. Likör. 10,8 × 6,6 cm. Lithographie, fünf Farben. Schweiz, XIX. Jahrhundert.
415. Arrak aus Goa. 10,4 × 6,5 cm. Lithographie, Gold. Deutschland, XIX. Jahrhundert.
416. Likör. 9,8 × 6,3 cm. Lithographie, vier Farben. Schweiz, XIX. Jahrhundert.

417

418

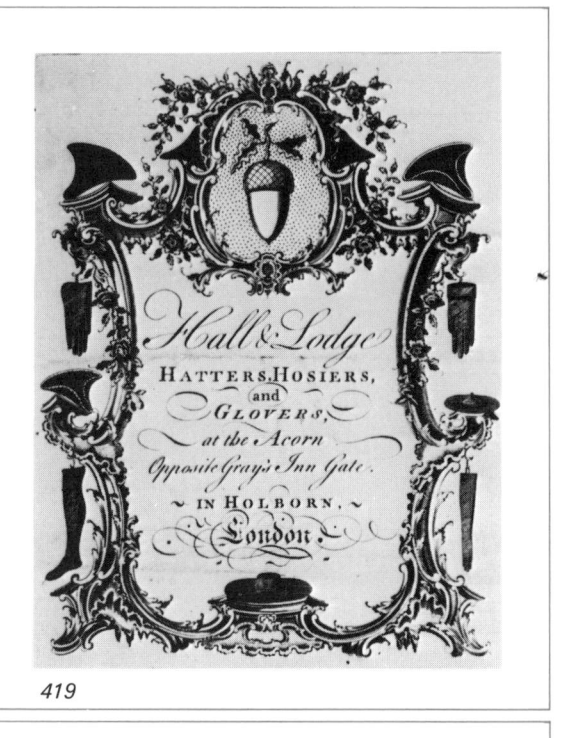

419

417. Organs. 5 ¹/₂ × 7 ¹/₈ in.   Copper plate engraving, monochrome.   'W. Darling fecit.' England, 1780.

418. Gift label.   2 ⁹/₁₆ × 2 ⁹/₁₆ in.   Offset, 4 colours.   Design and printing, A.B.C., Zurich.   Switzerland, 1971.

419. Hatters.   6 ⁵/₁₆ × 7 ⁷/₈ in.   Copper plate engraving, monochrome.   England, 1760.

420. Perfume. 1 ¹⁵/₁₆ × 2 ⁷/₁₆ in.   Litho, 3 colours and gold.   England, 19th century.

421. Groceries.   4 ¹⁵/₁₆ × 6 ¹/₂ in.   Copper plate engraving, monochrome.   Engraved by B. Coler.   England, 18th century.

417. Orgues. 14 × 18 cm. Gravure sur cuivre une coul. W. Darling fecit. Angleterre, 1780.

418. Etiquette pour cadeaux. 6,5 × 6,5 cm. Offset quatre coul. Créat. imp. A.B.C., Zurich. Suisse, 1971.

419. Chapellerie. 16 × 20 cm. Gravure sur cuivre une coul. Angleterre, 1760.

420. Parfum. 5 × 6,2 cm. Litho trois coul. et or. Angleterre, XIXᵉ siècle.

421. Epicerie. 12,5 × 16,5 cm. Gravure sur cuivre une coul. B. Coler sculptist. Angleterre, XVIIIᵉ siècle.

417. Orgeln. 14 × 18 cm. Kupferstich, eine Farbe. W. Darling fecit. England, 1780.

418. Geschenketikett. 6,5 × 6,5 cm. Offset, vier Farben. Urheber: Druckerei A.B.C., Zürich. Schweiz, 1971.

419. Hutmacherei. 16 × 20 cm. Kupferstich, eine Farbe. England, 1760.

420. Parfüm. 5 × 6,2 cm. Lithographie, drei Farben und Gold. England, XIX. Jahrhundert.

421. Lebensmittelgeschäft. 12,5 × 16,5 cm. Kupferstich, eine Farbe. Gestochen von B. Coler. England, XVIII. Jahrhundert.

420

421

422

ESSENCE
OF
VERBENA.

A DELICATE

APPENDAGE FOR

THE TOILET.

423

424

425

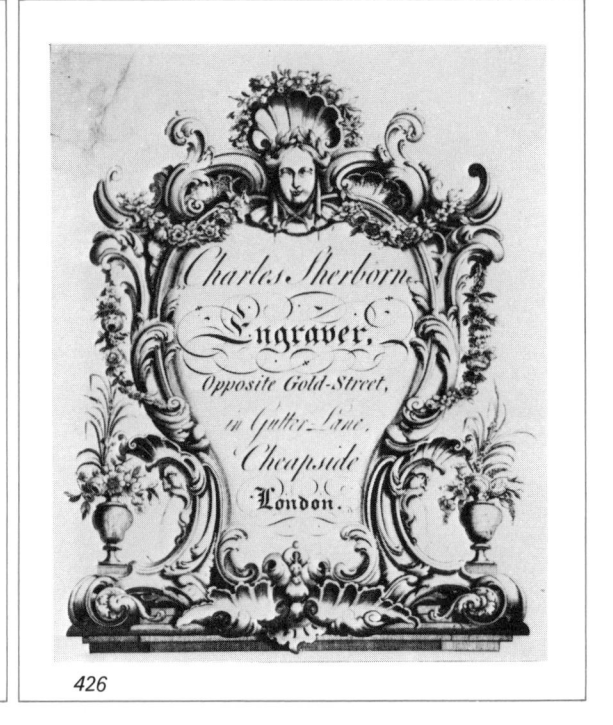

426

422. Brushes. $5\,5/16 \times 6\,13/16$ in. Copper plate engraving. England, 18th century.
423. Toilet water. $2\,3/16 \times 1\,7/16$ in. Litho, monochrome, on violet paper. England, 1930–1940.
424. Laces and silks. $5\,5/16 \times 6\,7/8$ in. Copper plate engraving, monochrome. England, 1765.
425. Rum. $3\,5/16 \times 4\,3/16$ in. Litho, 3 colours. Printing, Valnet, Besançon. France, 19th century.
426. Engraver. $5\,1/8 \times 5\,15/16$ in. Copper plate engraving, monochrome. England, 1760.

422. Brosses. 13,4 × 17,2 cm. Gravure sur cuivre une coul. Angleterre, XVIIIᵉ siècle.
423. Eau de toilette. 5,5 × 3,6 cm. Litho une coul., papier violet. Angleterre, 1930-1940.
424. Dentelles, soieries. 13,5 × 17,5 cm. Gravure sur cuivre une coul. Angleterre, 1765.
425. Rhum. 8,3 × 10,6 cm. Litho trois coul. Imp. Valnet, Besançon. France, XIXᵉ siècle.
426. Graveur. 13 × 15 cm. Gravure sur cuivre une coul. Angleterre, 1760.

422. Bürsten. 13,4 × 17,2 cm. Kupferstich, eine Farbe. England, XVIII. Jahrhundert.
423. Gesichtswasser. 5,5 × 3,6 cm. Lithographie, eine Farbe, violettes Papier. England, 1930–1940.
424. Spitzen- und Kantenwaren. 13,5 × 17,5 cm. Kupferstich, eine Farbe. England, 1765.
425. Rum. 8,3 × 10,6 cm. Lithographie, drei Farben. Druckerei Valnet, Besançon. Frankreich, XIX. Jahrhundert.
426. Bildstecher. 13 × 15 cm. Kupferstich, eine Farbe. England, 1760.

427

428

429

427. Blacklead. 3 1/16 × 4 15/16 in. Offset, 2 colours. England, 1935.
428. Starch. 2 1/4 × 4 in. Litho, monochrome, on ochre paper. England, 1900.
429. Vermouth. 3 9/16 × 6 in. Offset, 3 colours and gold. Design, Raul Rand, New York. USA, 1942.
430. Playing cards. 3 3/4 × 10 1/4 in. Copper plate engraving, monochrome. England, 18th century.
431. Oranges. 3 3/8 × 3 15/16 in. Rubber plate rotary, 2 colours. Spain, 1970.

427. *Plombs. 7,8 × 12,5 cm. Offset deux coul. Angleterre, 1935.*
428. *Amidon. 5,7 × 10,2 cm. Litho une coul., papier ocre. Angleterre, 1900.*
429. *Vermouth. 9 × 15,2 cm. Offset trois coul. et or. Créat. Raul Rand, New York. U.S.A., 1942.*
430. *Cartes à jouer. 9,5 × 26 cm. Gravure sur cuivre une coul. Angleterre, XVIIIe siècle.*
431. *Oranges. 8,5 × 10 cm. Rotative caoutchouc deux coul. Espagne, 1970.*

427. Bleisiegel. 7,8 × 12,5 cm. Offset, zwei Farben. England, 1935.
428. Stärke. 5,7 × 10,2 cm. Lithographie, eine Farbe, ockerfarbenes Papier. England, 1900.
429. Wermut. 9 × 15,2 cm. Offset, drei Farben und Gold. Urheber: Paul Rand, New York. U.S.A., 1942.
430. Spielkarten. 9,5 × 26 cm. Kupferstich, eine Farbe. England, XVIII. Jahrhundert.
431. Apfelsinen. 8,5 × 10 cm. Rotationsmaschine, Gummi, zwei Farben. Spanien, 1970.

430

431

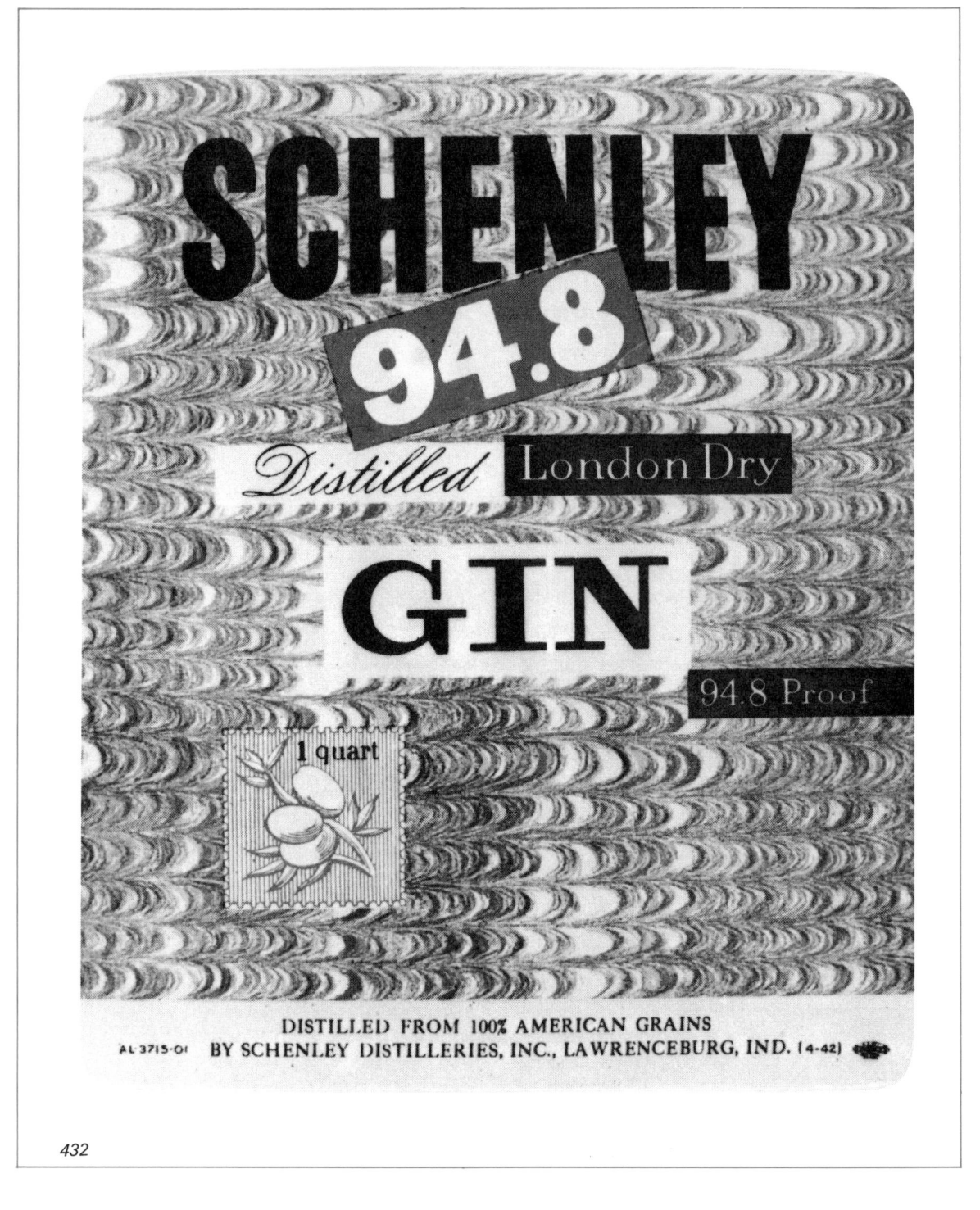

432

432. Gin. 4 × 4⁵/₈ in. Litho, 5 colours. Design, Paul Rand, New York. USA, 1942.

432. Gin. 10,1 × 11,7 cm. Litho cinq coul. Créat. Paul Rand, New York. U.S.A., 1942.

432. Gin. 10,1 × 11,7 cm. Lithographie, fünf Farben. Urheber: Paul Rand, New York. U.S.A., 1942.

433

434

435

433. Soap. 6 $^{13}/_{16}$ × 3 $^{5}/_{8}$ in. Litho, 2 colours and gold. France, 1900.
434. Cigarette papers. 2 $^{13}/_{16}$ × 1 $^{5}/_{8}$ in. Litho, gold. France, early 20th century.
435. Pomade hair dressing. 4 $^{3}/_{4}$ × 2 $^{5}/_{8}$ in. Copper plate engraving, monochrome. France, 19th century.
436. Jam. 4 $^{3}/_{8}$ × 2 $^{11}/_{16}$ in. Litho, monochrome. Design, Lowell. England, 19th century.
437. Chocolate. 5 $^{5}/_{16}$ × 2 $^{1}/_{2}$ in. Litho, 2 colours. England, 1900.

433. Savon. 17,2 × 9,2 cm. Litho deux coul. et or. France, 1900.
434. Papier à cigarettes. 7,2 × 4,2 cm. Litho or. France, début du XXᵉ siècle.
435. Pommade pour les cheveux. 12 × 6,7 cm. Gravure sur cuivre une coul. France, XIXᵉ siècle.
436. Confiture. 11 × 6,8 cm. Litho une coul. Créat. Lowell. Angleterre, XIXᵉ siècle.
437. Chocolat. 13,5 × 6,3 cm. Litho deux coul. Angleterre, 1900.

433. Seife. 17,2 × 9,2 cm. Lithographie, zwei Farben und Gold. Frankreich, 1900.
434. Zigarettenpapier. 7,2 × 4,2 cm. Lithographie, Gold. Frankreich, Beginn des XX. Jahrhunderts.
435. Haarsalbe. 12 × 6,7 cm. Kupferstich, eine Farbe. Frankreich, XIX. Jahrhundert.
436. Marmelade. 11 × 6,8 cm. Lithographie, eine Farbe. Urheber: Lowell. England, XIX. Jahrhundert.
437. Schokolade. 13,5 × 6,3 cm. Lithographie, zwei Farben. England, 1900.

436

437

438

439

440

441

442

438. Matches. 2 ³/₁₆ × 1 ¹/₂ in. Litho, 2 colours. Japan, 19th century.
439. Spirits. 6 ³/₄ × 2 ¹¹/₁₆ in. Litho, 2 colours and gold. Germany, 19th century.
440. Spirits. 4 ⁵/₁₆ × 2 ¹⁵/₁₆ in. Litho, 3 colours. Switzerland, 19th century.
441. Spirits. 3 ⁷/₈ × 3 ¹/₁₆ in. Litho, monochrome and gold, with rubber-stamped type. Germany, 19th century.
442. Textile. 4 ¹⁵/₁₆ × 3 ¹⁵/₁₆ in. Litho, 2 colours and gold. England, 19th century.

438. Allumettes. 5,6 × 3,8 cm. Litho deux coul. Japon, XIXᵉ siècle.
439. Alcool. 17,1 × 6,8 cm. Litho deux coul. et or. Allemagne, XIXᵉ siècle.
440. Eau-de-vie. 10,9 × 7,4 cm. Litho trois coul. Suisse, XIXᵉ siècle.
441. Eau-de-vie. 9,8 × 7,8 cm. Litho une coul. et or, caractère au tampon caoutchouc. Allemagne, XIXᵉ siècle.
442. Textile. 12,5 × 10 cm. Litho deux coul. et or. Angleterre, XIXᵉ siècle.

438. Streichhölzer. 5,6 × 3,8 cm. Lithographie, zwei Farben. Japan, XIX. Jahrhundert.
439. Alkohol. 17,1 × 6,8 cm. Lithographie, zwei Farben und Gold. Deutschland, XIX. Jahrhundert.
440. Branntwein. 10,9 × 7,4 cm. Lithographie, drei Farben. Schweiz, XIX. Jahrhundert.
441. Branntwein. 9,8 × 7,8 cm. Lithographie, eine Farbe und Gold, Gummistempel-Letter. Deutschland, XIX. Jahrhundert.
442. Textilware. 12,5 × 10 cm. Lithographie, zwei Farben und Gold. England, XIX. Jahrhundert.

443

444

445

446

447

443. Ginger wine. 3 $^9/_{16}$ × 4 $^3/_8$ in. Litho, 4 colours. England, late 19th century.
444. Textile. 2 $^{15}/_{16}$ × 4 $^1/_8$ in. Litho, 5 colours and embossing. England, early 19th century.
445. Hair oil. 2 $^7/_8$ × 4 $^1/_8$ in. Litho, 3 colours and gold. England, late 19th century.
446. Ink. 3 $^1/_{16}$ × 3 $^1/_{16}$ in. Litho, monochrome. England, 19th century.
447. Bookseller. 4 $^1/_2$ × 6 $^7/_8$ in. Copper plate engraving, monochrome. England, late 17th century.

443. Vin. 9 × 11,1 cm. Litho quatre coul. Angleterre, fin du XIXe siècle.
444. Textile. 7,5 × 10,5 cm. Litho cinq coul., gaufrage. Angleterre, début du XIXe siècle.
445. Huile pour cheveux. 7,3 × 10,5 cm. Litho trois coul. et or. Angleterre, fin du XIXe siècle.
446. Encre. 7,7 × 7,8 cm. Litho une coul. Angleterre, XIXe siècle.
447. Librairie. 11,3 × 17,4 cm. Gravure sur cuivre une coul. Angleterre, fin du XVIIe siècle.

443. Wein. 9 × 11,1 cm. Lithographie, vier Farben. England, Ende des XIX. Jahrhunderts.
444. Textilware. 7,5 × 10,5 cm. Lithographie, fünf Farben, Prägung. England, Beginn des XIX. Jahrhunderts.
445. Haaröl. 7,3 × 10,5 cm. Lithographie, drei Farben und Gold. England, Ende des XIX. Jahrhunderts.
446. Tinte. 7,7 × 7,8 cm. Lithographie, eine Farbe. England, XIX. Jahrhundert.
447. Buchhandlung. 11,3 × 17,4 cm. Kupferstich, eine Farbe. England, Ende des XVII. Jahrhunderts.

448

449

450

451

452

448. Fans. 4 $^{13}/_{16}$ × 6 $^{11}/_{16}$ in. Copper plate engraving, monochrome. England, 18th century.
449. Matches. 1 $^{7}/_{16}$ × 2 $^{3}/_{16}$ in. Litho, 4 colours. England, early 20th century.
450. Breeches. 4 $^{9}/_{16}$ × 6 $^{5}/_{16}$ in. Copper plate engraving, monochrome. England, 18th century.
451. Mustard. 4 $^{3}/_{8}$ × 9 $^{1}/_{16}$ in. Litho, 2 colours. England, 1894.
452. Pewterer. 2 $^{9}/_{16}$ × 3 $^{7}/_{16}$ in. Copper plate engraving, monochrome. England, 1746.

448. Eventails. 12,2 × 17 cm. Gravure sur cuivre une coul. Angleterre, XVIIIe siècle.
449. Allumettes. 3,6 × 5,6 cm. Litho quatre coul. Angleterre, début du XXe siècle.
450. Culottes. 11,6 × 16 cm. Gravure sur cuivre une coul. Angleterre, XVIIIe siècle.
451. Moutarde. 11 × 23 cm. Litho deux coul. Angleterre, 1894.
452. Fabricant d'objets en étain. 6,5 × 8,7 cm. Gravure sur cuivre une coul. Angleterre, 1746.

448. Fächer. 12,2 × 17 cm. Kupferstich, eine Farbe. England, XVIII. Jahrhundert.
449. Streichhölzer. 3,6 × 5,6 cm. Lithographie, vier Farben. England, Beginn des XX. Jahrhunderts.
450. Kniehosen. 11,6 × 16 cm. Kupferstich, eine Farbe. England, XVIII. Jahrhundert.
451. Senf. 11 × 23 cm. Lithographie, zwei Farben. England, 1894.
452. Zinnwarenhersteller. 6,5 × 8,7 cm. Kupferstich, eine Farbe. England, 1746.

453

454

455

453. Wine. 3 $^9/_{16}$ × 1 $^3/_4$ in. Litho, 3 colours. France, 19th century.
454. Trunks. 5 $^{15}/_{16}$ × 7 $^1/_2$ in. Copper plate engraving, monochrome. England, 1762.
455. Ink-powder. 4 $^{11}/_{16}$ × 2 $^5/_{16}$ in. Copper plate engraving. England, late 18th century.
456. Cigars. 2 $^3/_8$ × $^{11}/_{16}$ in. Litho, 2 colours. Spain, 20th century.
457. Wine. 3 $^1/_4$ × 1 $^{15}/_{16}$ in. Litho, gold, on black paper. France, 19th century.

453. Vin. 9 × 4,5 cm. Litho trois coul. France, XIXe siècle.
454. Coffres. 15 × 19 cm. Gravure sur cuivre une coul. Angleterre, 1762.
455. Encre en poudre. 11,8 × 5,9 cm. Gravure sur cuivre. Angleterre, fin du XVIIIe siècle.
456. Cigares. 6 × 1,7 cm. Litho deux coul. Espagne, XXe siècle.
457. Vin. 8,2 × 4,9 cm. Litho or, papier noir. France, XIXe siècle.

453. Wein. 9 × 4,5 cm. Lithographie, drei Farben. Frankreich, XIX. Jahrhundert.
454. Kästen. 15 × 19 cm. Kupferstich, eine Farbe. England, 1762.
455. Tintenpulver. 11,8 × 5,9 cm. Kupferstich. England, Ende des XVIII. Jahrhunderts.
456. Zigarren. 6 × 1,7 cm. Lithographie, zwei Farben. Spanien, XX. Jahrhundert.
457. Wein. 8,2 × 4,9 cm. Lithographie, Gold, schwarzes Papier. Frankreich, XIX. Jahrhundert.

456

457

458

459

460

461

462

458. Whisky. 4 $^7/_{16}$ × 3 $^1/_{16}$ in. Litho, monochrome and gold. England, 19th century.
459. Pins. 2 $^3/_8$ × 5 $^3/_4$ in. Litho, monochrome. England, 18th century.
460. Cigarette papers. 3 $^1/_8$ × 2 $^1/_8$ in. Litho, monochrome and gold. France, early 20th century.
461. Perfume. 1 $^{15}/_{16}$ × 1 $^{11}/_{16}$ in. Litho, 4 colours. France, 1900.
462. Coffins. 4 $^3/_8$ × 6 $^1/_{16}$ in. Copper plate engraving, monochrome. England, 18th century.

458. Whisky. 11,2 × 7,8 cm. Litho une coul. et or. Angleterre, XIXe siècle.
459. Epingles. 6 × 14,5 cm. Litho une coul. Angleterre, XVIIIe siècle.
460. Papier à cigarettes. 8 × 5,4 cm. Litho une coul. et or. France, début du XXe siècle.
461. Parfums. 5 × 4,3 cm. Litho quatre coul. France, 1900.
462. Cercueils. 11 × 15,4 cm. Gravure sur cuivre une coul. Angleterre, XVIIIe siècle.

458. Whisky. 11,2 × 7,8 cm. Lithographie, eine Farbe und Gold. England, XIX. Jahrhundert.
459. Nadeln. 6 × 14,5 cm. Lithographie, eine Farbe. England, XVIII. Jahrhundert.
460. Zigarettenpapier. 8 × 5,4 cm. Lithographie, eine Farbe und Gold. Frankreich, Beginn des XX. Jahrhunderts.
461. Parfüme. 5 × 4,3 cm. Lithographie, vier Farben. Frankreich, 1900.
462. Särge. 11 × 15,4 cm. Kupferstich, eine Farbe. England, XVIII. Jahrhundert.

463

464

465

466

467

463. Woollen goods. 4 $^{15}/_{16}$ × 6 $^9/_{16}$ in. Copper plate engraving, monochrome. England, 18th century.
464. Confectionery. 6 $^1/_4$ × 9 in. Litho, 2 colours. England, 1900.
465. Upholsterer. 5 $^1/_2$ × 7 $^{11}/_{16}$ in. Copper plate engraving, monochrome. England, 1770–1772.
466. Armagnac brandy. 3¾ × 5½ in. Litho, 2 colours, on buff paper. Printing, Guthrie. France, 1935.
467. Furs. 5 $^1/_2$ × 7 $^1/_8$ in. Copper plate engraving, monochrome. England, 1754.

463. Lainages. 12,5 × 16,7 cm. Gravure sur cuivre. Angleterre, XVIIIe siècle.
464. Confiserie. 15,8 × 22,8 cm. Litho deux coul. Angleterre, 1900.
465. Tapissier. 14 × 19,5 cm. Gravure sur cuivre une coul. Angleterre, 1770-1772.
466. Armagnac. 9,5 × 14 cm. Litho deux coul., papier chamois. Imp. Guthrie. France, 1935.
467. Fourrure. 14 × 18 cm. Gravure sur cuivre une coul. Angleterre, 1754.

463. Wollwaren. 12,5 × 16,7 cm. Kupferstich. England, XVIII. Jahrhundert.
464. Konditoreiware. 15,8 × 22,8 cm. Lithographie, zwei Farben. England, 1900.
465. Polsterer. 14 × 19,5 cm. Kupferstich, eine Farbe. England, 1770–1772.
466. Armagnac. 9,5 × 14 cm. Lithographie, zwei Farben, Chamois-Papier. Druckerei Guthrie. Frankreich, 1935.
467. Pelzware. 14 × 18 cm. Kupferstich, eine Farbe. England, 1754.

468

469

470

471

472

468. Clothing. 4 3/4 × 6 1/8 in. Copper plate engraving, monochrome. Engraved by B. Cole. England, 18th century.
469. Silk. 4 7/8 × 5 5/8 in. Litho, 4 colours. Printing, Guardian, Manchester. England, 1900.
470. Confectionery. 4 3/4 × 6 1/2 in. Copper plate engraving, monochrome. Engraved by James Wigler. England, 1748.
471. Paper. 6 7/8 × 7 1/8 in. Wood engraving, monochrome. England, 1885.
472. Gloves. 4 15/16 × 5 15/16 in. Copper plate engraving, monochrome. England, 1772.

468. *Vêtements. 12 × 15,5 cm. Gravure sur cuivre une coul. B. Cole sculptist. Angleterre, XVIIIe siècle.*
469. *Soie. 12,4 × 14,2 cm. Litho quatre coul. Imp. Guardian, Manchester. Angleterre, 1900.*
470. *Confiserie. 12 × 16,5 cm. Gravure sur cuivre une coul. James Wigler, graveur. Angleterre, 1748.*
471. *Papier. 17,5 × 18 cm. Gravure sur bois une coul. Angleterre, 1885.*
472. *Gants. 12,5 × 15 cm. Gravure sur cuivre une coul. Angleterre, 1772.*

468. Kleider. 12 × 15,5 cm. Kupferstich, eine Farbe. Gestochen von B. Coler. England, XVIII. Jahrhundert.
469. Seide. 12,4 × 14,2 cm. Lithographie, vier Farben. Druckerei Guardian, Manchester. England, 1900.
470. Konditoreiware. 12 × 16,5 cm. Kupferstich, eine Farbe. Stecher James Wigler. England, 1748.
471. Papier. 17,5 × 18 cm. Holzschnitt, eine Farbe. England, 1885.
472. Handschuhe. 12,5 × 15 cm. Kupferstich, eine Farbe. England, 1772.

473

474

475

476

477

478

479

480

473. Postcards. 2 ³/₁₆ × 3 ¹/₂ in. Letterpress, monochrome. England, 20th century.
474. Envelopes. 5 × 1 ¹/₂ in. Litho, 2 colours. England, 1860.
475. Wine. 4 ¹/₈ × 1 ³/₁₆ in. Litho, gold on black paper. France, 19th century.
476. Laundry-blue. 5 ¹/₄ × 5 ¹/₄ in. Litho, 4 colours. France, 19th century.
477. Cigarette papers. 2 ¹¹/₁₆ × ⁷/₈ in. Litho, monochrome and gold. Italy, early 20th century.
478. Cigars. 2 ³/₈ × ¹¹/₁₆ in. Offset, 2 colours. Holland, 20th century.
479. Writing paper. 5 × 1 ¹/₂ in. Litho, 2 colours. England, 1860.
480. Envelopes. 5 ⁵/₈ × 2 ¹/₁₆ in. Litho, 2 colours and embossing. England, 1890.

473. Cartes postales. 5,5 × 8,8 cm. Typo une coul. Angleterre, XXᵉ siècle.
474. Enveloppes. 12,6 × 3,8 cm. Litho deux coul. Angleterre, 1860.
475. Vin. 10,4 × 3,1 cm. Litho or, papier noir. France, XIXᵉ siècle.
476. Bleu pour lessive. 13,3 × 13,3 cm. Litho quatre coul. France, XIXᵉ siècle.
477. Papier à cigarettes. 6,8 × 2,3 cm. Litho une coul. et or. Italie, début du XXᵉ siècle.
478. Cigares. 6 × 1,7 cm. Offset deux coul. Hollande, XXᵉ siècle.
479. Papier à lettre. 12,6 × 3,8 cm. Litho deux coul. Angleterre, 1860.
480. Enveloppes. 14,2 × 5,2 cm. Litho deux coul., gaufrage. Angleterre, 1890.

473. Postkarten. 5,5 × 8,8 cm. Buchdruck, eine Farbe. England, XX. Jahrhundert.
474. Umschläge. 12,6 × 3,8 cm. Lithographie, zwei Farben. England, 1860.
475. Wein. 10,4 × 3,1 cm. Lithographie, Gold, schwarzes Papier. Frankreich, XIX. Jahrhundert.

476. Waschblau. 13,3 × 13,3 cm. Lithographie, vier Farben. Frankreich, XIX. Jahrhundert.
477. Zigarettenpapier. 6,8 × 2,3 cm. Lithographie, eine Farbe und Gold. Italien, Beginn des XX. Jahrhunderts.
478. Zigarren. 6 × 1,7 cm. Offset, zwei Farben. Holland, XX. Jahrhundert.
479. Briefpapier. 12,6 × 3,8 cm. Lithographie, zwei Farben. England, 1860.
480. Umschläge. 14,2 × 5,2 cm. Lithographie, zwei Farben, Prägung. England, 1890.

481

482

483

484

485

481. Cotton. 1 ³/₈ × 1 ³/₈ in. Litho, monochrome, on cream paper. England, 19th century.
482. Paste-board maker. 4 ¹/₂ × 6 ⁵/₁₆ in. Copper plate engraving, monochrome. England, 1761–1762.
483. Beer. 3 ¹/₈ × 2 ³/₁₆ in. Offset, 4 colours. Italy, 1969.
484. Optician. 3 ⁵/₈ × 2 ¹/₂ in. Copper plate engraving, monochrome. 'Dawson fecit.' England, late 18th century.
485. Cutler. 3 ¹⁵/₁₆ × 6 ⁵/₁₆ in. Copper plate engraving. England, 1740.

481. *Coton. 3,5 × 3,5 cm. Litho une coul., papier crème. Angleterre, XIXe siècle.*
482. *Cartonnier. 11,3 × 16 cm. Gravure sur cuivre une coul. Angleterre, 1761-1762.*
483. *Bière. 8 × 5,5 cm. Offset quatre coul. Italie, 1969.*
484. *Opticien. 9,2 × 6,3 cm. Gravure sur cuivre une coul. Dawson fecit. Angleterre, fin du XVIIIe siècle.*
485. *Coutelier. 10 × 16 cm. Gravure sur cuivre une coul. Angleterre, 1740.*

481. Baumwolle. 3,5 × 3,5 cm. Lithographie, eine Farbe, cremefarbenes Papier. England, XIX. Jahrhundert.
482. Pappwarenhersteller. 11,3 × 16 cm. Kupferstich, eine Farbe. England, 1761–1762.
483. Bier. 8 × 5,5 cm. Offset, vier Farben. Italien, 1969.
484. Optiker. 9,2 × 6,3 cm. Kupferstich, eine Farbe. Dawson fecit. England, Ende des XVIII. Jahrhunderts.
485. Messerschmied. 10 × 16 cm. Kupferstich, eine Farbe. England, 1740.

486

487

488

486. Writing paper. 4 $^1/_8$ × 6 $^{11}/_{16}$ in. Litho, 3 colours. England, 1900.
487. Ribbons. 3 $^1/_{16}$ × 6 $^{11}/_{16}$ in. Litho, 3 colours, on yellow paper. India, 19th century.
488. Rice starch. 4 $^3/_{16}$ × 5 $^3/_8$ in. Litho, 7 colours. England, late 19th century.
489. Textile. 3 $^1/_8$ × 4 in. Litho, 6 colours and embossed gold. England, 19th century.
490. Cigarette papers. 1 $^7/_8$ × 1 $^{11}/_{16}$ in. Litho, 2 colours and embossed gold. Spain, early 20th century.

486. *Papier à lettre. 10,5 × 17 cm. Litho trois coul. Angleterre, 1900.*
487. *Rubans. 7,7 × 16,9 cm. Litho trois coul., papier jaune. Inde, XIXe siècle.*
488. *Amidon de riz. 10,6 × 13,6 cm. Litho sept coul. Angleterre, fin du XIXe siècle.*
489. *Textile. 8 × 10,2 cm. Litho six coul. et or gaufré. Angleterre, XIXe siècle.*
490. *Papier à cigarettes. 4,8 × 4,3 cm. Litho deux coul. et or gaufré. Espagne, début du XXe siècle.*

486. Briefpapier. 10,5 × 17 cm. Lithographie, drei Farben. England, 1900.
487. Bänder. 7,7 × 16,9 cm. Lithographie, drei Farben, gelbes Papier. Indien, XIX. Jahrhundert.
488. Reisstärke. 10,6 × 13,6 cm. Lithographie, sieben Farben. England, Ende des XIX. Jahrhunderts.
489. Textilware. 8 × 10,2 cm. Lithographie, sechs Farben und Prägung in Gold. England, XIX. Jahrhundert.
490. Zigarettenpapier. 4,8 × 4,3 cm. Lithographie, zwei Farben und Prägung in Gold. Spanien, Beginn des XX. Jahrhunderts.

489

490

William Smith

Grocer,

AT

The Sugar Loaf in Aldersgate Street

LONDON

Sells all Sorts of Grocery with Teas, Coffee, Chocolate,

Snuff, Poland and Common Starch, and Tobacco,&c.

at the lowest Prices.

491

491. Grocery. 4 $\frac{15}{16}$ × 6 $\frac{7}{8}$ in. Copper plate engraving, monochrome. England, 18th century.

491. *Epicerie. 12,5 × 17,5 cm. Gravure sur cuivre une coul. Angleterre, XVIIIe siècle.*

491. Lebensmittelgeschäft. 12,5 × 17,5 cm. Kupferstich, eine Farbe. England, XVIII. Jahrhundert.

492

493

494

492. Pencils. 5 $^3/_4$ × 4 $^1/_8$ in. Litho, mono-chrome. Printing, Darling & Robinson, Newport & London. England, 1793.
493. Stove tiles. 2 $^{15}/_{16}$ × 4 $^{11}/_{16}$ in. Litho, 3 colours. Printing, Le Blond & Co., London. England, 1900.
494. Wine. 3 $^9/_{16}$ × 1 $^3/_4$ in. Litho, 3 colours. France, 19th century.
495. Jewellers. 5 $^5/_{16}$ × 6 $^{11}/_{16}$ in. Copper plate engraving, monochrome. England, 1734.
496. Soap. 3 $^{15}/_{16}$ × 3 $^{15}/_{16}$ in. Litho, 2 colours and gold. France, 1900.

492. Crayons. 14,5 × 10,5 cm. Litho une coul. Darling & Robinson fecit, Newport & London. Angleterre, 1793.
493. Carrelage pour poêles. 7,4 × 11,8 cm. Litho trois coul. Imp. Le Blond & Co., Londres. Angleterre, 1900.
494. Vin. 9 × 4,5 cm. Litho trois coul. France, XIXe siècle.
495. Joaillerie. 13,5 × 17 cm. Gravure sur cuivre une coul. Angleterre, 1734.
496. Savon. 10 × 8,3 cm. Litho deux coul. et or. France, 1900.

492. Bleistifte. 14,5 × 10,5 cm. Lithographie, eine Farbe. Darling & Robinson fecit, Newport & London. England, 1793.
493. Ofenkacheln. 7,4 × 11,8 cm. Lithographie, drei Farben. Druckerei Le Blond & Co., London. England, 1900.
494. Wein. 9 × 4,5 cm. Lithographie, drei Farben. Frankreich, XIX. Jahrhundert.
495. Juwelier. 13,5 × 17 cm. Kupferstich, eine Farbe. England, 1734.
496. Seife. 10 × 8,3 cm. Lithographie, zwei Farben und Gold. Frankreich, 1900.

495

496

497

498

499

500

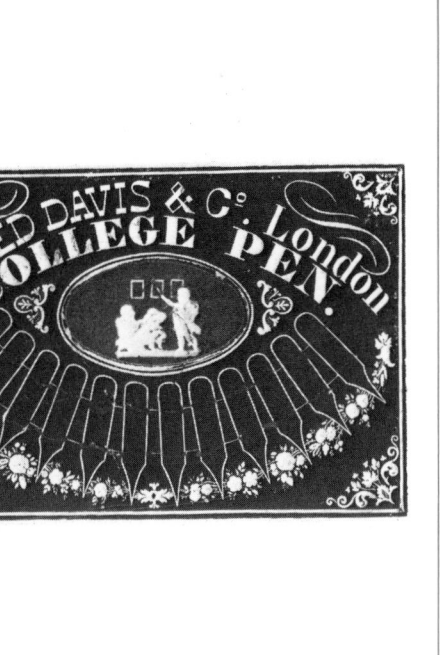

501

497. Champagne. 3 $^5/_8$ × 4 $^3/_8$ in. Litho, 4 colours. France, 1930.
498. Gingerbread. 4 $^3/_4$ × 3 $^1/_{16}$ in. Litho, 4 colours. Printing, Courbe-Rouget, Dôle. France, 19th century.
499. Ex-libris. 1 $^9/_{16}$ × 2 $^3/_8$ in. Letterpress, monochrome. England, 1900.
500. Shoes. 5 $^1/_2$ × 2 $^3/_8$ in. Litho, monochrome. England, 1860–1870.
501. Pens. 6 $^{11}/_{16}$ × 4 $^3/_4$ in. Litho, 2 colours and embossing. England, 19th century.

497. Champagne. 9,2 × 11 cm. Litho quatre coul. France, 1930.
498. Pain d'épices. 12 × 7,8 cm. Litho quatre coul. Imp. Courbe-Rouget, Dôle. France, XIXe siècle.
499. Ex-libris. 4 × 6,1 cm. Typo une coul. Angleterre, 1900.
500. Chaussures. 14 × 6 cm. Litho une coul. Angleterre, 1860-1870.
501. Plumes à écrire. 17 × 12 cm. Litho deux coul., gaufrage. Angleterre, XIXe siècle.

497. Champagner. 9,2 × 11 cm. Lithographie, vier Farben. Frankreich, 1930.
498. Lebkuchen. 12 × 7,8 cm. Lithographie, vier Farben. Druckerei Courbe-Rouget, Dôle. Frankreich, XIX. Jahrhundert.
499. Exlibris. 4 × 6,1 cm. Buchdruck, eine Farbe. England, 1900.
500. Schuhe. 14 × 6 cm. Lithographie, eine Farbe. England, 1860–1870.
501. Schreibfedern. 17 × 12 cm. Lithographie, zwei Farben, Prägung. England, XIX. Jahrhundert.

502

503

504

502. Jewellery. 4 $\frac{1}{8}$ × 6 $\frac{1}{2}$ in. Copper plate engraving, monochrome. England, 1750.

503. Stationery. 5 $\frac{13}{16}$ × 5 $\frac{3}{4}$ in. Litho, hand-coloured. England, 1860.

504. Buttons. 4 $\frac{3}{8}$ × 6 $\frac{1}{8}$ in. Copper plate engraving, monochrome. England, 18th century.

505. Cigarette papers. 1 $\frac{13}{16}$ × 1 $\frac{3}{4}$ in. Litho, monochrome, on pink paper. Spain, early 20th century.

506. Copper plate maker. 6 $\frac{11}{16}$ × 5 $\frac{5}{16}$ in. Copper plate engraving, monochrome. Engraved by H. Shepherd. England, early 19th century.

502. Bijouterie-joaillerie. 10,5 × 16,5 cm. Gravure sur cuivre une coul. Angleterre, 1750.

503. Papeterie. 14,8 × 14,6 cm. Litho coloriée à la main. Angleterre, 1860.

504. Boutons. 11 × 15,6 cm. Gravure sur cuivre. Angleterre, XVIIIe siècle.

505. Papier à cigarettes. 4,6 × 4,4 cm. Litho une coul. papier rose. Espagne, début du XXe siècle.

506. Graveur. 17 × 13,5 cm. Gravure sur cuivre une coul. H. Shepherd scripsit et sculptist. Angleterre, début du XIXe siècle.

502. Schmuck- und Juwelhändler. 10,5 × 16,5 cm. Kupferstich, eine Farbe. England, 1750.

503. Papiergeschäft. 14,8 × 14,6 cm. Lithographie, handkoloriert. England, 1860.

504. Knöpfe. 11 × 15,6 cm. Kupferstich. England, XVIII. Jahrhundert.

505. Zigarettenpapier. 4,6 × 4,4 cm. Lithographie, eine Farbe, Rosapapier. Spanien, Beginn des XX. Jahrhunderts.

506. Bildstecher. 17 × 13,5 cm. Kupferstich, eine Farbe. Geschrieben und gestochen von H. Shepherd. England, Beginn des XIX. Jahrhunderts.

505

506

507

508

509

510

511

512

507. Wine. 4 $\frac{1}{8}$ × 2 $\frac{1}{2}$ in. Litho, monochrome. Switzerland, 1863.
508. Watchmaker. 4 $\frac{15}{16}$ × 6 in. Copper plate engraving, monochrome. England, 1775.
509. Liqueur. 4 $\frac{9}{16}$ × 2 $\frac{3}{16}$ in. Litho, monochrome. France, 19th century.
510. Pewterer. 6 $\frac{7}{8}$ × 6 $\frac{1}{16}$ in. Copper plate engraving, monochrome. Engraved by J. Wigley. England, 1777.
511. Cigars. 2 $\frac{1}{2}$ × 1 $\frac{3}{16}$ in. Litho, monochrome and embossed gold. Mexico, 20th century.
512. Cigars. 2 $\frac{1}{2}$ × $\frac{7}{8}$ in. Offset, 3 colours and embossed gold. Europe, 20th century.

507. Vin. 10,4 × 6,3 cm. Litho une coul. Suisse, 1863.
508. Horlogerie. 12,5 × 15,2 cm. Gravure sur cuivre une coul. Angleterre, 1775.
509. Liqueur. 11,6 × 5,5 cm. Litho une coul. France, XIXe siècle.
510. Plats en étain. 17,5 × 15,4 cm. Gravure sur cuivre. J. Wigley sculptist. Angleterre, 1777.
511. Cigares. 6,3 × 3 cm. Litho une coul. et or gaufré. Mexique, XXe siècle.
512. Cigares. 6,3 × 2,3 cm. Offset trois coul. et or gaufré. Europe, XXe siècle.

507. Wein. 10,4 × 6,3 cm. Lithographie, eine Farbe. Schweiz, 1863.
508. Uhrengeschäft. 12,5 × 15,2 cm. Kupferstich, eine Farbe. England, 1775.
509. Likör. 11,6 × 5,5 cm. Lithographie, eine Farbe. Frankreich, XIX. Jahrhundert.
510. Zinngeschirr. 17,5 × 15,4 cm. Kupferstich. Gestochen von J. Wigley. England, 1777.
511. Zigarren. 6,3 × 3 cm. Lithographie, eine Farbe und Prägung in Gold. Mexiko, XX. Jahrhundert.
512. Zigarren. 6,3 × 2,3 cm. Offset, drei Farben und Prägung in Gold. Europa, XX. Jahrhundert.

513

514

515

516

517

513. Bookseller. 5 ³/₄ × 7 in. Copper plate engraving, monochrome. England 1747.
514. Needles. 3 ¹/₂ × 6 ¹⁵/₁₆ in. Wood engraving, monochrome, on buff paper. England, 1726.
515. Distillery. 5 ¹/₂ × 6 ⁷/₈ in. Copper plate engraving, monochrome. England, 18th century.
516. Jewellers. 5 ⁵/₁₆ × 6 ⁷/₈ in. Copper plate engraving, monochrome. England, 1760.
517. Stationery. 1 ³/₁₆ × 3 ¹⁵/₁₆ in. Litho, monochrome and gold, on embossed cream paper. England, 1851.

513. Librairie. 14,6 × 17,7 cm. Gravure sur cuivre une coul. Angleterre, 1747.
514. Aiguilles. 8,8 × 17,6 cm. Gravure sur bois une coul., papier chamois. Angleterre, 1726.
515. Distillerie. 14 × 17,5 cm. Gravure sur cuivre une coul. Angleterre, XVIIIᵉ siècle.
516. Bijouetrie-joaillerie. 13,5 × 17,5 cm. Gravure sur cuivre une coul. Angleterre, 1760.
517. Papeterie. 3,1 × 10 cm. Litho une coul. et or, papier crème gaufré. Angleterre, 1851.

513. Buchhandlung. 14,6 × 17,7 cm. Kupferstich, eine Farbe. England, 1747.
514. Nadeln. 8,8 × 17,6 cm. Holzschnitt, eine Farbe, Chamoispapier. England, 1726.
515. Brennerei. 14 × 17,5 cm. Kupferstich, eine Farbe. England, XVIII. Jahrhundert.
516. Schmuck- und Juwelhändler. 13,5 × 17,5 cm. Kupferstich, eine Farbe. England, 1760.
517. Papiergeschäft. 3,1 × 10 cm. Lithographie, eine Farbe und Gold, cremefarbenes Papier, geprägt. England, 1851.

IV. The label in everyday life

IV. La vie quotidienne à travers l'étiquette

IV. Das Etikett als Spiegel des täglichen Lebens

Work, food, clothing and leisure are essential elements of human life which are to be found in all ages and all societies. The labels grouped in this chapter illustrate these elements of our everyday existence.

Le travail, la nourriture, l'habillement et les loisirs sont les éléments indispensables à la vie de l'homme. Nous les retrouvons à toutes les époques et dans toutes les sociétés. A travers les étiquettes réunies dans ce quatrième chapitre, nous prenons ainsi contact avec la vie quotidienne.

Die Arbeit, die Nahrung, die Kleidung und die Freizeitgestaltung sind unentbehrliche Bestandteile des menschlichen Lebens. Wir finden sie in allen Epochen und allen Gesellschaften immer wieder. Durch die Etikette, die in diesem vierten Kapitel zusammengestellt sind, kommen wir also in Kontakt mit dem täglichen Leben.

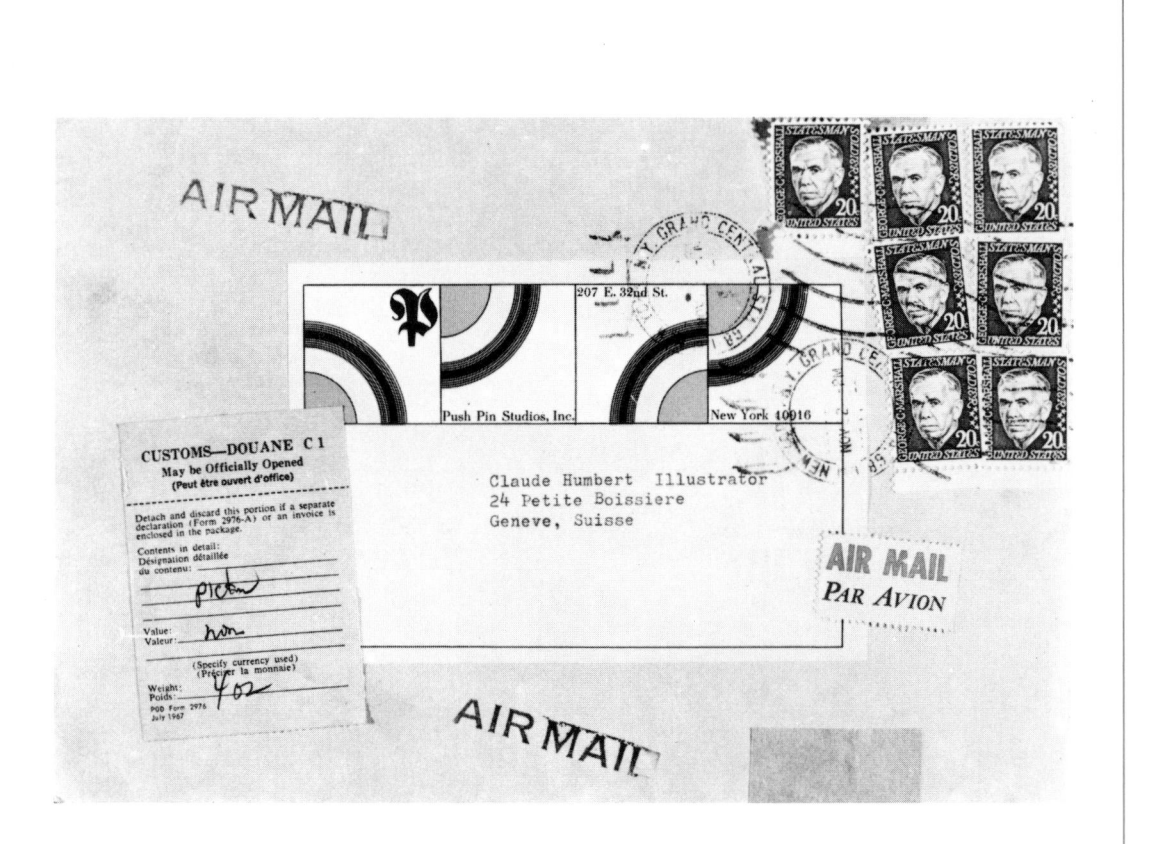

518

518. Envelope with various labels. 9 × 6 in. Address label from Push Pin Studios Inc./ New York. Design, Milton Glaser. USA, 1971.

518. *Enveloppe avec étiquettes diverses. 23 × 15 cm. Etiquette-adresse des Push Pin Studios Inc./ New York. Créat. Milton Glaser. U.S.A., 1971.*

518. Umschlag mit verschiedenen Etiketten. 23 × 15 cm. Adressenetikett der Push Pin Studios Inc./ New York. Urheber: Milton Glaser. U.S.A., 1971.

519

520

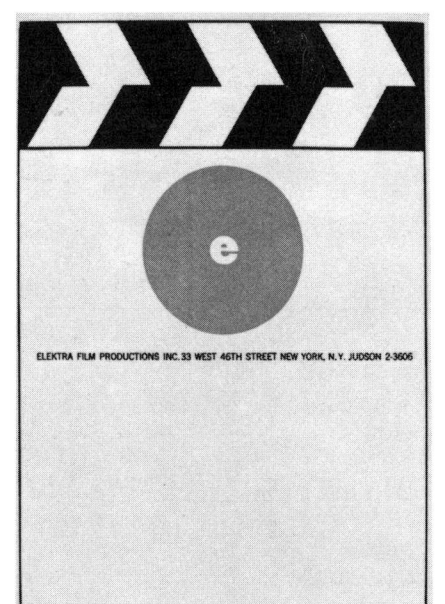

521

519. Tobacco. $^{61}/_{16} \times 1^{11}/_{16}$ in. Offset, 3 colours. France, 1971.
520. Address label. $3^1/_4 \times 4^3/_4$ in. Offset, 2 colours. Design, Push Pin Studios Inc. Milton Glaser, New York. USA, 1971.
521. Cigarette papers. $2^{13}/_{16} \times ^{15}/_{16}$ in. Litho, monochrome. France, early 20th century.
522. Synthetic rubber. $3^7/_{16} \times 17^3/_8$ in. Offset, 2 colours. Design, Plan Design A/S, Claus Rostrup. Denmark, 1971.
523. Spark plugs. $8^1/_8 \times 4^1/_8$ in. Offset, 3 colours and silver. Printing, J. Mc-Gavigan & Co. Ltd., Glasgow. Europe, 1971.

519. Tabac. 15,3 × 4,3 cm. Offset trois coul. France, 1971.
520. Etiquette-adresse. 8,2 × 12 cm. Offset deux coul. Créat. Push Pin Studios Inc., Milton Glaser. New York. U.S.A., 1971.
521. Papier à cigarettes. 7,2 × 2,4 cm. Litho une coul. France, début du XXᵉ siècle.
522. Caoutchouc synthétique. 8,7 × 44 cm. Offset deux coul. Créat. Plan Design A/S, Claus Rostrup. Danemark, 1971.
523. Bougies pour auto. 20,5 × 10,5 cm. Offset trois coul. et argent. Imp. J. McGavigan & Co. Ltd., Glasgow. Europe, 1971.

519. Tabak. 15,3 × 4,3 cm. Offset, drei Farben. Frankreich, 1971.
520. Adressenetikett. 8,2 × 12 cm. Offset, zwei Farben. Urheber: Push Pin Studios Inc./ Milton Glaser, New York. U.S.A., 1971.
521. Zigarettenpapier. 7,2 × 2,4 cm. Lithographie, eine Farbe. Frankreich, Beginn des XX. Jahrhunderts.
522. Synthetisches Gummi. 8,7 × 44 cm. Offset, zwei Farben. Urheber: Plan Design A/S, Claus Rostrup. Dänemark, 1971.
523. Autokerzen. 20,5 × 10,5 cm. Offset, drei Farben und Silber. Druckerei J. Mc Gavigan & Co. Ltd., Glasgow. Europa, 1971.

522

523

524

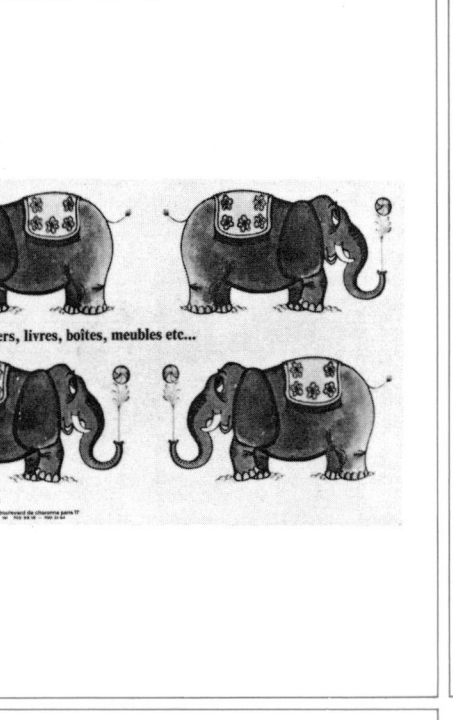

... sur vos cahiers, livres, boîtes, meubles etc...

525

526

527

FREE LABOR WILL WIN — LABOR DAY ★ 1942

FREE LABOR WILL WIN — LABOR DAY ★ 1942

FREE LABOR WILL WIN — LABOR DAY ★ 1942

FREE LABOR WILL WIN — LABOR DAY ★ 1942

528

524. Airline. 2 $^{11}/_{16}$ × 1 $^{13}/_{16}$ in. Offset, 2 colours. Italy, 1971.
525. Label for children (and grown-ups). 2 $^{3}/_{4}$ × 1 $^{1}/_{2}$ in. Offset, 4 colours. Design, Publistar, Paris. France, 1971.
526. Pens. 2 $^{7}/_{16}$ × 1 $^{3}/_{4}$ in. Litho, monochrome. England, early 20th century.
527. Textile. 1 $^{3}/_{8}$ × 2 $^{3}/_{16}$ in. Litho, 2 colours. USA, 1939.
528. Labour day. 2 $^{3}/_{8}$ × 1 $^{15}/_{16}$ in. Offset, 2 colours. USA, 1942.

524. Compagnie aérienne. 6,8 × 4,6 cm. Offset deux coul. Italie, 1971.
525. Etiquette pour enfants (et grandes personnes). 7 × 3,8 cm. Offset quatre coul. Créat. Publistar, Paris. France, 1971.
526. Plumes à écrire. 6,2 × 4,5 cm. Litho une coul. Angleterre, début du XXᵉ siècle.
527. Textile. 3,5 × 5,6 cm. Litho deux coul. U.S.A., 1939.
528. Journée de travail. 6 × 5 cm. Offset deux coul. U.S.A., 1942.

524. Fluggesellschaft. 6,8 × 4,6 cm. Offset, zwei Farben. Italien, 1971.
525. Etikette für Kinder (und Erwachsene). 7 × 3,8 cm. Offset, vier Farben. Urheber: Publistar, Paris. Frankreich, 1971.
526. Schreibfedern. 6,2 × 4,5 cm. Lithographie, eine Farbe. England, Beginn des XX. Jahrhunderts.
527. Textilware. 3,5 × 5,6 cm. Lithographie, zwei Farben. U.S.A., 1939.
528. Arbeitstag. 6 × 5 cm. Offset, zwei Farben. U.S.A., 1942.

529

530

531

529. Soap. 3 ¹/₄ × 4 ⁹/₁₆ in. Litho, 3 colours. USA, 1875.
530. Cigars. 7 ⁵/₈ × 6 ⁵/₁₆ in. Letterpress, 2 colours and gold. Design, Prof. L. Hohlwein. Germany, 1925.
531. Tobacco. 4 ¹/₈ × 4 ³/₈ in. Wood engraving and letterpress, monochrome. England, early 20th century.
532. Gift label. 1 ³/₁₆ × 2 ³/₄ in. Offset, 4 colours. Switzerland, 1971.
533. Soap for children. 5 × 4 ³/₄ in. Offset, 4 colours. Design, K & K Agency/ A. Katzourakis, Athens. Greece, 1969.

529. Savon. 8,2 × 11,5 cm. Litho trois coul. U.S.A., 1875.
530. Cigares. 19,4 × 16 cm. Typo deux coul. et or. Créat. Prof. L. Hohlwein. Allemagne, 1925.
531. Tabac. 10,5 × 11 cm. Bois et typo une coul. Angleterre, début du XXᵉ siècle.
532. Etiquette pour cadeaux. 3 × 7 cm. Offset quatre coul. Suisse, 1971.
533. Savon pour enfants. 12,7 × 12 cm. Offset quatre coul. Créat. Agence K & K, A. Katzourakis, Athènes. Grèce, 1969.

529. Seife. 8,2 × 11,5 cm. Lithographie, drei Farben. U.S.A., 1875.
530. Zigarren. 19,4 × 16 cm. Buchdruck, zwei Farben und Gold. Urheber: Professor L. Hohlwein. Deutschland, 1925.
531. Tabak. 10,5 × 11 cm. Holzschnitt und Buchdruck, eine Farbe. England, Beginn des XX. Jahrhunderts.
532. Geschenketikett. 3 × 7 cm. Offset, vier Farben. Schweiz, 1971.
533. Kinderseife. 12,7 × 12 cm. Offset, vier Farben. Urheber: Agentur K & K, A. Katzourakis, Athen. Griechenland, 1969.

532

533

534

535

536

537

538

534. Soap. 4 1/8 × 4 3/8 in. Offset, 4 colours. France, 1971.
535. Ex-libris. 4 9/16 × 8 1/8 in. Wood engraving, monochrome. Design, Prof. F. Hein. Germany, 1924.
536. Marmalade. 2 15/16 × 3 7/16 in. Litho, 8 colours. England, 20th century.
537. Cocoa. 4 9/16 × 6 1/16 in. Litho, 4 colours. England, late 19th century.
538. Writing paper. 7 11/16 × 6 7/8 in. Litho, 7 colours. England, 1887.

534. Savon. 10,4 × 11 cm. Offset quatre coul. France, 1971.
535. Ex-libris. 11,5 × 20,5 cm. Gravure sur bois une coul. Créat. Prof. F. Hein. Allemagne, 1924.
536. Marmelade. 7,5 × 8,7 cm. Litho huit coul. Angleterre, XXe siècle.
537. Cacao. 11,5 × 15,3 cm. Litho quatre coul. Angleterre, fin du XIXe siècle.
538. Papier à lettre. 19,5 × 17,4 cm. Litho sept coul. Angleterre, 1887.

534. Seife. 10,4 × 11 cm. Offset, vier Farben. Frankreich, 1971.
535. Exlibris. 11,5 × 20,5 cm. Holzschnitt, eine Farbe. Urheber: Professor F. Hein. Deutschland, 1924.
536. Marmelade. 7,5 × 8,7 cm. Lithographie, acht Farben. England, XX. Jahrhundert.
537. Kakao. 11,5 × 15,3 cm. Lithographie, vier Farben. England, Ende des XIX. Jahrhunderts.
538. Briefpapier. 19,5 × 17,4 cm. Lithographie, sieben Farben. England, 1887.

539

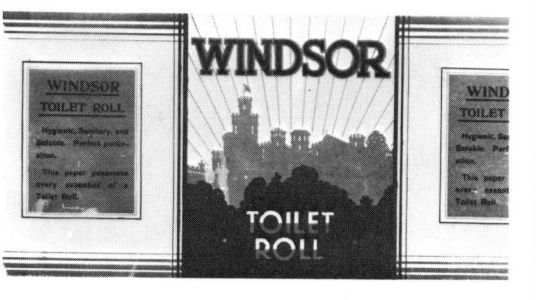

540

541

539. Wine. 4 ¹³/₁₆ × 2 ¹⁵/₁₆ in. Litho, monochrome and gold. Germany, 19th century.
540. Toilet paper. 7 ¹/₂ × 4 ³/₄ in. Litho, 2 colours. England, early 20th century.
541. Tobacco. 3 ¹/₂ × 2 ¹/₁₆ in. Offset, 2 colours. France, 1971.
542. Stationery. 4 ⁹/₁₆ × 5 ¹⁵/₁₆ in. Copper plate engraving, monochrome. England, 1676.
543. Beer. 7 ⁵/₈ × 4 ³/₈ in. Offset, 4 colours and gold. Germany, 1971.

539. Vin. 12,2 × 7,5 cm. Litho une coul. et or. Allemagne, XIXᵉ siècle.
540. Papier hygiénique. 19 × 12 cm. Litho deux coul. Angleterre, début du XXᵉ siècle.
541. Tabac. 8,8 × 5,2 cm. Offset deux coul. France, 1971.
542. Papeterie. 11,5 × 15 cm. Gravure sur cuivre une coul. Angleterre, 1676.
543. Bière. 19,3 × 11 cm. Offset quatre coul. et or. Allemagne, 1971.

539. Wein. 12,2 × 7,5 cm. Lithographie, eine Farbe und Gold. Deutschland, XIX. Jahrhundert.
540. Toilettenpapier. 19 × 12 cm. Lithographie, zwei Farben. England, Beginn des XX. Jahrhunderts.
541. Tabak. 8,8 × 5,2 cm. Offset, zwei Farben. Frankreich, 1971.
542. Papiergeschäft. 11,5 × 15 cm. Kupferstich, eine Farbe. England, 1676.
543. Bier. 19,3 × 11 cm. Offset, vier Farben und Gold. Deutschland, 1971.

542

543

544

545

546

547

548

544. Porcelain. 4 $^9/_{16}$ × 3 $^5/_{16}$. Copper plate engraving, monochrome. England, 1779.
545. Café de l'Europe. 3 $^{11}/_{16}$ × 3 $^7/_8$ in. Design, C. Toplis; printing, W. Alexander, London. England, 19th century.
546. Mercers. 9 $^{13}/_{16}$ × 6 $^1/_8$ in. Copper plate engraving, monochrome. England, 18th century.
547. Tea, coffee and chocolate seller. 3 $^5/_8$ × 4 $^1/_4$ in. Copper plate engraving, monochrome. England, 18th century.
548. Wine. 4 $^5/_8$ × 3 $^9/_{16}$ in. Offset, 2 colours and gold. Design, O. Ecksell, Stockholm. Sweden, 1952.

544. *Porcelaine. 11,5 × 8,4 cm. Gravure sur cuivre une coul. Angleterre, 1779.*
545. *Café de l'Europe. 9,3 × 9,8 cm. Créat. C. Toplis, imp. W. Alexander, Londres. Angleterre, XIXe siècle.*
546. *Mercerie. 25 × 15,5 cm. Gravure sur cuivre une coul. Angleterre, XVIIIe siècle.*
547. *Débit de thé, café, chocolat. 9,2 × 10,8 cm. Gravure sur cuivre une coul. Angleterre, XVIIIe siècle.*
548. *Vin. 11,7 × 9 cm. Offset deux coul. et or. Créat. O. Ecksell, Stockholm. Suède, 1952.*

544. Porzellan. 11,5 × 8,4 cm. Kupferstich, eine Farbe. England, 1779.
545. Europa-Café. 9,3 × 9,8 cm. Urheber: C. Toplis, Druckerei W. Alexander, London. England, XIX. Jahrhundert.
546. Kurzwarenhandel. 25 × 15,5 cm. Kupferstich, eine Farbe. England, XVIII. Jahrhundert.
547. Tee-, Kaffee- und Schokoladenstube. 9,2 × 10,8 cm. Kupferstich, eine Farbe. England, XVIII. Jahrhundert.
548. Wein. 11,7 × 9 cm. Offset, zwei Farben und Gold. Urheber: O. Ecksell, Stockholm. Schweden, 1952.

549

550

551

549. Salt. 1 ¹/₂ × ⁷/₈ in. Litho, monochrome. England, early 19th century.
550. Petrol. 4 ³/₁₆ × 2 ¹/₂ in. Silk-screen, 3 colours. Printing, Marzck, Vienna. International, 20th century.
551. Cigarette papers. 2 ¹³/₁₆ × 1 ⁹/₁₆ in. Litho, monochrome and gold. France, early 20th century.
552. Address label. 5 ⁷/₈ × 3 in. Offset, 3 colours. Design, Push Pin Studios Inc Milton Glaser, New York. USA, 1971.
553. Mineral water. 5 ¹/₂ × 4 ⁷/₁₆ in. Offset, 2 colours. Design, K & K Agency/F. Carabott, Athens. Greece. 1968.

549. Sel. 3,8 × 2,2 cm. Litho une coul. Angleterre, début du XIXᵉ siècle.
550. Essence. 10,6 × 6,4 cm. Sérigraphie trois coul. Imp. Marzck, Vienne. International, XXᵉ siècle.
551. Papier à cigarettes. 7,2 × 4 cm. Litho une coul. et or. France, début du XXᵉ siècle.
552. Etiquette-adresse. 14,9 × 7,6 cm. Offset trois coul. Créat. Push Pin Studios Inc./ Milton Glaser, New York. U.S.A., 1971.
553. Eau minérale. 14 × 11,2 cm. Offset deux coul. Créat. Agence K & K, F. Carabott, Athènes. Grèce, 1968.

549. Salz. 3,8 × 2,2 cm. Lithographie, eine Farbe. England, Beginn des XIX. Jahrhunderts.
550. Benzin. 10,6 × 6,4 cm. Siebdruck, drei Farben. Druckerei Marzck, Wien. International, XX. Jahrhundert.
551. Zigarettenpapier. 7,2 × 4 cm. Lithographie, eine Farbe und Gold. Frankreich, Beginn des XX. Jahrhunderts.
552. Adressenetikett. 14,9 × 7,6 cm. Offset, drei Farben. Urheber: Push Pin Studios Inc./ Milton Glaser, New York. U.S.A., 1971.

552

553. Mineralwasser. 14 × 11,2 cm. Offset, zwei Farben. Urheber: Agentur K & K, F. Carabott, Athen. Griechenland, 1968.

553

554

555

556

557

558

554. Fruit preserve. 3 9/16 × 2 9/16 in. Litho, 5 colours. USA, early 20th century.
555. Department store. 2 3/4 × 4 3/4 in. Letterpress, monochrome. Switzerland, 1971.
556. Wine. 4 1/8 × 2 9/16 in. Litho, monochrome, on embossed gold paper. France, 19th century.
557. Chemist. 2 13/16 × 2 13/16 in. Copper plate engraving, monochrome. England, 20th century.
558. Stationery. 4 9/16 × 2 15/16 in. Litho, monochrome and gold. France, 19th century.

554. Confiture. 9 × 6,5 cm. Litho cinq coul. U.S.A., début du XXᵉ siècle.
555. Grand magasin. 7 × 12 cm. Typo une coul. Suisse, 1971.
556. Vin. 10,5 × 6,5 cm. Litho une coul., papier or gaufré. France, XIXᵉ siècle.
557. Pharmacie. 7,2 × 7,2 cm. Gravure sur cuivre une coul. Angleterre, XXᵉ siècle.
558. Papeterie. 11,5 × 7,5 cm. Litho une coul. et or. France, XIXᵉ siècle.

554. Marmelade. 9 × 6,5 cm. Lithographie, fünf Farben. U.S.A., Beginn des XX. Jahrhunderts.
555. Kaufzentrum. 7 × 12 cm. Buchdruck, eine Farbe. Schweiz, 1971.
556. Wein. 10,5 × 6,5 cm. Lithographie, eine Farbe und Goldpapier, geprägt. Frankreich, XIX. Jahrhundert.
557. Apotheke. 7,2 × 7,2 cm. Kupferstich, eine Farbe. England, XX. Jahrhundert.
558. Papiergeschäft. 11,5 × 7,5 cm. Lithographie, eine Farbe und Gold. Frankreich, XIX. Jahrhundert.

559

560

561

562

563

559. Shoe cream. 3 $^1/_8$ × 5 $^3/_{16}$ in. Litho, 3 colours and gold. USA, 19th century.
560. Printer's mark. 1 $^5/_{16}$ × 2 $^1/_4$ in. Design and printing, Robert Estienne, Paris. France, 1503–1559.
561. Honey. 4 $^3/_4$ × 7 $^5/_8$ in. Copper plate engraving, monochrome. England, 18th century.
562. Dyers. 4 $^1/_8$ × 6 $^1/_2$ in. Copper plate engraving, monochrome. England, 1747.
563. Oil merchant. 6 $^5/_{16}$ × 4 $^1/_8$ in. Wood engraving and letterpress, monochrome. England, early 19th century.

559. Crème pour chaussures. 7,9 × 13,2 cm. Litho trois coul. et or. U.S.A., XIXe siècle.
560. Marque d'imprimeur. 3,4 × 5,7 cm. Créat. imp. Robert Estienne, Paris. France, 1503-1559.
561. Miel. 12 × 19,3 cm. Gravure sur cuivre une coul. Angleterre, XVIIIe siècle.
562. Teinturerie. 10,5 × 16,5 cm. Gravure sur cuivre une coul. Angleterre, 1747.
563. Marchand d'huile. 16 × 10,5 cm. Bois et typo une coul. Angleterre, début du XIXe siècle.

559. Schuhcreme. 7,9 × 13,2 cm. Lithographie, drei Farben und Gold. U.S.A., XIX. Jahrhundert.
560. Druckereimarke. 3,4 × 5,7 cm. Urheber: Druckerei Robert Estienne, Paris. Frankreich, 1503–1559.
561. Honig. 12 × 19,3 cm. Kupferstich, eine Farbe. England, XVIII. Jahrhundert.
562. Färberei. 10,5 × 16,5 cm. Kupferstich, eine Farbe. England, 1747.
563. Ölhändler. 16 × 10,5 cm. Holzschnitt und Buchdruck, eine Farbe. England, Beginn des XIX. Jahrhunderts.

564

565

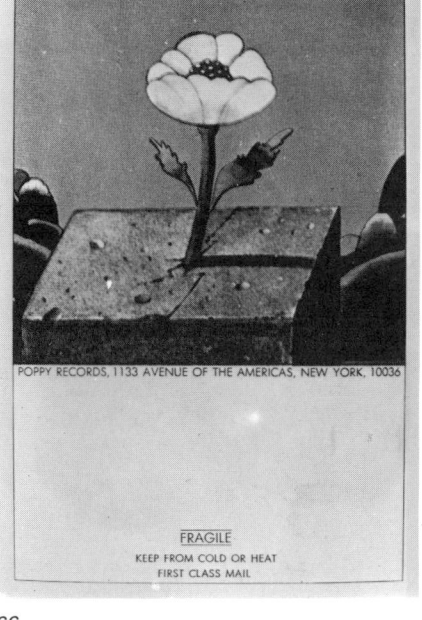

POPPY RECORDS, 1133 AVENUE OF THE AMERICAS, NEW YORK, 10036

FRAGILE
KEEP FROM COLD OR HEAT
FIRST CLASS MAIL

566

567

568

564. Rose water. 1 $^{11}/_{16}$ × 2 $^{7}/_{16}$ in. Litho, monochrome, on pink paper. England, 19th century.
565. Perfume. 1 $^{5}/_{8}$ in. diameter. Letterpress, 3 colours. Design, E. Blankenburg. Germany, 1924.
566. Address label. 5 $^{3}/_{4}$ × 4 in. Offset, 4 colours. Design, Push Pin Studios Inc./ Milton Glaser, New York. USA, 1971.
567. Tea. 3 $^{15}/_{16}$ × 2 $^{3}/_{16}$ in. Litho, 4 colours. England, 1900.
568. Matches. 2 $^{1}/_{2}$ × 2 $^{3}/_{8}$ in. Litho, 5 colours. Japan, 1969.

564. *Eau de rose. 4,3 × 6,2 cm. Litho une coul., papier rose. Angleterre, XIXe siècle.*
565. *Parfum. Diam. 4,2 cm. Typo trois coul. Créat. E. Blankenburg. Allemagne, 1924.*
566. *Etiquette-adresse. 14,5 × 10,2 cm. Offset quatre coul. Créat. Push Pin Studios Inc./ Milton Glaser, New York. U.S.A., 1971.*
567. *Thé. 10 × 5,5 cm. Litho quatre coul. Angleterre, 1900.*
568. *Allumettes. 6,3 × 6 cm. Litho cinq coul. Japon, 1969.*

564. Rosenwasser. 4,3 × 6,2 cm. Lithographie, eine Farbe, Rosapapier. England, XIX. Jahrhundert.
565. Parfüm. Durchmesser 4,2 cm. Buchdruck, drei Farben. Urheber: E. Blankenburg. Deutschland, 1924.
566. Adressenetikett. 14,5 × 10,2 cm. Offset, vier Farben. Urheber: Push Pin Studios Inc./Milton Glaser, New York. U.S.A., 1971.
567. Tee. 10 × 5,5 cm. Lithographie, vier Farben. England, 1900.
568. Streichhölzer. 6,3 × 6 cm. Lithographie, fünf Farben. Japan, 1969.

569

570

571

572

573

569. Carpenter. 5 $^{15}/_{16}$ × 7 $^{1}/_{8}$ in. Copper plate engraving, monochrome. England, 1730.
570. Graphic designer. 4 $^{3}/_{4}$ × 2 $^{5}/_{8}$ in. Offset, monochrome. Design, C. Dussauge, Ambilly. France, 1971.
571. Cutlery. 3 $^{9}/_{16}$ × 5 $^{1}/_{2}$ in. Copper plate engraving, monochrome. Engraved by I. Clark. England, 1670.
572. Perfume. 1 $^{3}/_{4}$ in. diameter. Letterpress, 3 colours. Design, E. Blankenburg. Germany, 1942.
573. Aperitif. 4 $^{5}/_{8}$ × 3 $^{9}/_{16}$ in. Letterpress, 4 colours. Design, O. Ecksell, Stockholm. Sweden, 1952.

569. Charpentier. 15 × 18 cm. Gravure sur cuivre une coul. Angleterre, 1730.
570. Graphiste. 12 × 6,6 cm. Offset une coul. Créat. C. Dussauge, Ambilly. France, 1971.
571. Coutellerie. 9 × 14 cm. Gravure sur cuivre une coul. Gravure I. Clark. Angleterre, 1670.
572. Parfum. Diam. 4,5 cm. Typo trois coul. Créat. E. Blankenburg. Allemagne, 1942.
573. Apéritif. 11,7 × 9 cm. Typo quatre coul. Créat. O. Ecksell, Stockholm. Suède, 1952.

569. Zimmermann. 15 × 18 cm. Kupferstich, eine Farbe. England, 1730.
570. Grafikerin. 12 × 6,6 cm. Offset, eine Farbe. Urheber: C. Dussauge, Ambilly. Frankreich, 1971.
571. Messerschmied. 9 × 14 cm. Kupferstich, eine Farbe. Gestochen von I. Clark. England, 1670.
572. Parfüm. Durchmesser 4,5 cm. Buchdruck, drei Farben. Urheber: E. Blankenburg. Deutschland, 1942.
573. Aperitif. 11,7 × 9 cm. Buchdruck, vier Farben. Urheber: O. Ecksell, Stockholm. Schweden, 1952.

574

575

576

PULV.
GLYCYRRH DECORT.

This beautiful Powder is prepared from the inner portions only of the finest Liquorice Root, carefully selected, and deprived of the cortical parts.

It possesses in a high degree the peculiar well-known sweetness of the Root; and being infinitely superior to the Liquorice Powder commonly sold, it will be found decidedly preferable for Pharmaceutical purposes,—more especially for the covering of pills, for which it is excellently adapted, not merely for the sake of preventing their adhesion, but also for the purpose of completely avoiding by the sweetness of the coating the unpleasant taste and nausea frequently experienced from taking aloetic and other medicines, when given without this adjunct, even in the form of pills.

Prepared by
MANDER, WEAVER, AND CO.,
CHEMICAL LABORATORY,
WOLVERHAMPTON.
(Established 1773.)

General Depot for choice Chemical and Galenical Preparations, and for every article connected with Scientific and Operative Chemistry.

577

CRAINT L'HUMIDITÉ

FUMEURS : Le papier LA✠ à bord Gommé est de qualité supérieure son perfectionnement le fait apprécier de tous les fumeurs.

BREVETÉ S.G.D.G.

PAPIER PUR FIL
GOMMAGE PERFECTIONNÉ
QUALITÉ SUPÉRIEURE

RIZ LA ✠
GOMMÉ

N°   121

DIPLÔMES D'HONNEUR
MÉDAILLES   OR & ARGENT

578

574. Bicarbonate of soda. $2\,^7/_8 \times 3\,^1/_2$ in. Litho, monochrome. England, early 20th century.

575. Wine. $3\,^3/_4 \times 4\,^{15}/_{16}$ in. Offset, 3 colours. England, early 20th century.

576. Epsom salts. $3 \times 3\,^{15}/_{16}$ in. Litho, monochrome. England, early 20th century.

577. Pharmaceutical products. $2\,^3/_8 \times 2\,^7/_{16}$ in. Letterpress, monochrome. England, 19th century.

578. Cigarette papers. $3\,^1/_{16} \times 3\,^3/_4$ in. Litho, monochrome. France, early 20th century.

574. Bicarbonate. $7,3 \times 8,8$ cm. Litho une coul. Angleterre, début du XXe siècle.

575. Vin. $9,6 \times 12,5$ cm. Offset trois coul. Angleterre, début du XXe siècle.

576. Sels purifiés. $7,6 \times 10$ cm. Litho une coul. Angleterre, début du XXe siècle.

577. Produits pharmaceutiques. $6 \times 6,2$ cm. Typo une coul. Angleterre, XIXe siècle.

578. Papier à cigarettes. $7,7 \times 9,5$ cm. Litho une coul. France, début du XXe siècle.

574. Bikarbonat. $7,3 \times 8,8$ cm. Lithographie, eine Farbe. England, Beginn des XX. Jahrhunderts.

575. Wein. $9,6 \times 12,5$ cm. Offset, drei Farben. England, Beginn des XX. Jahrhunderts.

576. Gereinigte Salze. $7,6 \times 10$ cm. Lithographie, eine Farbe. England. Beginn des XX. Jahrhunderts.

577. Pharmazeutische Produkte. $6 \times 6,2$ cm. Buchdruck, eine Farbe. England, XIX. Jahrhundert.

578. Zigarettenpapier. $7,7 \times 9,5$ cm. Lithographie, eine Farbe. Frankreich, Beginn des XX. Jahrhunderts.

579

580

581

582

583

579. Wigs. 4 $^3/_{16}$ × 6 $^5/_{16}$ in. Copper plate engraving, monochrome. England, 18th century.
580. Pencils. 6 $^1/_2$ × 5 $^1/_8$ in. Litho, monochrome. England, 1893.
581. Stockings and gloves. 4 $^1/_4$ × 6 $^7/_8$ in. Copper plate engraving, monochrome. England, 1742.
582. Jewellery. 3 $^{15}/_{16}$ × 3 $^1/_2$ in. Copper plate engraving, monochrome. England 1773.
583. Licensed valuers. 4 $^1/_{16}$ × 2 $^{15}/_{16}$ in. Copper plate engraving, monochrome. England, 1756.

579. Perruques. 10,6 × 16 cm. Gravure sur cuivre une coul. Angleterre, XVIIIe siècle.
580. Crayons. 16,5 × 13 cm. Litho une coul. Angleterre, 1893.
581. Bas et gants. 10,7 × 17,4 cm. Gravure sur cuivre une coul. Angleterre, 1742.
582. Bijouterie-joaillerie. 10 × 8,8 cm. Gravure sur cuivre une coul. Angleterre, 1773.
583. Commissaire-priseur. 10,3 × 7,5 cm. Gravure sur cuivre une coul. Angleterre, 1756.

579. Perücken. 10,6 × 16 cm. Kupferstich, eine Farbe. England, XVIII. Jahrhundert.
580. Bleistifte. 16,5 × 13 cm. Lithographie, eine Farbe. England, 1893.
581. Strümpfe und Handschuhe. 10,7 × 17,4 cm. Kupferstich, eine Farbe. England, 1742.
582. Schmuck- und Juwelhändler. 10 × 8,8 cm. Kupferstich, eine Farbe. England, 1773.
583. Versteigerer. 10,3 × 7,5 cm. Kupferstich, eine Farbe. England, 1756.

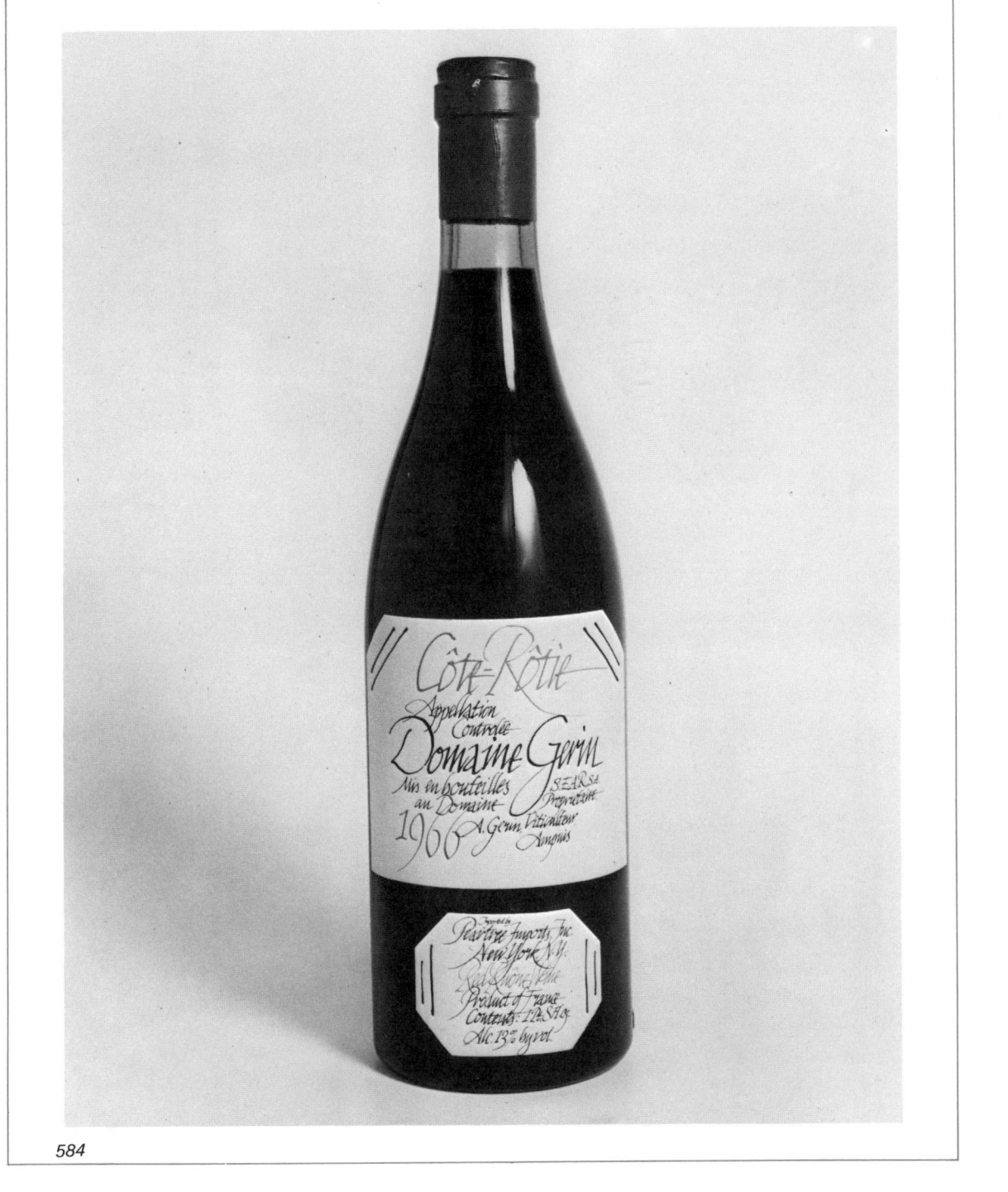

584

584. Wine. 2 $^{15}/_{16}$ × 3 $^{15}/_{16}$ in. / 1 $^{3}/_{16}$ × 2 $^{7}/_{16}$ in. Offset, 2 colours. Design, Chermayeff & Geismar Associates Inc., New York. USA, 1971.

584. Vin. 7,5 × 10 cm / 3 × 6,2 cm. Offset deux coul. Créat. Chermayeff & Geismar Associates Inc., New York. U.S.A., 1971.

584. Wein. 7,5 × 10 cm / 3 × 6,2 cm. Offset, zwei Farben. Urheber: Chermayeff & Geismar Associates Inc., New York. U.S.A., 1971.

585

TIME INCORPORATED

586

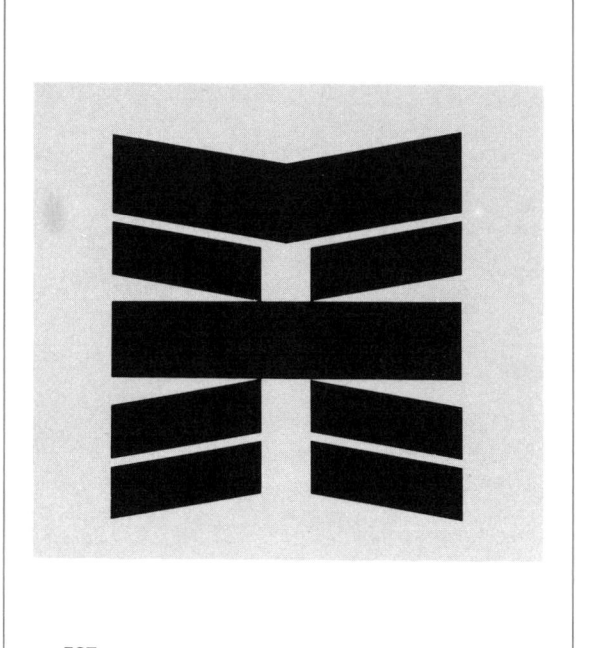

587

585. Magazines. 4 $^3/_4$ × 4 $^3/_4$ in. Offset, 2 colours. Design, A. Saks Inc., New York.
USA, 1971.
586. Ex-libris. 1 $^{15}/_{16}$ × 1 $^{15}/_{16}$ in. Letterpress, monochrome. Germany, 1924.
587. Paper industry. 1 $^3/_{16}$ × 1 $^1/_4$ in. Offset,
monochrome. Design, T. Vellve, Barce-
lona. Spain, 1970.
588. Ex-libris. 2 $^{15}/_{16}$ × 4 $^9/_{16}$ in. Wood engraving, 2 colours. Design, H. Pape,
Munich. Germany, 1925.
589. Ex-libris. 1 $^{11}/_{16}$ × 1 $^{11}/_{16}$ in. Letterpress, monochrome. France, 1900.

585. *Magazines. 12 × 12 cm. Offset deux coul.
Créat. A. Saks Inc., New York. U.S.A., 1971.*
586. *Ex-libris. 5 × 5 cm. Typo une coul. Allemagne, 1924.*
587. *Industrie du papier. 3 × 3,2 cm. Offset une
coul. Créat. T. Vellve, Barcelone. Espagne,
1970.*
588. *Ex-libris. 7,5 × 11,5 cm. Gravure sur bois
deux coul. Créat. H. Pape, Munich.
Allemagne, 1925.*
589. *Ex-libris. 4,3 × 4,3 cm. Typo une coul.
France, 1900.*

585. Magazine. 12 × 12 cm. Offset, zwei Farben.
Urheber: A. Saks Inc., New York. U.S.A.,
1971.
586. Exlibris. 5 × 5 cm. Buchdruck, eine Farbe.
Deutschland, 1924.
587. Papierindustrie. 3 × 3,2 cm. Offset, eine
Farbe. Urheber: T. Vellve, Barcelona.
Spanien, 1970.
588. Exlibris. 7,5 × 11,5 cm. Holzschnitt, zwei
Farben. Urheber: H. Pape, München.
Deutschland, 1925.
589. Exlibris. 4,3 × 4,3 cm. Buchdruck, eine
Farbe. Frankreich, 1900.

588

589

590

GREAT BRITAIN

591

592

593

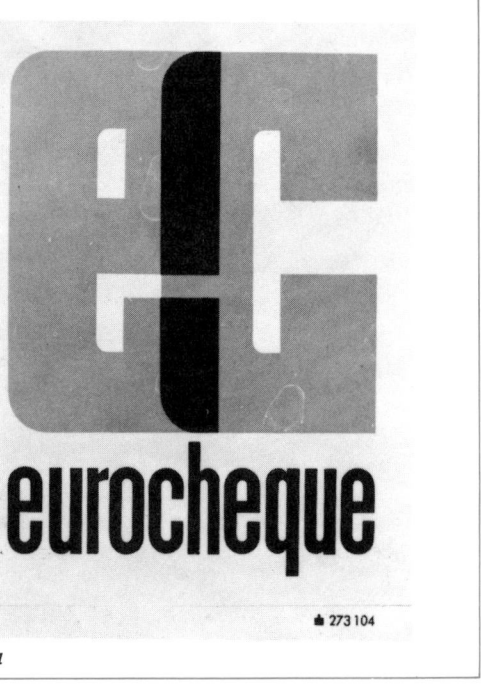

eurocheque

594

590. Motor tyres. 5 1/8 × 3 15/16 in. Litho, 2 colours, on transparent paper. USA, 1940.
591. Badge. 2 1/4 × 2 15/16 in. Silk-screen, 3 colours and gold. England, 1971.
592. Wine. 5 1/8 × 2 3/8 in. Litho, 4 colours. Design, Gerstung. Germany, 1936–1937.
593. Motor cars. 2 3/8 in. diameter. Letter-press, monochrome. Italy, 1971.
594. Bank. 4 3/4 × 5 1/8 in. Offset, 3 colours. Europe, 1971.

590. *Pneumatiques. 13 × 10 cm. Litho deux coul. papier transparent. U.S.A., 1940.*
591. *Ecusson. 5,7 × 7,5 cm. Sérigraphie trois coul. et or. Angleterre, 1971.*
592. *Vin. 13 × 6 cm. Litho quatre coul. Créat. Gerstung. Allemagne, 1936-1937.*
593. *Automobiles. Diam. 6 cm. Typo une coul. Italie, 1971.*
594. *Banque. 12 × 13 cm. Offset trois coul. Europe, 1971.*

590. Reifen. 13 × 10 cm. Lithographie, zwei Farben, durchsichtiges Papier. U.S.A., 1940.
591. Wappenschild. 5,7 × 7,5 cm. Siebdruck, drei Farben und Gold. England, 1971.
592. Wein. 13 × 6 cm. Lithographie, vier Farben. Urheber: Gerstung. Deutschland, 1936–1937.
593. Automobile. Durchmesser 6 cm. Buchdruck, eine Farbe. Italien, 1971.
594. 12 × 13 cm. Offset, drei Farben. Europa, 1971.

595

596

597

595. Rice starch. 4 $^{13}/_{16}$ × 5 $^{3}/_{8}$ in. Litho, 7 colours. England, late 19th century.
596. Confectionery. 1 $^{1}/_{2}$ × 2 $^{1}/_{8}$ in. Litho, 5 colours. Italy, 1971.
597. Textile. 6 $^{7}/_{8}$ × 9 $^{1}/_{16}$ in. Litho, 8 colours. India, late 19th century.
598. Matches. 2 $^{9}/_{16}$ × 3 $^{9}/_{16}$ in. Litho, 3 colours. Norway, early 20th century.
599. Ex-libris. 3 $^{15}/_{16}$ × 5 $^{15}/_{16}$ in. Wood engraving, monochrome. Design, H. Pape, Munich. Germany, 1924.

595. *Amidon de riz. 10,6 × 13,6 cm. Litho sept coul. Angleterre, fin du XIXe siècle.*
596. *Confiserie. 3,8 × 5,4 cm. Litho cinq coul. Italie, 1971.*
597. *Textile. 17,5 × 23 cm. Litho huit coul. Inde, fin du XIXe siècle.*
598. *Allumettes. 6,5 × 9 cm. Litho trois coul. Norvège, début du XXe siècle.*
599. *Ex-libris. 10 × 15 cm. Gravure sur bois une coul. Créat. H. Pape, Munich. Allemagne, 1924.*

595. Reisstärke. 10,6 × 13,6 cm. Lithographie, sieben Farben. England, Ende des XIX. Jahrhunderts.
596. Konditoreiware. 3,8 × 5,4 cm. Lithographie, fünf Farben. Italien, 1971.
597. Textilware. 17,5 × 23 cm. Lithographie, acht Farben. Indien, Ende des XIX. Jahrhunderts.
598. Streichhölzer. 6,5 × 9 cm. Lithographie, drei Farben. Norwegen, Beginn des XX. Jahrhunderts.
599. Exlibris. 10 × 15 cm. Holzschnitt, eine Farbe. Urheber: H. Pape, München. Deutschland, 1924.

598

599

600

601

602

603

604

600. Anchovy essence. 2 $^1/_2$ × 3 $^5/_8$ in. Litho, monochrome. England, 19th century.
601. Vegetables. 2 $^3/_{16}$ × 3 $^1/_8$ in. Litho, 6 colours. France, 19th century.
602. Pickles. 2 $^{15}/_{16}$ × 4 $^3/_8$ in. Litho, 6 colours. England, 1900.
603. Confectionery. 3 $^{11}/_{16}$ × 5 $^1/_8$ in. Copper plate engraving, monochrome. England, 18th century.
604. Patent medicine. 3 $^1/_8$ × 5 $^3/_4$ in. Wood engraving and letterpress, 2 colours. Germany, 19th century.

600. *Concentré d'anchois. 6,3 × 9,2 cm. Litho une coul. Angleterre, XIXe siècle.*
601. *Primeurs. 5,6 × 8 cm. Litho six coul. France, XIXe siècle.*
602. *Légumes au vinaigre. 7,5 × 11 cm. Litho six coul. Angleterre, 1900.*
603. *Confiserie. 9,3 × 13 cm. Gravure sur cuivre une coul. Angleterre, XVIIIe siècle.*
604. *Remède. 8 × 14,5 cm. Gravure sur bois et typo deux coul. Allemagne, XIXe siècle.*

600. Sardellenkonzentrat. 6,3 × 9,2 cm. Lithographie, eine Farbe. England, XIX. Jahrhundert.
601. Frühobst und Frühgemüse. 5,6 × 8 cm. Lithographie, sechs Farben. Frankreich, XIX. Jahrhundert.
602. Essiggemüse. 7,5 × 11 cm. Lithographie, sechs Farben. England, 1900.
603. Konditoreiware. 9,3 × 13 cm. Kupferstich, eine Farbe. England, XVIII. Jahrhundert.
604. Heilmittel. 8 × 14,5 cm. Holzschnitt und Buchdruck, zwei Farben. Deutschland, XIX. Jahrhundert.

605

606

607

605. Shirts. 7 $^1/_2$ × 4 $^9/_{16}$ in. Silk-screen, 3 colours. France, 1971.
606. Drapery. 3 $^7/_8$ × 6 $^1/_{16}$ in. Copper plate engraving, monochrome. England, 19th century.
607. Tobacco. 4 $^1/_8$ × 3 $^5/_{16}$ in. Letterpress, monochrome. Design, Prof. C.O. Czeschka, Hamburg. Germany, 1924.
608. Fish-hooks. 1 $^3/_4$ × 1 $^1/_{16}$ in. Litho, monochrome. England, 19th century.
609. Cigars. 7 $^{11}/_{16}$ × 4 $^9/_{16}$ in. Letterpress, 4 colours. Design, Prof. C.O. Czeschka, Hamburg. Germany, 1924.

605. Chemises. 19 × 11,5 cm. Sérigraphie trois coul. France, 1971.
606. Draperie. 9,8 × 15,4 cm. Gravure sur cuivre une coul. Angleterre, XIXe siècle.
607. Tabac. 10,4 × 8,3 cm. Typo une coul. Créat. prof. C.O. Czeschka, Hambourg. Allemagne, 1924.
608. Hameçons. 4,5 × 2,7 cm. Litho une coul. Angleterre, XIXe siècle.
609. Cigares. 19,5 × 11,5 cm. Typo quatre coul. Créat. prof. C.O. Czeschka, Hambourg. Allemagne, 1924.

605. Hemden. 19 × 11,5 cm. Siebdruck, drei Farben. Frankreich, 1971.
606. Tuchwaren. 9,8 × 15,4 cm. Kupferstich, eine Farbe. England, XIX. Jahrhundert.
607. Tabak. 10,4 × 8,3 cm. Buchdruck, eine Farbe. Urheber: Professor C.O. Czeschka, Hamburg. Deutschland, 1924.
608. Angelhaken. 4,5 × 2,7 cm. Lithographie, eine Farbe. England, XIX. Jahrhundert.
609. Zigarren. 19,5 × 11,5 cm. Buchdruck, vier Farben. Urheber: Professor C.O. Czeschka, Hamburg. Deutschland, 1924.

608

609

610

611

612

613

614

610. Bootmaker. 2 1/8 × 2 11/16 in. Copper plate engraving, monochrome. England, 18th century.
611. Ski boots. 3 7/8 × 4 3/8 in. Silk-screen, 3 colours. Switzerland, 1971.
612. Matches. 1 1/4 × 2 1/16 in. Litho, 4 colours. Sweden early 20th century.
613. Ski fasteners. 3 1/8 × 4 13/16 in. Offset, 3 colours. France, 1971.
614. Boot polish. 2 15/16 × 4 3/8 in. Wood engraving and letterpress, monochrome. England, 19th century.

610. Fabricant de chaussures. 5,4 × 6,8 cm. Gravure sur cuivre une coul. Angleterre, XVIIIe siècle.
611. Chaussures de ski. 9,8 × 11 cm. Sérigraphie trois coul. Suisse, 1971.
612. Allumettes. 3,2 × 5,3 cm. Litho quatre coul. Suède, début du XXe siècle.
613. Fixations de skis. 8 × 12,2 cm. Offset trois coul. France, 1971.
614. Cirage. 7,5 × 11 cm. Gravure sur bois et typo une coul. Angleterre, XIXe siècle.

610. Schuhfabrikant. 5,4 × 6,8 cm. Kupferstich, eine Farbe. England, XVIII. Jahrhundert.
611. Schistiefel. 9,8 × 11 cm. Siebdruck, drei Farben. Schweiz, 1971.
612. Streichhölzer. 3,2 × 5,3 cm. Lithographie, vier Farben. Schweden, Beginn des XX. Jahrhunderts.
613. Schibindung. 8 × 12,2 cm. Offset, drei Farben. Frankreich, 1971.
614. Schuhcreme. 7,5 × 11 cm. Holzschnitt und Buchdruck, eine Farbe. England, XIX. Jahrhundert.

615

616

617

615. Lemonade.   3 ¹/₈ × 2 ¹/₁₆   in.   Offset, 2 colours.   Design, K & K Agency/F. Carabott, Athens.   Greece, 1968.
616. Optician.   3 ¹/₄ × 2 ³/₁₆   in.   Letterpress, monochrome.   England, 19th century.
617. Orangeade.   3 ¹/₈ × 2 ¹/₁₆   in.   Offset, 2 colours.   Design, K & K Agency/ F. Carabott, Athens.   Greece, 1968.
618. Biscuits.   10 ¹/₄ × 5 ⁵/₈   in.   Litho, monochrome and gold.   England, 20th century.
619. Cigars.   9 ¹/₄ × 5 ¹⁵/₁₆   in.   Letterpress, 3 colours.   Design, Prof. C.O. Czeschka, Hamburg.   Germany, 1924.

615. *Limonade.   8 × 5,3 cm. Offset deux coul. Créat. agence K & K, F. Carabott, Athènes. Grèce, 1968.*
616. *Opticien.   8,2 × 5,5 cm.   Typo une coul. Angleterre, XIXᵉ siècle.*
617. *Orangeade.   8 × 5,3 cm. Offset deux coul. Créat. agence K & K, F. Carabott, Athènes. Grèce, 1968.*
618. *Biscuits.   26 × 14,2 cm. Litho une coul. et or. Angleterre, XXᵉ siècle.*
619. *Cigares.   23,5 × 15 cm. Typo trois coul. Créat. Prof. C.O. Czeschka, Hambourg. Allemagne, 1924.*

615. Limonade. 8 × 5,3 cm. Offset, zwei Farben. Urheber: Agentur K & K, F. Carabott, Athen. Griechenland, 1968.
616. Optiker. 8,2 × 5,5 cm. Buchdruck, eine Farbe. England, XIX. Jahrhundert.
617. Orangeade. 8 × 5,3 cm. Offset, zwei Farben. Urheber: Agentur K & K, F. Carabott, Athen. Griechenland, 1968.
618. Zwieback. 26 × 14,2 cm. Lithographie, eine Farbe und Gold. England, XX. Jahrhundert.
619. Zigarren. 23,5 × 15 cm. Buchdruck, drei Farben. Urheber: Professor C.O. Czeschka, Hamburg. Deutschland, 1924.

618

619

620

621

622

623

624

620. Lemons. 6 $^{13}/_{16}$ × 3 $^9/_{16}$ in. Offset, 4 colours. K & K Agency/J. Angelopoulos, Athens. Greece, 1969.

621. Fruit juice. 1 $^7/_8$ × 3 $^1/_2$ in. Offset, 4 colours. Design, Plan Design A/S/C. Rostrup. Denmark, 1971.

622. Lemon syrup. 4 $^9/_{16}$ × 3 in. Litho, 4 colours. Design, Gerstung. Germany, 1936–1937.

623. Fruit juice. 9 $^1/_{16}$ × 8 $^3/_{16}$ in. Offset, 4 colours. France, 1971.

624. Orange flower water. 1 $^5/_8$ × 2 $^7/_{16}$ in. Litho, monochrome. England, 19th century.

620. Citrons. 17,2 × 9 cm. Offset quatre coul. Agence K & K, J. Angelopoulos, Athènes. Grèce, 1969.

621. Jus de fruit. 4,8 × 8,8 cm. Offset quatre coul. Créat. Plan Design A/S, C. Rostrup. Danemark, 1971.

622. Sirop de citron. 11,6 × 7,6 cm. Litho quatre coul. Créat. Gerstung. Allemagne, 1936-1937.

623. Jus de fruit. 23 × 20,8 cm. Offset quatre coul. France, 1971.

624. Eau de fleur d'oranger. 4,2 × 6,2 cm. Litho une coul. Angleterre, XIXᵉ siècle.

620. Zitronen. 17,2 × 9 cm. Offset, vier Farben. Agentur K & K, J. Angelopoulos, Athen. Griechenland, 1969.

621. Fruchtsaft. 4,8 × 8,8 cm. Offset, vier Farben. Urheber: Plan Design A/S, C. Rostrup. Dänemark, 1971.

622. Zitronensirup. 11,6 × 7,6 cm. Lithographie, vier Farben. Urheber: Gerstung. Deutschland, 1936–1937.

623. Fruchtsaft. 23 × 20,8 cm. Offset, vier Farben. Frankreich, 1971.

624. Orangenblütenwasser. 4,2 × 6,2 cm. Lithographie, eine Farbe. England, XIX. Jahrhundert.

625. Rice starch. $4\,^3/_{16} \times 5\,^3/_8$ in. Litho, 7 colours. England, late 19th century.
626. Upholsterer. $4\,^{13}/_{16} \times 6\,^5/_{16}$ in. Wood engraving and letterpress, monochrome. England, 1753.
627. Textile. $3\,^5/_8 \times 5$ in. Litho, 5 colours. England, 19th century.
628. Mathematical instruments. $4\,^3/_8 \times 7\,^1/_8$ in. Copper plate engraving, monochrome. Engraved by Th. Platt. England, 1730.
629. Instruments. $4\,^9/_{16} \times 6$ in. Copper plate engraving, monochrome. England, 18th century.

625. *Amidon de riz. 10,6 × 13,6 cm. Litho sept coul. Angleterre, fin du XIXe siècle.*
626. *Tapissier. 12,2 × 16 cm. Bois et typo une coul. Angleterre, 1753.*
627. *Textile. 9,2 × 12,7 cm. Litho cinq coul. Angleterre, XIXe siècle.*
628. *Instruments. 11 × 18 cm. Gravure sur cuivre une coul. Grav. Th. Platt. Angleterre, 1730.*
629. *Instruments. 11,5 × 15,2 cm. Gravure sur cuivre une coul. Angleterre, XVIIIe siècle.*

625. Reisstärke. 10,6 × 13,6 cm. Lithographie, sieben Farben. England, Ende des XIX. Jahrhunderts.
626. Polsterer. 12,2 × 16 cm. Holzschnitt und Buchdruck, eine Farbe. England, 1753.
627. Textilware. 9,2 × 12,7 cm. Lithographie, fünf Farben. England, XIX. Jahrhundert.
628. Instrumente. 11 × 18 cm. Kupferstich, eine Farbe. Gestochen von Th. Platt. England, 1730.
629. Instrumente. 11,5 × 15,2 cm. Kupferstich, eine Farbe. England, XVIII. Jahrhundert.

630

631

632

633

634

630. Perfume. 1 5/8 in. diameter. Letterpress, 3 colours. Design, E. Blankenburg. Germany, 1924.
631. Dessert wine. 4 5/8 × 3 9/16 in. Offset, 4 colours. Design, O. Eksell, Stockholm. Sweden, 1952.
632. Perfume. 1 5/8 in. diameter. Letterpress, 3 colours. Design, E. Blankenburg. Germany, 1924.
633. Lace-maker. 6 1/8 × 7 1/2 in. Litho, monochrome. England, 19th century.
634. Spirits. 4 3/8 × 2 15/16 in. Litho, 3 colours. Switzerland, 19th century.

630. *Parfum. Diam. 4,2 cm. Typo trois coul. Créat. E. Blankenburg. Allemagne, 1924.*
631. *Vin de dessert. 11,7 × 9 cm. Offset quatre coul. Créat. O. Eksell, Stockholm. Suède, 1952.*
632. *Parfum. Diam. 4,2 cm. Typo trois coul. Créat. E. Blankenburg. Allemagne, 1924.*
633. *Dentellier. 15,5 × 19 cm. Litho une coul. Angleterre, XIXe siècle.*
634. *Eau-de-vie. 11 × 7,5 cm. Litho trois coul. Suisse, XIXe siècle.*

630. Parfüm. Durchmesser 4,2 cm. Buchdruck, drei Farben. Urheber: E. Blankenburg. Deutschland, 1924.
631. Dessertwein. 11,7 × 9 cm. Offset, vier Farben. Urheber: O. Eksell, Stockholm. Schweden, 1952.
632. Parfüm. Durchmesser 4,2 cm. Buchdruck, drei Farben. Urheber: E. Blankenburg. Deutschland, 1924.
633. Spitzenfabrikant. 15,5 × 19 cm. Lithographie, eine Farbe. England, XIX. Jahrhundert.
634. Branntwein. 11 × 7,5 cm. Lithographie, drei Farben. Schweiz, XIX. Jahrhundert.

635

636

637

635. Hotel. 6 $^1/_4$ × 4 $^{15}/_{16}$ in. Litho, 5 colours.
Printing, Richter & Co., Naples. Italy,
20th century.
636. Pickles. 6 × 4 in. Litho, 2 colours.
England, 1900.
637. Soap. 2 × 2 $^{15}/_{16}$ in. Litho, monochrome,
hand-coloured. France, 19th century.
638. Jam. 9 $^1/_{16}$ × 3 $^9/_{16}$ in. Litho, 6 colours.
England, late 19th century.
639. Hotel. 6 $^5/_{16}$ × 4 $^3/_4$ in. Litho, 3 colours.
Printing, Richter & Co., Naples. Italy,
early 20th century.

635. Hôtel. 15,8 × 12,5 cm. Litho cinq coul.
Imp. Richter & Co., Naples. Italie, XXe siècle.
636. Légumes au vinaigre. 15,2 × 10,2 cm.
Litho deux coul. Angleterre, 1900.
637. Savon. 5,1 × 7,4 cm. Litho une coul.
coloriée à la main. France, XIXe siècle.
638. Confiture. 23 × 9 cm. Litho six coul. Angleterre, fin du XIXe siècle.
639. Hôtel. 16 × 12 cm. Litho trois coul. Imp.
Richter & Co., Naples. Italie, début du
XXe siècle.

635. Hotel. 15,8 × 12,5 cm. Lithographie, fünf
Farben. Druckerei Richter & Co., Neapel.
Italien, XX. Jahrhundert.
636. Essiggemüse. 15,2 × 10,2 cm. Lithographie, zwei Farben. England, 1900.
637. Seife. 5,1 × 7,4 cm. Lithographie, eine
Farbe, handkoloriert. Frankreich, XIX. Jahrhundert.
638. Marmelade. 23 × 9 cm. Lithographie, sechs
Farben. England, Ende des XIX. Jahrhunderts.
639. Hotel. 16 × 12 cm. Lithographie, drei Farben. Druckerei Richter & Co., Neapel.
Italien, Beginn des XX. Jahrhunderts.

638

639

640

641

642

643

644

640. Hotel. 4 ³/₄ × 4 ³/₄ in. Litho, 2 colours. Printing, Schwob & Richard, Paris. France, early 20th century.
641. Trunks. 7 ⁷/₈ × 6 ¹¹/₁₆ in. Copper plate engraving, monochrome. England, 18th century.
642. Biscuits. 8 ⁷/₈ × 9 ¹/₈ in. Litho, 8 colours. England, early 20th century.
643. Tonic. 12 ¹⁵/₁₆ × 6 ¹³/₁₆ in. Litho, 3 colours and gold. England, 1900.
644. Cigars. 5 ⁵/₁₆ × 2 ¹³/₁₆ in. Offset, 5 colours and embossed gold. Holland, 20th century.

640. Hôtel. 12 × 12 cm. Litho deux coul. Imp. Schwob & Richard, Paris. France, début du XXᵉ siècle.
641. Coffres. 21 × 17 cm. Gravure sur cuivre une coul. Angleterre, XVIIIᵉ siècle.
642. Biscuits. 22,5 × 23,2 cm. Litho huit coul. Angleterre, début du XXᵉ siècle.
643. Tonique. 32,8 × 17,2 cm. Litho trois coul. et or. Angleterre, 1900.
644. Cigares. 13,5 × 7,2 cm. Offset cinq coul. et or gaufré. Hollande, XXᵉ siècle.

640. Hotel. 12 × 12 cm. Lithographie, zwei Farben. Druckerei Schwob & Richard, Paris. Frankreich, Beginn des XX. Jahrhunderts.
641. Kästen. 21 × 17 cm. Kupferstich, eine Farbe. England, XVIII. Jahrhundert.
642. Zwieback. 22,5 × 23,2 cm. Lithographie, acht Farben. England, Beginn des XX. Jahrhunderts.
643. Tonikum. 32,8 × 17,2 cm. Lithographie, drei Farben und Gold. England, 1900.
644. Zigarren. 13,5 × 7,2 cm. Offset, fünf Farben und Prägung in Gold. Holland, XX. Jahrhundert.

645

646

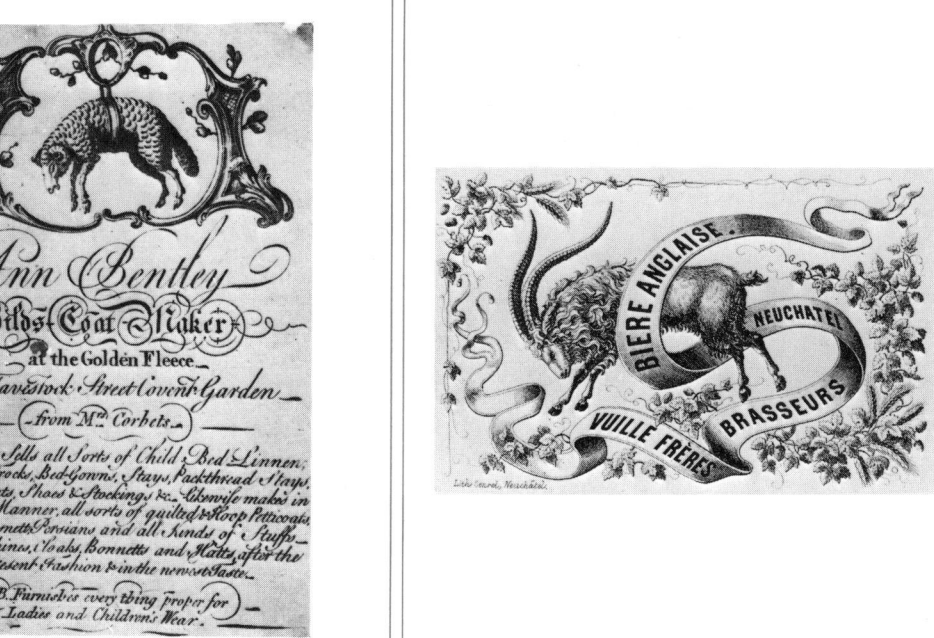

647

645. Cigarettes (matches). 1 $^7/_{16}$ × 1 $^7/_8$ in. Offset, 3 colours. USA, 1971.
646. Children's coats. 4 $^3/_8$ × 6 $^5/_{16}$ in. Copper plate engraving, monochrome. England, 1753.
647. Beer. 5 × 3 $^1/_{16}$ in. Litho, monochrome. Printing, Sonrel, Neuchâtel. Switzerland, 19th century.
648. Cigars. 10 $^7/_{16}$ × 5 $^{11}/_{16}$ in. Letterpress, 4 colours. Design, Prof. C. O. Czeschka, Hamburg. Germany, 1924.
649. Motor cars. 2 $^3/_{16}$ × 2 $^9/_{16}$ in. Silkscreen, 4 colours and gold. Germany, 1971.

645. *Cigarettes (allumettes). 3,6 × 4,8 cm. Offset trois coul. U.S.A., 1971.*
646. *Manteaux pour enfants. 11 × 16 cm. Gravure sur cuivre une coul. Angleterre, 1753.*
647. *Bière. 12,7 × 7,8 cm. Litho une coul. Imp. Sonrel, Neuchâtel. Suisse, XIXe siècle.*
648. *Cigares. 26,5 × 14,4 cm. Typo quatre coul. Créat. prof. C.O. Czeschka, Hambourg. Allemagne, 1924.*
649. *Automobiles. 5,5 × 6,5 cm. Sérigraphie quatre coul. et or. Allemagne, 1971.*

645. Zigaretten (Streichhölzer). 3,6 × 4,8 cm. Offset, drei Farben. U.S.A., 1971.
646. Kindermäntel. 11 × 16 cm. Kupferstich, eine Farbe. England, 1753.
647. Bier. 12,7 × 7,8 cm. Lithographie, eine Farbe. Druckerei Sonrel, Neuchâtel. Schweiz, XIX. Jahrhundert.
648. Zigarren. 26,5 × 14,4 cm. Buchdruck, vier Farben. Urheber: Professor C. O. Czeschka, Hamburg. Deutschland, 1924.
649. Automobile. 5,5 × 6,5 cm. Siebdruck, vier Farben und Gold. Deutschland, 1971.

648

649

650

651

652

653

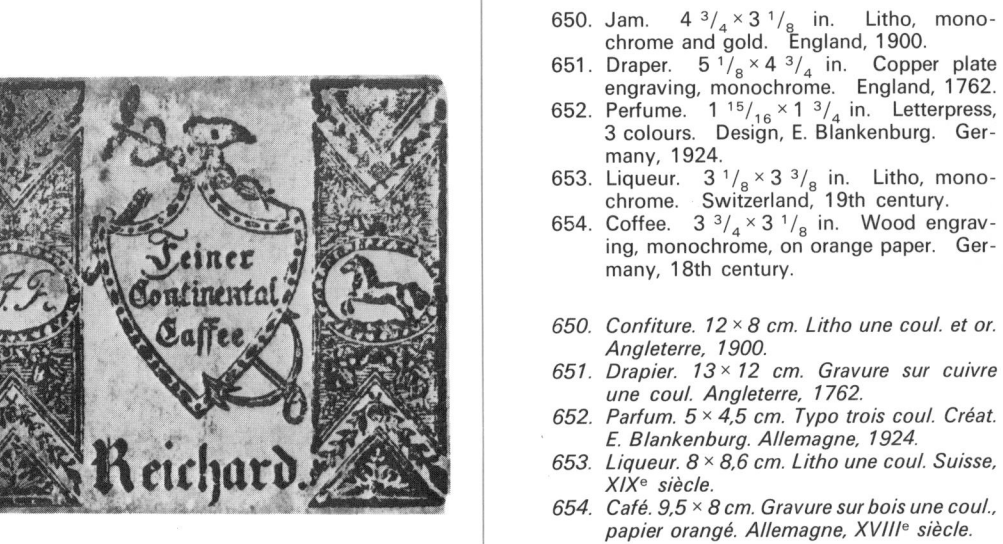

654

650. Jam. 4 ³/₄ × 3 ¹/₈ in. Litho, mono-chrome and gold. England, 1900.
651. Draper. 5 ¹/₈ × 4 ³/₄ in. Copper plate engraving, monochrome. England, 1762.
652. Perfume. 1 ¹⁵/₁₆ × 1 ³/₄ in. Letterpress, 3 colours. Design, E. Blankenburg. Germany, 1924.
653. Liqueur. 3 ¹/₈ × 3 ³/₈ in. Litho, mono-chrome. Switzerland, 19th century.
654. Coffee. 3 ³/₄ × 3 ¹/₈ in. Wood engraving, monochrome, on orange paper. Germany, 18th century.

650. Confiture. 12 × 8 cm. Litho une coul. et or. Angleterre, 1900.
651. Drapier. 13 × 12 cm. Gravure sur cuivre une coul. Angleterre, 1762.
652. Parfum. 5 × 4,5 cm. Typo trois coul. Créat. E. Blankenburg. Allemagne, 1924.
653. Liqueur. 8 × 8,6 cm. Litho une coul. Suisse, XIXᵉ siècle.
654. Café. 9,5 × 8 cm. Gravure sur bois une coul., papier orangé. Allemagne, XVIIIᵉ siècle.

650. Marmelade. 12 × 8 cm. Lithographie, eine Farbe und Gold. England, 1900.
651. Tuchhändler. 13 × 12 cm. Kupferstich, eine Farbe. England, 1762.
652. Parfüm. 5 × 4,5 cm. Buchdruck, drei Farben. Urheber: E. Blankenburg. Deutschland, 1924.
653. Likör. 8 × 8,6 cm. Lithographie, eine Farbe. Schweiz, XIX. Jahrhundert.
654. Kaffee. 9,5 × 8 cm. Holzschnitt, eine Farbe, orangefarbiges Papier. Deutschland, XVIII. Jahrhundert.

655

656

657

655, 656, 657. Sugar. 1 3/4 × 2 3/4 in. Offset, 4 colours. Italy, 1969.
658. Airline. 3 15/16 × 3 1/8 in. Silk-screen, 5 colours. Algeria, 1971.
659. Packed spaghetti. 8 11/16 × 4 1/8 in. Litho, 5 colours. Printing, Stecher-Traung, Roch, New York. USA, 20th century.

655, 656, 657. Sucre cristallisé. 4,5 × 7cm. Offset quatre coul. Italie, 1969.
658. Compagnie aérienne. 10 × 8 cm. Sérigraphie cinq coul. Algérie, 1971.
659. Spaghetti en boîte. 22 × 10,5 cm. Litho cinq coul. Imp. Stecher-Traung, Roch, New York. U.S.A., XXe siècle.

655, 656, 657. Kristallzucker. 4,5 × 7 cm. Offset, vier Farben. Italien, 1969.
658. Fluggesellschaft. 10 × 8 cm. Siebdruck, fünf Farben. Algerien, 1971.
659. Spaghetti, verpackt. 22 × 10,5 cm. Lithographie, fünf Farben. Druckerei Stecher-Traung, Roch, New York. U.S.A., XX. Jahrhundert.

658

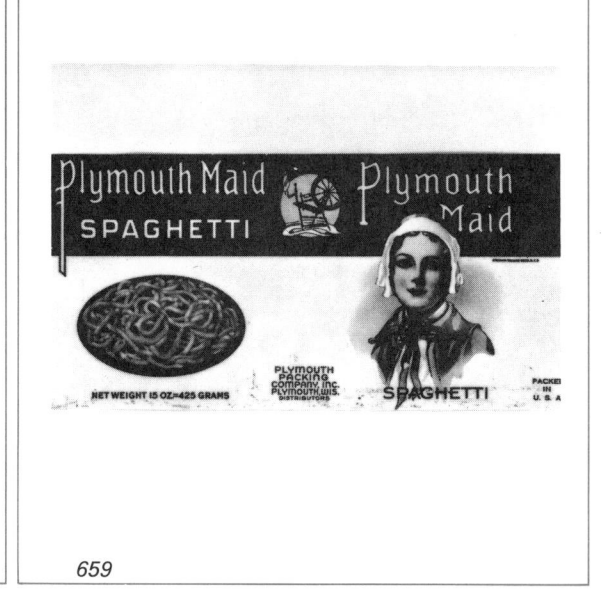

659

660

660. Tomatoes. 8 9/16 × 7 1/8 in. Litho, 6 colours. USA, 20th century.

660. Tomates. 21,8 × 18 cm. Litho six coul. U.S.A., XXᵉ siècle.

660. Tomaten. 21,8 × 18 cm. Lithographie, sechs Farben. U.S.A., XX. Jahrhundert.

661

663

661. Ex-libris. 1 $^1/_{16}$ × 1 $^7/_8$ in. Letterpress, monochrome. Design, J. Claverie, Lyons. France, 1971.
662. Ex-libris. 1 $^3/_4$ × 2 $^1/_2$ in. Letterpress, monochrome. England, 1900.
663. Ex-libris. 1 $^9/_{16}$ × 2 $^{11}/_{16}$ in. Letterpress, monochrome. England, 1900.
664. Cigars. 10 $^9/_{16}$ × 4 $^{11}/_{16}$ in. Letterpress, 3 colours. Design, Prof. C. O. Czeschka, Hamburg. Germany, 1924.
665. Textile. 1 $^{13}/_{16}$ × 2 $^{11}/_{16}$ in. Offset, 2 colours. Greece, 1970.

661. Ex-libris. 2,7 × 4,8 cm. Typo une coul. Créat. J. Claverie, Lyon. France, 1971.
662. Ex-libris. 4,5 × 6,3 cm. Typo une coul. Angleterre, 1900.
663. Ex-libris. 4 × 6,8 cm. Typo une coul. Angleterre, 1900.
664. Cigares. 26,8 × 11,8 cm. Typo trois coul. Créat. prof. C.O. Czeschka, Hambourg. Allemagne, 1924.
665. Textile. 4,6 × 6,8 cm. Offset deux coul. Grèce, 1970.

661. Exlibris. 2,7 × 4,8 cm. Buchdruck, eine Farbe. Urheber: J. Claverie, Lyon. Frankreich, 1971.
662. Exlibris. 4,5 × 6,3 cm. Buchdruck, eine Farbe. England, 1900.
663. Exlibris. 4 × 6,8 cm. Buchdruck, eine Farbe. England, 1900.
664. Zigarren. 26,8 × 11,8 cm. Typographie, drei Farben. Urheber: Professor C.O. Czeschka, Hamburg. Deutschland, 1924.
665. Textilware. 4,6 × 6,8 cm. Offset, zwei Farben. Griechenland, 1970.

664

665

666

667

668

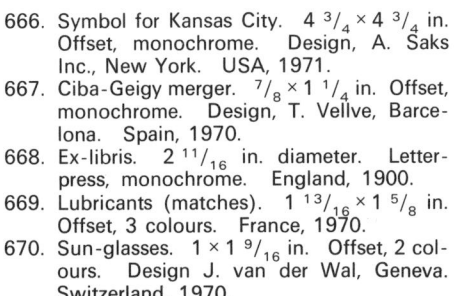

669

670

666. Symbol for Kansas City. 4 $3/4$ × 4 $3/4$ in. Offset, monochrome. Design, A. Saks Inc., New York. USA, 1971.
667. Ciba-Geigy merger. $7/8$ × 1 $1/4$ in. Offset, monochrome. Design, T. Vellve, Barcelona. Spain, 1970.
668. Ex-libris. 2 $11/16$ in. diameter. Letterpress, monochrome. England, 1900.
669. Lubricants (matches). 1 $13/16$ × 1 $5/8$ in. Offset, 3 colours. France, 1970.
670. Sun-glasses. 1 × 1 $9/16$ in. Offset, 2 colours. Design J. van der Wal, Geneva. Switzerland, 1970.

666. Symbole pour Kansas City. 12 × 12 cm. Offset une coul. Créat. A. Saks Inc., New York. U.S.A., 1971.
667. Fusion Ciba-Geigy. 2,2 × 3,2 cm. Offset une coul. Créat. T. Vellve, Barcelone. Espagne, 1970.
668. Ex-libris. Diam. 6,8 cm. Typo une coul. Angleterre, 1900.
669. Lubrifiants (allumettes). 4,6 × 4,2 cm. Offset trois coul. France, 1970.
670. Lunettes de soleil. 2,5 × 4 cm. Offset deux coul. Créat. J. van der Wal, Genève. Suisse, 1970.

666. Symbol für Kansas City. 12 × 12 cm. Offset, eine Farbe. Urheber: A. Saks Inc., New York. U.S.A., 1971.
667. Fusion Ciba-Geigy. 2,2 × 3,2 cm. Offset, eine Farbe (Urheber: T. Vellve, Barcelona. Spanien, 1970.
668. Exlibris. Durchmesser 6,8 cm. Buchdruck, eine Farbe. England, 1900.
669. Schmiermittel (Streichhölzer). 4,6 × 4,2 cm. Offset, drei Farben. Frankreich, 1970.
670. Sonnenbrille. 2,5 × 4 cm. Offset, zwei Farben. Urheber: J. van der Wal, Genf. Schweiz, 1970.

671

672

673

671. Wine. 3 $^3/_8$ × 7/$_8$ in.   Offset, monochrome. Italy, 1968.
672. Cigars. 2 $^1/_2$ × $^3/_4$ in.   Litho, 2 colours
and embossed gold.   Brazil, 20th century.
673. Wine. 4 $^1/_{16}$ × 1 $^{11}/_{16}$ in.   Offset, 4 colours and gold. Italy, 1967.
674. Sweet corn. 9 $^1/_{16}$ × 3 $^7/_{16}$ in.   Litho,
4 colours. England, 1800.
675. Fizzy drink. 4 $^3/_8$ × 2 in.   Offset, 3 colours.   Italy, 20th century.

671. Vin. 8,5 × 2,2 cm. Offset une coul. Italie,
1968.
672. Cigares. 6,3 × 2 cm. Litho deux coul. et or
gaufré. Brésil, XXᵉ siècle.
673. Vin. 10,3 × 4,3 cm. Offset quatre coul. et
or. Italie, 1967.
674. Maïs. 23 × 8,7 cm. Litho quatre coul.
Angleterre, 1800.
675. Boisson gazeuse. 11 × 5,1 cm. Offset trois
coul. Italie, XXᵉ siècle.

671. Wein. 8,5 × 2,2 cm. Offset, eine Farbe.
Italien, 1968.
672. Zigarren. 6,3 × 2 cm. Lithographie, zwei
Farben und Prägung in Gold. Brasilien,
XX. Jahrhundert.
673. Wein. 10,3 × 4,3 cm. Offset, vier Farben
und Gold. Italien, 1967.
674. Maïs. 23 × 8,7 cm. Lithographie, vier Farben. England, 1800.
675. Kohlensäurehaltiges Getränk. 11 × 5,1 cm.
Offset, drei Farben. Italien, XX. Jahrhundert.

674

675

676

677

678

679

680

676. Cigars. 2 $^9/_{16}$ × 1 $^1/_8$ in. Litho, 4 colours and embossed gold. Brazil, 20th century.
677. News. 5 $^1/_2$ × 2 $^5/_8$ in. Letterpress, monochrome. Design, Prof. C.O. Czeschka, Hamburg. Germany, 1924.
678. Cigars. 2 $^1/_2$ × $^7/_8$ in. Offset, monochrome and embossed gold. Cuba, 20th century.
679. Sauce. 2 $^9/_{16}$ × 1 $^5/_{16}$ in. Litho, 2 colours. England, 1900.
680. Cigars. 5 $^{15}/_{16}$ × 2 $^9/_{16}$ in. Offset, 5 colours and embossed gold. Holland, 20th century.

676. Cigares. 6,5 × 2,9 cm. Litho quatre coul. et or gaufré. Brésil, XXe siècle.
677. Informations. 14 × 6,7 cm. Typo une coul. Créat. prof. C.O. Czeschka, Hambourg. Allemagne, 1924.
678. Cigares. 6,3 × 2,3 cm. Offset une coul. et or gaufré. Cuba, XXe siècle.
679. Sauce. 6,5 × 3,3 cm. Litho deux coul. Angleterre, 1900.
680. Cigares. 15 × 6,5 cm. Offset cinq coul. et or gaufré. Hollande, XXe siècle.

676. Zigarren. 6,5 × 2,9 cm. Lithographie, vier Farben und Prägung in Gold. Brasilien, XX. Jahrhundert.
677. Nachrichten. 14 × 6,7 cm. Buchdruck, eine Farbe. Urheber: Professor. C.O. Czeschka, Hamburg. Deutschland, 1924.
678. Zigarren. 6,3 × 2,3 cm. Offset, eine Farbe und Prägung in Gold. Kuba, XX. Jahrhundert.
679. Sosse. 6,5 × 3,3 cm. Lithographie, zwei Farben. England, 1900.
680. Zigarren. 15 × 6,5 cm. Offset, fünf Farben und Prägung in Gold. Holland, XX. Jahrhundert.

681

682

683

681. Cigars. 2 ³/₄ × 1 in. Litho, monochrome and embossed gold. Cuba, 20th century.
682. Cigars. 2 ³/₈ × ¹¹/₁₆ in. Litho, monochrome. Mexico, 20th century.
683. Wine. 3 ¹³/₁₆ × 1 ³/₄ in. Offset, 3 colours and gold. Italy, 1968.
684. Wine. 3 ¹³/₁₆ × 1 ³/₄ in. Offset, 4 colours. Italy, 1968.
685. Fruit. 4 ¹/₂ × 1 ¹/₈ in. Offset, 2 colours, on plastic. Italy, 1970.

681. Cigares. 7 × 2,6 cm. Litho une coul. et or gaufré. Cuba, XXᵉ siècle.
682. Cigares. 6 × 1,7 cm. Litho une coul. Mexique, XXᵉ siècle.
683. Vin. 9,7 × 4,5 cm. Offset trois coul. et or. Italie, 1968.
684. Vin. 9,7 × 4,5 cm. Offset quatre coul. Italie, 1968.
685. Fruits. 11,3 × 2,8 cm. Offset deux coul., matière plastique. Italie, 1970.

681. Zigarren. 7 × 2,6 cm. Lithographie, eine Farbe und Prägung in Gold. Kuba, XX. Jahrhundert.
682. Zigarren. 6 × 1,7 cm. Lithographie, eine Farbe. Mexiko, XX. Jahrhundert.
683. Wein. 9,7 × 4,5 cm. Offset, drei Farben und Gold. Italien, 1968.
684. Wein. 9,7 × 4,5 cm. Offset, vier Farben. Italien, 1968.
685. Früchte. 11,3 × 2,8 cm. Offset, zwei Farben, Kunststoff. Italien, 1970.

684

685

686

687

Bela Cubana

688

689

690

686. Cigars. 2 $^9/_{16}$ × $^{11}/_{16}$ in. Litho, 3 colours. Brazil, 20th century.
687. Skis. 9 $^1/_4$ × 2 $^3/_4$ in. Silk-screen, 4 colours. Europe, 1971.
688. Cigars. 2 $^9/_{16}$ × $^{11}/_{16}$ in. Litho, 3 colours. Brazil, 20th century.
689. Wine. 4 $^3/_8$ × 1 $^5/_{16}$ in. Offset, 3 colours and gold. Italy, 1968.
690. Cigars. 2 $^3/_4$ × $^{11}/_{16}$ in. Litho, monochrome, on green paper. Manila, 20th century.

686. Cigares. 6,5 × 1,7 cm. Litho trois coul. Brésil, XXᵉ siècle.
687. Skis. 23,5 × 7 cm. Sérigraphie quatre coul. Europe, 1971.
688. Cigares. 6,5 × 1,7 cm. Litho trois coul. Brésil, XXᵉ siècle.
689. Vin. 11 × 3,4 cm. Offset trois coul. et or. Italie, 1968.
690. Cigares. 7 × 1,8 cm. Litho une coul., papier vert. Manille, XXᵉ siècle.

686. Zigarren. 6,4 × 1,7 cm. Lithographie, drei Farben. Brasilien, XX. Jahrhundert.
687. Schier. 23,5 × 7 cm. Siebdruck, vier Farben. Europa, 1971.
688. Zigarren. 6,5 × 1,7 cm. Lithographie, drei Farben. Brasilien, XX. Jahrhundert.
689. Wein. 11 × 3,4 cm. Offset, drei Farben und Gold. Italien, 1968.
690. Zigarren. 7 × 1,8 cm. Lithographie, eine Farbe, grünes Papier. Manila, XX. Jahrhundert.

691

692

693

691. Wine. 3 $^{13}/_{16}$ × 4 $^{7}/_{16}$ in. Offset, 4 colours. Italy, 1968.
692. Matches. 1 $^{3}/_{4}$ × 1 $^{15}/_{16}$ in. Offset, monochrome. Italy, 1970.
693. Wine. 3 $^{9}/_{16}$ × 4 $^{9}/_{16}$ in. Design in 4 colours by B. Gratecap, Paris. France, 1971.
694. Matches. 1 $^{15}/_{16}$ × 1 $^{15}/_{16}$ in. Offset, 4 colours. Italy, 1968.
695. Wine. 4 $^{15}/_{16}$ × 3 $^{11}/_{16}$ in. Offset, monochrome. France, early 20th century.

691. Vin. 9,7 × 11,2 cm. Offset quatre coul. Italie, 1968.
692. Allumettes. 4,5 × 5 cm. Offset une coul. Italie, 1970.
693. Vin. 9 × 11,5 cm. Maquette quatre coul. Créat. B. Gratecap, Paris. France, 1971.
694. Allumettes. 5 × 5 cm. Offset quatre coul. Italie, 1968.
695. Vin. 12,5 × 9,3 cm. Offset une coul. France, début du XXe siècle.

691. Wein. 9,7 × 11,2 cm. Offset, vier Farben. Italien, 1968.
692. Streichhölzer. 4,5 × 5 cm. Offset, eine Farbe. Italien, 1970.
693. Wein. 9 × 11,5 cm. Entwurf, vier Farben. Urheber: B. Gratecap, Paris. Frankreich, 1971.
694. Streichhölzer. 5 × 5 cm. Offset, vier Farben. Italien, 1968.
695. Wein. 12,5 × 9,3 cm. Offset, eine Farbe. Frankreich, Beginn des XX. Jahrhunderts.

694

695

696

697

698

699

700

696. Tea.　5 $\frac{1}{2}$ × 3 $\frac{3}{4}$ in.　Offset, 4 colours and gold.　India, 1971.
697. Panettone.　9 $\frac{13}{16}$ × 8 $\frac{5}{16}$ in.　Offset, 4 colours and gold.　Italy, 1971.
698. Vitamins.　5 $\frac{1}{2}$ × 3 $\frac{3}{4}$ in.　Offset, 2 colours.　Design, K & K Agency/J. Angelopoulos, Athens.　Greece, 1969.
699. Matches.　3 $\frac{9}{16}$ × 2 $\frac{13}{16}$ in.　Offset, 2 colours.　Printing, Solo, Austria.　Egypt, early 20th century.
700. Tobacco.　4 $\frac{1}{8}$ × 3 $\frac{5}{16}$ in.　Letterpress, monochrome.　Design, Prof. C.O. Czeschka, Hamburg.　Germany, 1924.

696. Thé. 14 × 9,5 cm. Offset quatre coul. et or. Inde, 1971.
697. Panettone. 25 × 21 cm. Offset quatre coul. et or. Italie, 1971.
698. Vitamines. 14 × 9,5 cm. Offset deux coul. Créat. Agence K & K, J. Angelopoulos, Athènes. Grèce, 1969.
699. Allumettes. 9 × 7,2 cm. Offset deux coul. Imp. Solo, Autriche. Egypte, début du XXᵉ siècle.
700. Tabac. 10,4 × 8,3 cm. Typo une coul. Créat. Prof. C.O. Czeschka, Hambourg. Allemagne, 1924.

696. Tee. 14 × 9,5 cm. Offset, vier Farben und Gold. Indien, 1971.
697. Teigkörbchen. 25 × 21 cm. Offset, vier Farben und Gold. Italien, 1971.
698. Vitamine. 14 × 9,5 cm. Offset, zwei Farben. Urheber: Agentur K & K, J. Angelopoulos, Athen. Griechenland, 1969.
699. Streichhölzer. 9 × 7,2 cm. Offset, zwei Farben. Druckerei Solo, Österreich. Ägypten, Beginn des XX. Jahrhunderts.
700. Tabak. 10,4 × 8,3 cm. Buchdruck, eine Farbe. Urheber: Professor C.O. Czeschka, Hamburg. Deutschland, 1924.

701

702

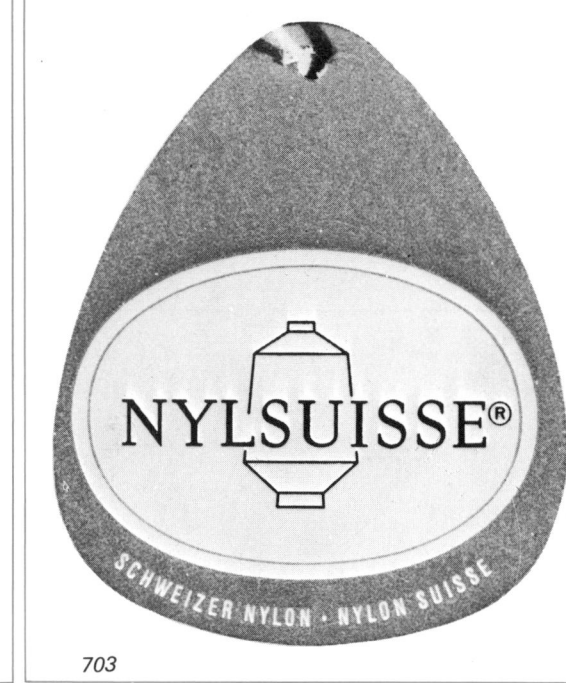

703

701. Airline. 3 $^{1}/_{16}$ × 3 $^{1}/_{2}$ in. Offset, 3 colours. Algeria, 1971.
702. Watchmaker's trademark. 1 $^{5}/_{16}$ × 1 $^{1}/_{2}$ in.
Offset, 2 colours and embossed gold.
Design, J. Van der Wal, Geneva. Switzerland, 1971.
703. Textile. 1 $^{15}/_{16}$ × 2 $^{1}/_{4}$ in. Offset, 2 colours. Switzerland, 1970.
704. Skis. 9 $^{1}/_{4}$ × 5 $^{1}/_{8}$ in. Silk-screen, 3 colours. Europe, 1971.
705. Air filters. 2 $^{1}/_{16}$ in. diameter. Letterpress, monochrome. Germany, 1924.

701. *Compagnie aérienne. 7,7 × 8,9 cm. Offset*
trois coul. Algérie, 1971.
702. *Horlogerie, marque d'authenticité. 3,4 ×*
3,8 cm. Offset deux coul. et or gaufré.
Créat. J. Van der Wal, Genève. Suisse,
1971.
703. *Textile. 5 × 5,8 cm. Offset deux coul.*
Suisse, 1970.
704. *Skis. 23,5 × 13 cm. Sérigraphie trois coul.*
Europe, 1971.
705. *Filtres à air. Diam. 5,2 cm. Typo une coul.*
Allemagne, 1924.

701. Fluggesellschaft. 7,8 × 8,9 cm. Offset, drei
Farben. Algerien, 1971.
702. Uhrengeschäft, Echtheitsmerkzeichen.
3,4 × 3,8 cm. Offset, zwei Farben und
Prägung in Gold. Urheber: J. Van der Wal,
Genf. Schweiz, 1971.
703. Textilware. 5 × 5,8 cm. Offset, zwei Farben.
Schweiz, 1970.
704. Schier. 23,5 × 13 cm. Siebdruck, drei Farben. Europa, 1971.
705. Luftfilter. Durchmesser 5,2 cm. Buchdruck,
eine Farbe. Deutschland, 1924.

704

705

706

707

708

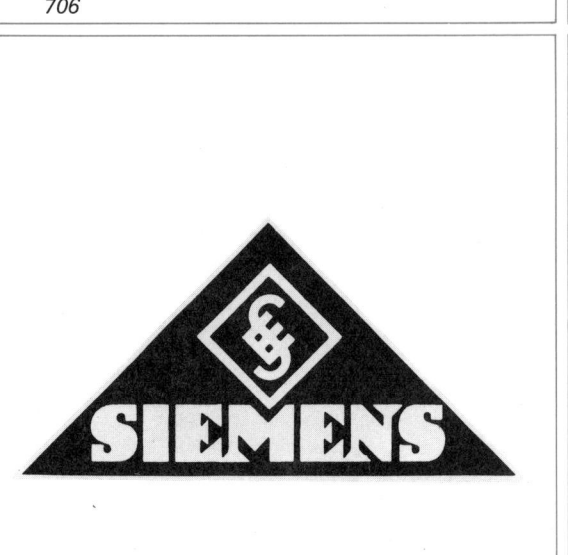

709

710

706. Apéritif. 2 ³/₈ × 1 ³/₁₆ in. Offset, 3 colours. Italy, 1971.
707. Biscuits. 4 ¹/₂ × 7 ¹/₈ in. Offset, 4 colours. Italy, 1971.
708. Tobacco. 4 ³/₈ × 2 ¹⁵/₁₆ in. Letterpress, monochrome. Design, Prof. C.O. Czeschka, Hamburg. Germany, 1924.
709. Electrical appliances. 2 ⁹/₁₆ × 1 ³/₁₆ in. Letterpress, monochrome. Germany, 1922.
710. Cigars. 9 ¹/₈ × 6 ¹/₈ in. Letterpress, 4 colours and gold. Design, Prof. C. O. Czeschka, Hamburg. Germany, 1924.

706. Apéritif. 6 × 3 cm. Offset trois coul. Italie, 1971.
707. Biscuits. 11,3 × 18 cm. Offset quatre coul. Italie, 1971.
708. Tabac. 11,1 × 7,4 cm. Typo une coul. Créat. Prof. C. O. Czeschka, Hambourg. Allemagne, 1924.
709. Appareils électriques. 6,5 × 3,1 cm. Typo une coul. Allemagne, 1922.
710. Cigares. 23,2 × 13,5 cm. Typo quatre coul, et or. Créat. Prof. C. O. Czeschka, Hambourg. Allemagne, 1924.

706. Aperitif. 6 × 3 cm. Offset, drei Farben. Italien, 1971.
707. Zwieback. 11,3 × 18 cm. Offset, vier Farben. Italien, 1971.
708. Tabak. 11,1 × 7,4 cm. Buchdruck, eine Farbe. Urheber: Professor C.O. Czeschka, Hamburg. Deutschland, 1924.
709. Elektrische Geräte. 6,5 × 3,1 cm. Buchdruck, eine Farbe. Deutschland, 1922.
710. Zigarren. 23,2 × 13,5 cm. Buchdruck, vier Farben und Gold. Urheber: Professor C. O. Czeschka, Hamburg. Deutschland, 1924.

711

712

713

711. Textile. 1 $^{15}/_{16}$ × $^9/_{16}$ in. Woven, monochrome. Italy, 1969.
712. Textile. 1 $^3/_{16}$ × 2 $^3/_4$ in. Woven, 3 colours. Italy, 1969.
713. Textile. 2 $^3/_{16}$ × $^9/_{16}$ in. Woven, monochrome. Italy, 1969.
714. Textile. Litho, monochrome. England,
19th century.
715. Tapestry. 8 $^{11}/_{16}$ × 2 $^{15}/_{16}$ in. Letterpress, monochrome. Printing, J. Cha-
lande, Geneva. Switzerland, 1969.

711. Textile. 5 × 1,5 cm. Tissage une coul.
Italie, 1959.
712. Textile. 3 × 7 cm. Tissage trois coul. Italie,
1969.
713. Textile. 5,5 × 1,5 cm. Tissage une coul.
Italie, 1969.
714. Textile. Litho une coul. Angleterre, XIXe
siècle.
715. Tapisserie. Typo une coul. 22 × 7,5 cm.
Imp. J. Chalande, Genève. Suisse, 1969.

711. Textilware. 5 × 1,5 cm. Gewebe, eine
Farbe. Italien, 1969.
712. Textilware. 3 × 7 cm. Gewebe, drei Farben.
Italien, 1969.
173. Textilware. 5,5 × 1,5 cm. Gewebe, eine
Farbe. Italien, 1969.
714. Textilware. Lithographie, eine Farbe. England, XIX. Jahrhundert.
715. Tapeziergeschäft. Buchdruck, eine Farbe.
22 × 7,5 cm. Druckerei J. Chalande, Genf.
Schweiz, 1969.

714

715

722

723

724

725

726

722. Clementines. 4 $^1/_{16}$ × 4 $^1/_4$ in. Rubber plate rotary, 4 colours. Tunisia, 1969.
723. Confectionery. 6 $^5/_{16}$ in. diameter. Offset, 4 colours and gold. Italy, 1971.
724. Peaches. 7 $^7/_8$ × 7 $^9/_{16}$ in. Litho, 4 colours. USA, 20th century.
725. Lemons. 2 $^3/_{16}$ × 5 $^1/_8$ in. Rubber plate rotary, 3 colours. Italy, 1970.
726. Apple juice. Offset, 3 colours. Design, E. & U. Hiestand, Zurich. Switzerland, 1963–1967.

722. Mandarines. 10,3 × 10,7 cm. Rotative caoutchouc quatre coul. Tunisie, 1969.
723. Confiserie. Diam. 16 cm. Offset quatre coul. et or. Italie, 1971.
724. Pêches. 20 × 19,2 cm. Lithographie quatre coul. U.S.A., XXᵉ siècle.
725. Citrons. 5,5 × 13 cm. Rotative caoutchouc trois coul. Italie, 1970.
726. Jus de pommes. Offset trois coul. Créat. E. & U. Hiestand, Zurich. Suisse, 1963-1967.

721. Mandarinen. 10,3 × 10,7 cm. Rotationsmaschine, Gummi, vier Farben. Tunesien, 1969.
723. Konditoreiware. Durchmesser 16 cm. Offset, vier Farben und Gold. Italien, 1971.
724. Pfirsiche. 20 × 19,2 cm. Lithographie, vier Farben. U.S.A., XX. Jahrhundert.
725. Zitronen. 5,5 × 13 cm. Rotationsmaschine, Gummi, drei Farben. Italien, 1970.
726. Apfelsaft. Offset, drei Farben. Urheber: E. & U. Hiestand, Zürich. Schweiz, 1963–1967.

727

728

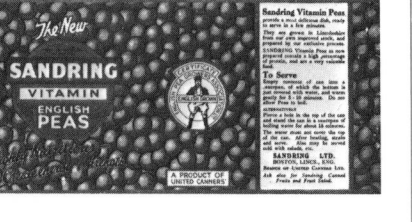

729

727. Vegetables.   8 ¹/₈ × 4 ¹/₁₆ in.   Litho,
    4 colours.   UAR, 1970.
728. Pineapple.   12 ¹³/₁₆ × 4 ³/₈ in.   Litho,
    7 colours.   England, 1900.
729. Sauce. 6 ¹/₈ × 2 ³/₈ in. Offset, 4 colours.
    Hong Kong, 1971.
730. Peas.   11 × 4 ³/₁₆ in.   Litho, 5 colours.
    England, 20th century.
731. Raspberries. Litho, 2 colours.   Printing,
    Kynock Press.   England, 1934.

727. *Légumes. 20,5 × 10,3 cm. Litho quatre*
    coul. R.A.U., 1970.
728. *Ananas. 32,5 × 11 cm. Litho sept coul.*
    Angleterre, 1900.
729. *Sauce. 15,5 × 6 cm. Offset quatre coul.*
    Hong-Kong, 1971.
730. *Petits pois. 28 × 10,6 cm. Litho cinq coul.*
    Angleterre, XXᵉ siècle.
731. *Framboises. Litho deux coul. Imp. Kynock*
    Press. Angleterre, 1934.

727. Gemüse. 20,5 × 10,3 cm. Lithographie,
    vier Farben. V.A.R., 1970.
728. Ananas. 32,5 × 11 cm. Lithographie, sieben
    Farben. England, 1900.
729. Sosse. 15,5 × 6 cm. Offset, vier Farben.
    Hongkong, 1971.
730. Erbsen. 28 × 10,6 cm. Lithographie, fünf
    Farben. England, XX. Jahrhundert.
731. Himbeeren. Lithographie, zwei Farben.
    Druckerei Kynock Press. England, 1934.

730

731

732

733

734

735

736

732. Bamboo shoots. 10 $^3/_8$ × 4 $^1/_4$ in. Offset, 4 colours. Hong Kong, 1971.
733. Plums. 11 $^5/_8$ × 3 $^5/_8$ in. Litho, 7 colours. England, 1900.
734. Salami. 5 $^3/_{16}$ × 2 $^3/_4$ in. Offset, 4 colours. Italy, 1971.
735. Mangoes. 7 $^1/_2$ × 2 $^3/_4$ in. Offset, 4 colours. India, 1971.
736. Cannelloni. 11 × 3 $^1/_8$ in. Offset, 4 colours. Italy, 1971.

732. Pousses de bambou. 26,3 × 10,7 cm. Offset quatre coul. Hong-Konh, 1971.
733. Pruneaux. 29,5 × 9,2 cm. Litho sept coul. Angleterre, 1900.
734. Salami. 13,2 × 6,9 cm. Offset quatre coul. Italie, 1971.
735. Fruits. 19 × 6,9 cm. Offset quatre coul. Inde, 1971.
736. Cannelloni. 28 × 8 cm. Offset quatre coul. Italie, 1971.

732. Bambus-Schösslinge. 26,3 × 10,7 cm. Offset, vier Farben. Hongkong, 1971.
733. Gedörrte Pflaumen. 29,5 × 9,2 cm. Lithographie, sieben Farben. England, 1900.
734. Salami. 13,2 × 6,9 cm. Offset, vier Farben. Italien, 1971.
735. Früchte. 19 × 6,9 cm. Offset, vier Farben. Indien, 1971.
736. Cannelloni 28 × 8 cm. Offset, vier Farben. Italien, 1971.

737

738

739

737. Bean sprouts. 9 $^1/_{16}$ × 4 $^3/_{16}$ in. Offset, 4 colours. Canada, 1971.

738. Apéritif. 3 $^3/_8$ × 5 $^3/_{16}$ in. Offset, 4 colours and gold. Design, Paul Rand, New York. USA, 1950.

739. Tripe. 7 $^1/_8$ × 4 $^3/_8$ in. Offset, 4 colours. France, 1971.

740. Clam sauce. 3 $^9/_{16}$ × 3 $^9/_{16}$ in. Offset, 4 colours. Italy, 1971.

741. Pasta. 5 $^{11}/_{16}$ × 2 $^9/_{16}$ in. Offset, 4 colours. Italy, 1971.

737. Pousses de haricots. 23 × 10,6 cm. Offset quatre coul. Canada, 1971.

738. Vin apéritif. 8,6 × 13,1 cm. Offset quatre coul. et or. Créat. Paul Rand, New York. U.S.A., 1950.

739. Tripes. 18 × 11 cm. Offset quatre coul. France, 1971.

740. Sugo. 9 × 9 cm. Offset quatre coul. Italie, 1971.

741. Pâtes alimentaires. 14,4 × 6,5 cm. Offset quatre coul. Italie, 1971.

737. Bohnenschösslinge. 23 × 10,6 cm. Offset, vier Farben. Kanada, 1971.

738. Aperitif-Wein. 8,6 × 13,1 cm. Offset, vier Farben und Gold. Urheber: Paul Rand, New York. U.S.A., 1950.

739. Eingeweide. 18 × 11 cm. Offset, vier Farben. Frankreich, 1971.

740. Sugo. 9 × 9 cm. Offset, vier Farben. Italien, 1971.

741. Teigwaren. 14,4 × 6,5 cm. Offset, vier Farben. Italien, 1971.

740

741

742. Beer. 3 7/8 × 2 9/16 in. Offset, 2 colours and silver. Germany, 1961.
743. Apple juice. 4 3/4 × 2 15/16 in. Offset, 4 colours. Design, E. & U. Hiestand, Zurich. Switzerland, 1963–1967.
744. Coppa. 7 7/8 × 3 3/4 in. Offset, 4 colours. Italy, 1971.
745. Mangoes. 6 7/8 × 1 7/8 in. Litho, 5 colours. UAR, 1971.
746. Olives. 8 3/16 × 5 5/8 in. Litho, 5 colours. USA, 20th century.

742. Bière. 9,8 × 6,5 cm. Offset deux coul. et argent. Allemagne, 1961.
743. Jus de pommes. 12 × 7,5 cm. Offset quatre coul. Créat. E. & U. Hiestand, Zurich. Suisse, 1963-1967.
744. Coppa. 20 × 9,5 cm. Offset quatre coul. Italie, 1971.
745. Mangues. 17,5 × 4,8 cm. Litho cinq coul. R.A.U., 1971.
746. Olives. 20,8 × 14,2 cm. Litho cinq coul. U.S.A., XXᵉ siècle.

742. Bier. 9,8 × 6,5 cm. Offset, zwei Farben und Silber. Deutschland, 1961.
743. Apfelsaft. 12 × 7,5 cm. Offset, vier Farben. Urheber: E. & U. Hiestand, Zürich. Schweiz, 1963–1967.
744. Coppa. 20 × 9,5 cm. Offset, vier Farben. Italien, 1971.
745. Mangonen. 17,5 × 4,8 cm. Lithographie, fünf Farben. V.A.R., 1971.
746. Oliven. 20,8 × 14,2 cm. Lithographie, fünf Farben. U.S.A., XX. Jahrhundert.

747

748

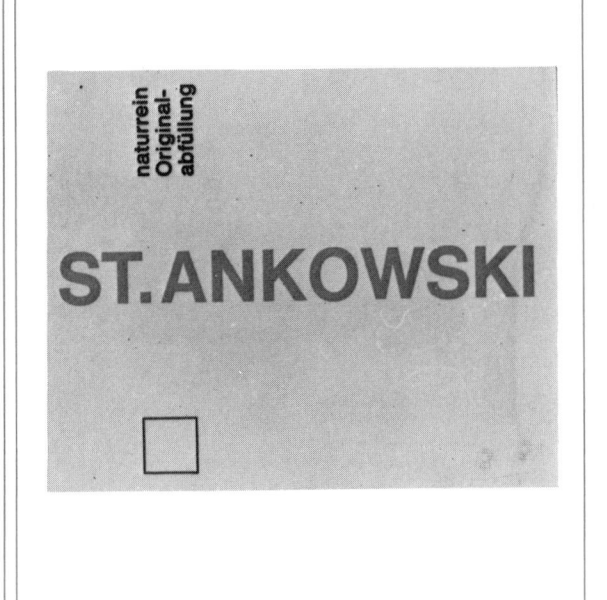

749

747. Silcarbo paper. 9 $^1/_8$ × 2 $^{15}/_{16}$ in. Offset, 3 colours. Design, E. & U. Hiestand, Zurich. Switzerland, 1963.
748. Address label. 2 $^1/_{16}$ × 3 $^1/_2$ in. Offset, 3 colours. Design, Herb Lubalin, New York. USA, 1971.
749. Wine. 4 $^1/_8$ × 3 $^3/_8$ in. Offset, 2 colours. Design, A. Stankowski, Stuttgart. Germany, 1971.
750. Cosmetics. 2 $^{11}/_{16}$ × 4 $^9/_{16}$ in. Letterpress, 3 colours. Design, W. Schwerdiner. Germany, 1924.
751. Address label. 6 $^{15}/_{16}$ × 3 $^3/_8$ in. Offset, 3 colours. Design, Push Pin Studios Inc./Milton Glaser, New York. USA, 1971.

747. Papier silcarbo. 23,1 × 7,5 cm. Offset trois coul. Créat. E. & U. Hiestand, Zurich. Suisse, 1963.
748. Etiquette-adresse. 5,2 × 8,9 cm. Offset trois coul. Créat. Herb Lubalin, New York. U.S.A., 1971.
749. Vin. 10,5 × 8,5 cm. Offset deux coul. Créat. A. Stankowski, Stuttgart. Allemagne, 1791.
750. Parfumerie. 6,8 × 11,6 cm. Typo trois coul. Créat. W. Schwerdiner. Allemagne, 1924.
751. Etiquette-adresse. 17,6 × 8,5 cm. Offset trois coul. irisées. Créat. Push Pin Studios Inc., Milton Glaser, New York. U.S.A., 1971.

747. Silcarbopapier. 23,1 × 7,5 cm. Offset, drei Farben. Urheber: E. & U. Hiestand, Zürich. Schweiz, 1963.
748. Adressenetikett. 5,2 × 8,9 cm. Offset, drei Farben. Urheber: Herb. Lubalin, New York. U.S.A., 1971.
749. Wein. 10,5 × 8,5 cm. Offset, zwei Farben. Urheber: A. Stankowski, Stuttgart. Deutschland, 1971.

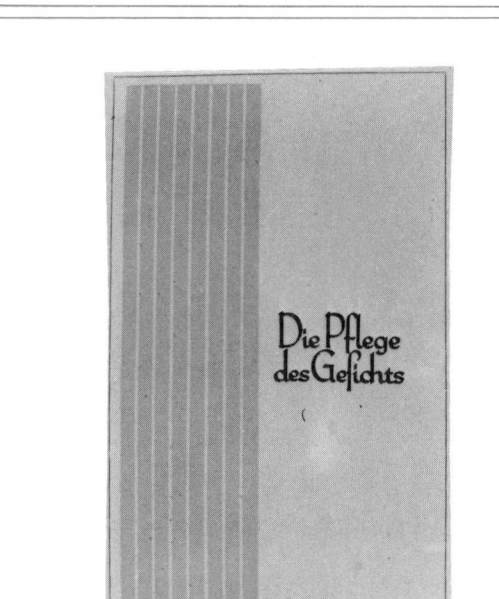

750

751

750. Parfümhandlung. 6,8 × 11,6 cm. Buchdruck, drei Farben. Urheber: W. Schwerdiner. Deutschland, 1924.
751. Adressenetikett. 17,6 × 8,5 cm. Offset, drei irisierte Farben. Urheber: Push Pin Studios Inc., Milton Glaser, New York. U.S.A., 1971.

752

753

754

755

756

752. Airline. 2 $^{15}/_{16}$ × 3 $^3/_4$ in. Offset, 2 colours. Germany, 1971.
753. Address label. 4 $^1/_2$ × 4 $^3/_{16}$ in. Offset, 2 colours. Design, Push Pin Studios Inc./ S. Chwast, New York. USA, 1971.
754. Skin cream. 3 $^1/_2$ × 4 $^1/_8$ in. Offset, 3 colours. Design, K & K Agency/ I. Emirza, Athens. Greece, 1970.
755. Medicament. 5 × 3 $^5/_{16}$ in. Offset, 3 colours. Switzerland, 1971.
756. Address label. 6 × 3 $^1/_{16}$ in. Offset, 3 colours. Design, Herb Lubalin, New York. USA, 1971.

752. Compagnie aérienne. 7,5 × 9,6 cm. Offset deux coul. Allemagne, 1971.
753. Etiquette-adresse. 11,4 × 10,6 cm. Offset deux coul. Créat. Push Pin Studios Inc., S. Chwast, New York. U.S.A., 1971.
754. Crème pour la peau. 8,8 × 10,5 cm. Offset trois coul. Créat. Agence K & K, I. Emirza, Athènes. Grèce, 1970.
755. Médicament. 12,7 × 8,4 cm. Offset trois coul. Suisse, 1971.
756. Etiquette-adresse. 15,2 × 7,8 cm. Offset trois coul. Créat. Herb Lubalin, New York. U.S.A., 1971.

752. Fluggesellschaft. 7,5 × 9,6 cm. Offset, zwei Farben. Deutschland, 1971.
753. Adressenetikett. 11,4 × 10,6 cm. Offset, zwei Farben. Urheber: Push Pin Studios Inc., S. Chwast, New York. U.S.A., 1971.
754. Hautcreme. 8,8 × 10,5 cm. Offset, drei Farben. Urheber: Agentur K & K, I. Emirza, Athen. Griechenland, 1970.
755. Arzneimittel. 12,7 × 8,4 cm. Offset, drei Farben. Schweiz, 1971.
756. Adressenetikett. 15,2 × 7,8 cm. Offset, drei Farben. Urheber: Herb Lubalin, New York. U.S.A., 1971.

757

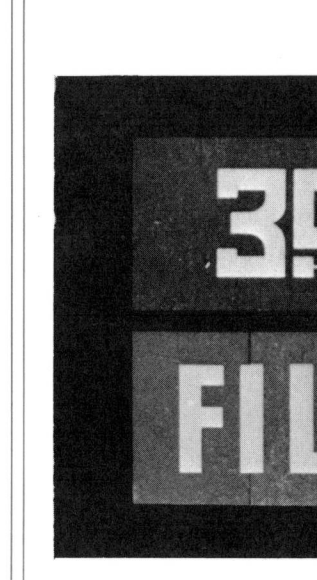

758

759

757. Computer programming. 4 $^3/_4$ × 4 $^3/_4$ in.
Offset, monochrome. Design, A. Saks
Inc., New York. USA, 1971.
758. Printed fabrics. 2 $^1/_2$ × 3 $^7/_8$ in. Offset,
3 colours. Design, Push Pin Studios Inc.,
New York. USA, 1971.
759. Film (matches). 1 $^5/_8$ × 1 $^3/_4$ in. Offset,
4 colours. Switzerland, 1969.
760. Monogram. 1 $^1/_4$ × 1 $^1/_8$ in. Offset,
monochrome. Design, T. Vellve, Barcelona. Spain, 1969.
761. Wine. 4 $^5/_8$ × 3 $^9/_{16}$ in. Offset, 2 colours.
Design, O. Ecksell, Stockholm. Sweden,
1952.

*757. Programmation (computer). 12 × 12 cm.
Offset une coul. Créat. A. Saks. Inc., New
York. U.S.A., 1971.*
*758. Tissus imprimés. 6,3 × 9,8 cm. Offset trois
coul. Créat. Push Pin Studios Inc., New
York. U.S.A., 1971.*
*759. Films (allumettes). 4,2 × 4,5 cm. Offset
quatre coul. Suisse, 1969.*
*760. Monogramme. 3,2 × 2,9 cm. Offset une
coul. Créat. T. Vellve, Barcelone. Espagne,
1969.*
*761. Vin. 11,7 × 9 cm. Offset deux coul. Créat.
O. Ecksell, Stockholm. Suède, 1952.*

760

761

757. Programmierung (Computer). 12 × 12 cm.
Offset, eine Farbe. Urheber: A. Saks Inc.,
U.S.A., 1971.
758. Bedruckte Gewebe. 6,3 × 9,8 cm. Offset,
drei Farben. Urheber: Push Pin Studios
Inc., New York. U.S.A., 1971.
759. Filme (Streichhölzer). 4,2 × 4,5 cm. Offset,
vier Farben. Schweiz, 1969.
760. Monogramm. 3,2 × 2,9 cm. Offset, eine
Farbe. Urheber: T. Vellve, Barcelona.
Spanien, 1969.

761. Wein. 11,7 × 9 cm. Offset, zwei Farben.
Urheber: O. Ecksell, Stockholm. Schweden,
1952.

762

763

764

STOKES & DALTON'S
PREPARED
SWEET HERBS
THYME

NEW SEASON'S HERBS
CAREFULLY PREPARED AND
DRIED BY OUR SPECIAL
PROCESS, THEREBY
PRESERVING THEIR NATURAL
AROMA AND FLAVOUR

STOKES & DALTON LTD
VICTORIA SPICE MILLS,
LEEDS, 9.

NEED

Pelikan
ENCRE
DE CHINE
pour héliographies
17 NOIR

765

ALL NEW
MATERIALS
SLEEPYHEAD
REGD
INNER SPRING MATTRESS
THE CENTRE OF THIS MATTRESS HAS BEEN
SPECIALLY HEAT TREATED AFTER
ASSEMBLY & IS PRACTICALLY INDESTRUCTIBLE
GUARANTEED
FIVE YEARS
SLEEPYHEAD MATTRESS CO. LTD. BIRMINGHAM   MADE UNDER ONE OR MORE OF THE FOLLOWING PATENTS.
382993, 390694, 396652, 399652, 431038 & OTHERS.
INSPECTOR

766

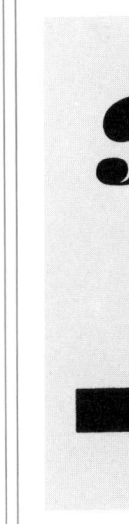

SCHENLEY
CLUB GIN
*Distilled
London dry
Gin*
100% NEUTRAL SPIRITS
DISTILLED
FROM AMERICAN GRAIN
4/5 QUART
80.9 PROOF
Distilled by Schenley Distilleries, Inc.
LAWRENCEBURG, INDIANA

762. Thyme. 3 $^{11}/_{16}$ × 4 in. Litho, 3 colours. England, 20th century.
763. Refugee aid organisation. 4 $^3/_4$ × 4 $^3/_4$ in. Offset, monochrome. Design, A. Saks Inc., New York. USA, 1971.
764. Ink. 1 $^1/_2$ × 2 $^5/_8$ in. Offset, 2 colours. Germany, 1971.
765. Mattresses. 8 $^1/_2$ × 5 $^1/_2$ in. Litho, 2 colours and gold thread. England, 20th century.
766. Gin. 4 $^{11}/_{16}$ × 4 $^9/_{16}$ in. Offset, 7 colours. Design, Paul Rand, New York. USA, 1942.

762. Thym. 9,4 × 10,2 cm. Litho trois coul. Angleterre, XXᵉ siècle.
763. Organisation d'aide aux réfugiés. 12 × 12 cm. Offset une coul. Créat. A. Saks Inc., New York. U.S.A., 1971.
764. Encre. 3,8 × 6,6 cm. Offset deux coul. Allemagne, 1971.
765. «Sleepy Head». 21,5 × 14 cm. Litho deux coul., tissu or. Angleterre, XXᵉ siècle.
766. Gin. 11,8 × 11,6 cm. Offset sept coul. Créat. Paul Rand, New York. U.S.A., 1942.

762. Thymian. 9,4 × 10,2 cm. Lithographie, drei Farben. England, XX. Jahrhundert.
763. Organisation für Flüchtlingshilfe. 12 × 12 cm. Offset, eine Farbe. Urheber: A. Saks Inc., New York. U.S.A., 1971.
764. Tinte. 3,8 × 6,6 cm. Offset, zwei Farben. Deutschland, 1971.
765. «Sleepy Head». 21,5 × 14 cm. Lithographie, zwei Farben, Goldgewebe. England, XX. Jahrhundert.
766. Gin. 11,8 × 11,6 cm. Offset, sieben Farben. Urheber: Paul Rand, New York. U.S.A., 1942.

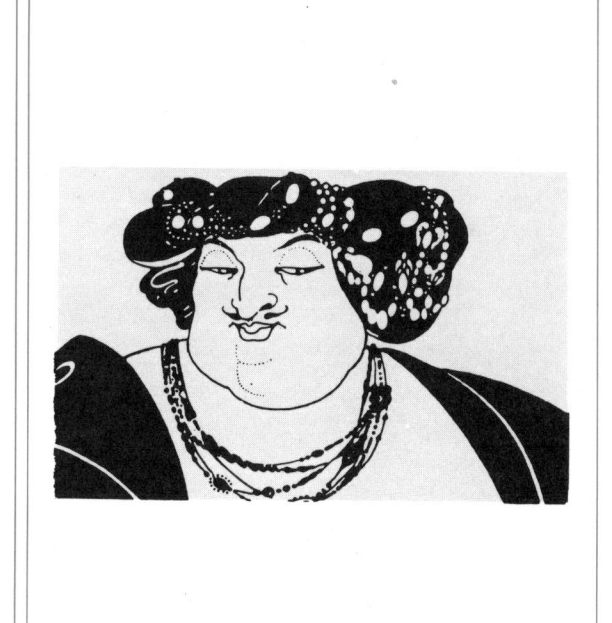

767

768

769

767. World nature fund. 1 $^9/_{16}$ × 1 $^9/_{16}$ in. Offset, 2 colours. International, 1968.
768. Propaganda label. 6 $^1/_2$ × 9 $^1/_4$ in. Wood engraving, monochrome. Design, R. Koch, Offenbach. Germany, 1924.
769. Matches. 2 $^3/_{16}$ × 1 $^3/_8$ in. Offset, monochrome. Japan, 1968.
770. Label for children (and grown-ups). 2 $^3/_4$ × 1 $^9/_{16}$ in. Design, Publistar, Paris. France, 1971.
771. Soap. 5 $^{15}/_{16}$ × 3 $^3/_8$ in. Litho, 7 colours. France, early 20th century.

767. *Fonds mondial pour la nature. 4 × 4 cm. Offset deux coul. International, 1968.*
768. *Etiquette de propagande. 16,5 × 23,5 cm. Gravure sur bois une coul. Créat. R. Koch, Offenbach. Allemagne, 1924.*
769. *Allumettes. 5,6 × 3,5 cm. Offset une coul. Japon, 1968.*
770. *Etiquette pour enfants (et grandes personnes). 7 × 3,9 cm. Créat. Publistar, Paris. France, 1971.*
771. *Savon. 15 × 8,5 cm. Litho sept coul. France, début du XXᵉ siècle.*

767. Weltkasse für die Natur. 4 × 4 cm. Offset, zwei Farben. International, 1968.
768. Propagandaetikett. 16,5 × 23,5 cm. Holzschnitt, eine Farbe. Urheber: R. Koch, Offenbach. Deutschland, 1924.
769. Streichhölzer. 5,6 × 3,5 cm. Offset, eine Farbe. Japan, 1968.
770. Etikett für Kinder (und Erwachsene). 7 × 3,9 cm. Urheber: Publistar, Paris. Frankreich, 1971.
771. Seife. 15 × 8,5 cm. Lithographie, sieben Farben. Frankreich, Beginn des XX. Jahrhunderts.

770

771

772

774

776

775

772. Cigarette papers. 1 $^9/_{16}$ × 2 $^1/_{16}$ in. Litho, 7 colours. France, early 20th century.
773. Propaganda label. 6 $^1/_2$ × 9 $^1/_4$ in. Wood engraving, monochrome. Design, Prof. Böhm, Berlin. Germany, 1924.
774. Matches. 3 $^9/_{16}$ × 2 $^{13}/_{16}$ in. Offset, 2 colours. Near East, 19th century.
775. Cigars. 8 $^1/_2$ × 5 $^{15}/_{16}$ in. Letterpress, 3 colours. Design, Prof. L. Hohlwein. Germany, 1925.
776. Mustard. 2 $^{15}/_{16}$ × 4 $^3/_8$ in. Litho, monochrome. England, 1880.

772. *Papier à cigarettes. 4 × 5,2 cm. Litho sept coul. France, début du XXe siècle.*
773. *Etiquette de propagande. 16,5 × 23,5 cm. Gravure sur bois une coul. Créat. prof. Böhm, Berlin. Allemagne, 1924.*
774. *Allumettes. 9 × 7,2 cm. Offset deux coul. Moyen-Orient, XIXe siècle.*
775. *Cigares. 21,5 × 15 cm. Typo trois coul. Créat. prof. L. Hohlwein. Allemagne, 1925.*
776. *Moutarde. 7,5 × 11 cm. Litho une coul. Angleterre, 1880.*

772. Zigarettenpapier. 4 × 5,2 cm. Lithographie, sieben Farben. Frankreich, Beginn des XX. Jahrhunderts.
773. Propagandaetikett. 16,5 × 23,5 cm. Holzschnitt, eine Farbe. Urheber: Professor Böhm, Berlin. Deutschland, 1924.
774. Streichhölzer. 9 × 7,2 cm. Offset, zwei Farben. Mittlerer Orient, XIX. Jahrhundert.
775. Zigarren. 21,5 × 15 cm. Buchdruck, drei Farben. Urheber: Professor L. Hohlwein. Deutschland, 1925.
776. Senf. 7,5 × 11 cm. Lithographie, eine Farbe. England, 1880.

777

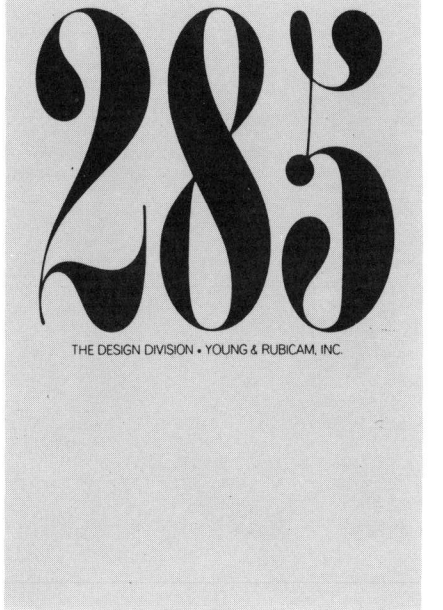

THE DESIGN DIVISION • YOUNG & RUBICAM, INC.

778

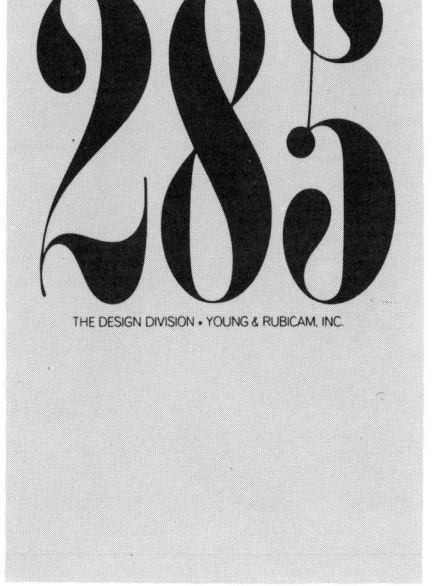

779

777. Cigarette papers.   2 $^{15}/_{16}$ × 1 $^{9}/_{16}$ in. Litho, monochrome.   France, early 20th century.

778. Address label.   3 $^{5}/_{16}$ × 4 $^{11}/_{16}$ in.   Offset, 2 colours.   Design, Herb Lubalin, New York.   USA, 1971.

779. Mineral water.   6 $^{3}/_{16}$ × 4 $^{5}/_{8}$ in.   Offset, 2 colours.   Italy, 1969.

780. Cigarette papers.   2 $^{15}/_{16}$ × 1 $^{3}/_{8}$ in. Litho, gold.   France, early 20th century.

781. Address label.   5 × 3 $^{3}/_{8}$ in.   Design, Push Pin Studios Inc./Milton Glaser/S. Chwast, New York.   USA, 1971.

777. Papier à cigarettes. 7,5 × 4 cm. Litho une coul. France, début du XXe siècle.

778. Etiquette-adresse. 8,3 × 11,8 cm. Offset deux coul. Créat. Herb Lubalin, New York. U.S.A., 1971.

779. Eau minérale. 15,7 × 11,7 cm. Offset deux coul. Italie, 1969.

780. Papier à cigarettes. 7,5 × 3,5 cm. Litho or. France, début du XXe siècle.

781. Etiquette-adresse. 12,7 × 8,5 cm. Créat. Push Pin Studios Inc., Milton Glaser/ S. Chwast, New York. U.S.A., 1971.

777. Zigarettenpapier. 7,5 × 4 cm. Lithographie, eine Farbe. Frankreich, Beginn des XX. Jahrhunderts.

778. Adressenetikett. 8,3 × 11,8 cm. Offset, zwei Farben. Urheber: Herb Lubalin, New York. U.S.A., 1971.

779. Mineralwasser. 15,7 × 11,7 cm. Offset, zwei Farben. Italien, 1969.

780. Zigarettenpapier. 7,5 × 3,5 cm. Lithographie, Gold. Frankreich, Beginn des XX. Jahrhunderts.

781. Adressenetikett. 12,7 × 8,5 cm. Urheber: Push Pin Studios Inc., Milton Glaser/ S. Chwast, New York. U.S.A., 1971.

TUBES
JOB

780

781

782. Men's toiletries. 22 × 19 ⁵/₈ in. Silk-
screen, 2 colours. Design, Plan Design
A/S/Orn Vidarsson. Denmark, 1971.

782. *Produits de toilette pour hommes. 56 ×
50 cm. Sérigraphie deux coul. Créat. Plan
Design A/S, Ørn Vidarsson. Danemark,
1971.*

782. Toilettenerzeugnisse für Herren. 56 × 50 cm.
Siebdruck, zwei Farben. Urheber: Plan
Design A/S, Ørn Vidarsson. Dänemark,
1971.

783

784

785

783. Paper mill. 4 × 1 $^{15}/_{16}$ in. Offset, monochrome. USA, 1971.

784. Tobacco. 5 × 1 $^{3}/_{4}$ in. Offset, 2 colours. France, 20th century.

785. Cigarettes. 1 $^{13}/_{16}$ × $^{15}/_{16}$ in. Offset, monochrome. France, 1971.

786. Cigars. 9 $^{3}/_{16}$ × 5 $^{15}/_{16}$ in. Letterpress, 3 colours. Design, Prof. C.O. Czeschka, Hamburg. Germany, 1924.

787. Cigars. 8 $^{11}/_{16}$ × 5 $^{1}/_{8}$ in. Letterpress, 3 colours. Design, Prof. C.O. Czeschka, Hamburg. Germany, 1924.

783. Fabrique de papier. 10,2 × 4,9 cm. Offset une coul. U.S.A., 1971.

784. Tabac. 12,7 × 4,5 cm. Offset deux coul. France, XXe siècle.

785. Cigarettes. 4,6 × 2,4 cm. Offset une coul. France, 1971.

786. Cigares. 23,3 × 15 cm. Typo trois coul. Créat. prof. C.O. Czeschka, Hambourg. Allemagne, 1924.

787. Cigares. 22 × 13 cm. Typo trois coul. Créat. prof. C.O. Czeschka, Hambourg. Allemagne, 1924.

783. Papierfabrik. 10,2 × 4,9 cm. Offset, eine Farbe. U.S.A., 1971.

784. Tabak. 12,7 × 4,5 cm. Offset, zwei Farben. Frankreich, XX. Jahrhundert.

785. Zigaretten. 4,6 × 2,4 cm. Offset, eine Farbe. Frankreich, 1971.

786. Zigarren. 23,3 × 15 cm. Buchdruck, drei Farben. Urheber: Professor C.O. Czeschka, Hamburg. Deutschland, 1924.

787. Zigarren. 22 × 13 cm. Buchdruck, drei Farben. Urheber: C.O. Czeschka, Hamburg. Deutschland, 1924.

786

787

788

789

790

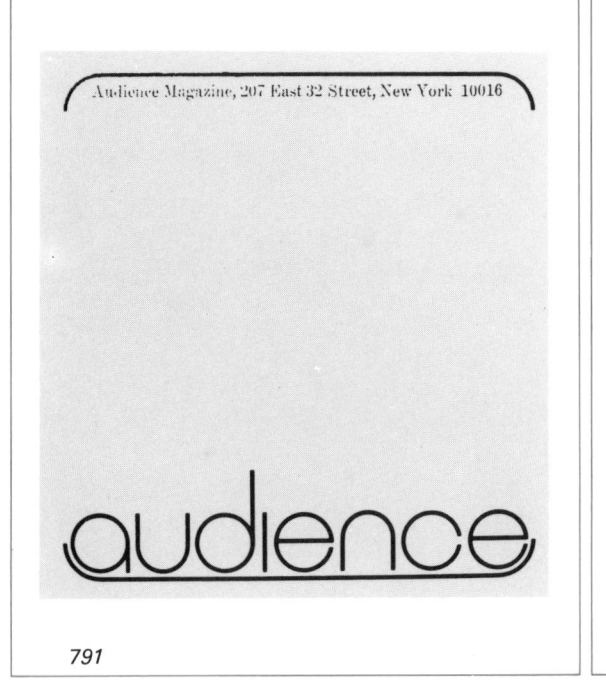

791

GOOD BOOK

792

788. Airline. $2^{11}/_{16} \times 4^1/_8$ in. Offset, 2 colours. Germany, 1962.
789. Perfume. $1^{15}/_{16}$ in. diameter. Letterpress, 3 colours. Design, E. Blankenburg. Germany, 1924.
790. Address label. $6 \times 4^1/_2$ in. Design, Push Pin Studios Inc., New York. USA, 1971.
791. Address label. $3^{13}/_{16} \times 3^{15}/_{16}$ in. Offset, monochrome. Design, Push Pin Studios Inc./Milton Glaser/S. Chwast, New York. USA, 1971.
792. Address label. $3^5/_{16} \times 6$ in. Offset, 2 colours. Design, Herb Lubalin, New York. USA, 1971.

788. Compagnie aérienne. 6,8 × 10,5 cm. Offset deux coul. Allemagne, 1962.
789. Parfum. Diam. 5 cm. Typo trois coul. Créat. E. Blankenburg. Allemagne, 1924.
790. Etiquette-adresse. 15,2 × 11,4 cm. Créat. Push Pin Studios Inc., New York. U.S.A., 1971.
791. Etiquette-adresse. 9,7 × 10 cm. Offset une coul. Créat. Push Pin Studios Inc., Milton Glaser/S. Chwast, New York. U.S.A., 1971.
792. Etiquette-adresse. 8,3 × 15,2 cm. Offset deux coul. Créat. Herb Lubalin, New York. U.S.A., 1971.

788. Fluggesellschaft. 6,8 × 10,5 cm. Offset, zwei Farben. Deutschland, 1962.
789. Parfüm. Durchmesser 5 cm. Buchdruck, drei Farben. Urheber: E. Blankenburg. Deutschland, 1924.
790. Adressenetikett. 15,2 × 11,4 cm. Urheber: Push Pin Studios Inc., New York. U.S.A., 1971.
791. Adressenetikett. 9,7 × 10 cm. Offset, eine Farbe. Urheber: Push Pin Studios Inc., Milton Glaser/S. Chwast, New York. U.S.A., 1971.

792. Adressenetikett. 8,3 × 15,2 cm. Offset, zwei Farben Urheber: Herb Lubalin, New York. U.S.A., 1971.

793

794

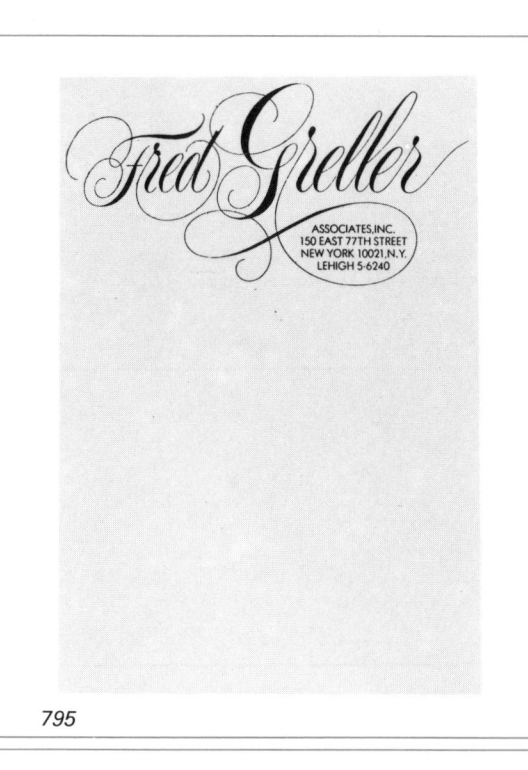

795

793. Address label. 3 $^9/_{16}$ × 4 $^3/_4$ in. Offset, monochrome. Design, Push Pin Studios Inc./Milton Glaser, New York. USA, 1971.
794. Cigarette papers. 1 $^{13}/_{16}$ × 1 $^9/_{16}$ in. Litho, monochrome and silver. Spain, early 20th century.
795. Address label. 3 $^5/_8$ × 5 $^1/_{16}$ in. Relief impression, monochrome. Design, Herb Lubalin, New York. USA, 1971.
796. Soap. 6 $^3/_{16}$ × 3 $^1/_8$ in. Litho, 2 colours and gold. France, early 20th century.
797. Address label. 3 $^9/_{16}$ × 3 $^9/_{16}$ in. Design, Push Pin Studios Inc./Milton Glaser, New York. USA, 1971.

793. *Etiquette-adresse. 9 × 12 cm. Offset une coul. Créat. Push Pin Studios Inc., Milton Glaser, New York. U.S.A., 1971.*
794. *Papier à cigarettes. 4,6 × 4 cm. Litho une coul. et argent. Espagne, début du XXᵉ siècle.*
795. *Etiquette-adresse. 9,1 × 12,8 cm. Imp. relief une coul. Créat. Herb Lubalin, New York. U.S.A., 1971.*
796. *Savon. 15,7 × 8 cm. Litho deux coul. et or. France, début du XXᵉ siècle.*
797. *Etiquette-adresse. 9 × 9 cm. Créat. Push Pin Studios Inc., Milton Glaser, New York. U.S.A., 1971.*

793. Adressenetikett. 9 × 12 cm. Offset, eine Farbe. Urheber: Push Pin Studios Inc., Milton Glaser, New York. U.S.A., 1971.
794. Zigarettenpapier. 4,6 × 4 cm. Lithographie, eine Farbe und Silber. Spanien, Beginn des XX. Jahrhunderts.
795. Adressenetikett. 9,1 × 12,8 cm. Prägedruck, eine Farbe. Urheber: Herb Lubalin, New York. U.S.A., 1971.

796

797

796. Seife. 15,7 × 8 cm. Lithographie, zwei Farben und Gold. Frankreich, Beginn des XX. Jahrhunderts.
797. Adressenetikett. 9 × 9 cm. Urheber: Push Pin Studios Inc., Milton Glaser, New York. U.S.A., 1971.

798

799

800

801

802

798. Address label. 5 $^1/_8$ × 3 $^9/_{16}$ in. Offset, monochrome and silver. Design, Push Pin Studios Inc./Milton Glaser/S. Chwast, New York. USA, 1971.
799. Cigarette papers. 1 $^{13}/_{16}$ × 1 $^5/_8$ in. Litho, monochrome. Spain, early 20th century.
800. Publication. 4 $^3/_4$ × 1 $^{15}/_{16}$ in. Offset, 3 colours, on green paper. France, 1970.
801. Cigars. 6 $^{11}/_{16}$ × 5 in. Letterpress, 3 colours. Design, Prof. C.O. Czeschka, Hamburg. Germany, 1924.
802. Label for parcels. 5 $^1/_8$ × 1 $^{15}/_{16}$ in. France, 1970.

798. Etiquette-adresse. 13 × 9 cm. Offset une coul. et argent. Créat. Push Pin Studios Inc., Milton Glaser/S. Chwast, New York. U.S.A., 1971.
799. Papier à cigarettes. 4,6 × 4,2 cm. Litho une coul. Espagne, début du XXe siècle.
800. Edition. 12 × 5 cm. Offset trois coul., papier vert. France, 1970.
801. Cigares. 17 × 12,7 cm. Typo trois coul. Créat. prof. C.O. Czeschka, Hambourg. Allemagne, 1924.
802. Etiquette pour paquets. 13 × 5 cm. France, 1970.

798. Adressenetikett. 13 × 9 cm. Offset, eine Farbe und Silber. Urheber: Push Pin Studios Inc., Milton Glaser/S. Chwast, New York. U.S.A., 1971.
799. Zigarettenpapier. 4,6 × 4,2 cm. Lithographie, eine Farbe. Spanien, Beginn des XX. Jahrhunderts.
800. Verlag. 12 × 5 cm. Offset, drei Farben, grünes Papier. Frankreich, 1970.
801. Zigarren. 17 × 12,7 cm. Buchdruck, drei Farben. Urheber: Professor C.O. Czeschka, Hamburg. Deutschland, 1924.
802. Etikett für Pakete. 13 × 5 cm. Frankreich, 1970.

803

804

805

806

807

803. Tonic. 2 3/4 × 2 15/16 in. Offset, 3 colours. Design, K & K Agency/J. Angelopoulos, Athens. Greece, 1969.
804. Sauce. 2 3/4 × 3 15/16 in. Offset, 4 colours and gold. Japan, 1971.
805. Address label. 6 3/8 × 3 5/16 in. Design, Herb Lubalin, New York. USA, 1971.
806. Investment fund. 3 1/8 × 1 3/8 in. Silkscreen, monochrome, on gold paper. Printing, P. Terbois, Geneva. International, 1968.
807. Shop. 3 15/16 × 1 11/16 in. Offset, 2 colours. Switzerland, 1970.

803. Fortifiant. 7 × 7,5 cm. Offset trois coul. Créat. Agence K & K, J. Angelopoulos, Athènes. Grèce, 1969.
804. Sauce. 7 × 10 cm. Offset quatre coul. et or. Japon, 1971.
805. Etiquette-adresse. 16,2 × 8,3 cm. Créat. Herb Lubalin, New York. U.S.A., 1971.
806. Fonds de placement. 8 × 3,5 cm. Sérigraphie une coul., papier or. Imp. P. Terbois, Genève. International, 1968.
807. Boutique. 10 × 4,3 cm. Offset deux coul. Suisse, 1970.

803. Stärkungsmittel. 7 × 7,5 cm. Offset, drei Farben. Urheber: Agentur K & K, J. Angelopoulos, Athen. Griechenland, 1969.
804. Sosse. 7 × 10 cm. Offset, vier Farben und Gold. Japan, 1971.
805. Adressenetikett. 16,2 × 8,3 cm. Urheber: Herb. Lubalin, New York. U.S.A., 1971.
806. Investitionsgelder. 8 × 3,5 cm. Siebdruck, eine Farbe, Goldpapier. Druckerei P. Terbois, Genf. International, 1968.
807. Kaufladen. 10 × 4,3 cm. Offset, zwei Farben. Schweiz, 1970.

808

809

810

811

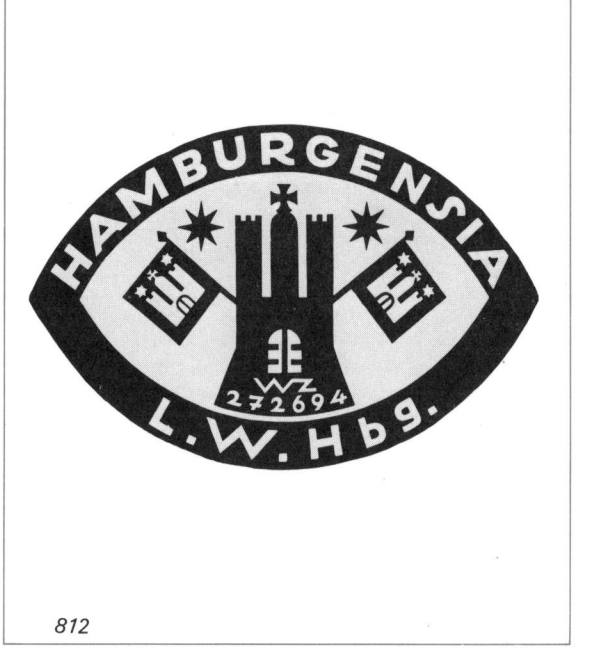

812

808. Vitamins. 4 ³/₄ × 3 ⁹/₁₆ in. Offset, 3 colours. Design, K & K Agency/A. Katzourakis, Athens. Greece, 1969.
809. Perfumery. ⁷/₈ × 1 ¹/₈ in. Letterpress, monochrome. Design, F. H. Ehmcke. Germany, 1924.
monochrome. Design, F. H. Ehmcke. Germany, 1924.
810. Perfumery. 1¹/₄ × 1 in. Letterpress, monochrome. Design, F. H. Ehmcke. Germany, 1924.
811. Hors-d'œuvre. 3 ¹⁵/₁₆ in. diameter. Offset, 4 colours. Italy, 1971.
812. Tourism. 5 ¹/₈ × 3 ⁵/₁₆ in. Letterpress, monochrome. Design, Prof. C.O. Czeschka, Hamburg. Germany, 1924.

808. Vitamines. 12 × 9 cm. Offset trois coul. Créat. Agence K & K, A. Katzourakis, Athènes. Grèce, 1969.
809. Parfumerie. 2,3 × 2,8 cm. Typo une coul. Créat. F. H. Ehmcke, Allemagne, 1924.
810. Parfumerie. 3,2 × 2,5 cm. Typo une coul. Créat. F. H. Ehmcke. Allemagne, 1924.
811. Hors-d'œuvre. Diam. 10 cm. Offset quatre coul. Italie, 1971.
812. Tourisme. 13 × 8,4 cm. Typo une coul. Créat. prof. C.O. Czeschka, Hambourg. Allemagne, 1924.

808. Vitamine. 12 × 9 cm. Offset, drei Farben. Urheber: Agentur K & K, A. Katzourakis, Athen. Griechenland, 1969.
809. Parfümhandlung. 2,3 × 2,8 cm. Buchdruck, eine Farbe. Urheber: F. H. Ehmcke. Deutschland, 1924.
810. Parfümhandel. 3,2 × 2,5 cm. Buchdruck, eine Farbe. Urheber: F. H. Ehmcke. Deutschland, 1924.
811. Vorspeise. Durchmesser 10 cm. Offset, vier Farben. Italien, 1971.

812. Tourismus. 13 × 8,4 cm. Buchdruck, eine Farbe. Urheber: Professor C.O. Czeschka, Hamburg. Deutschland, 1924.

813

814

815

816

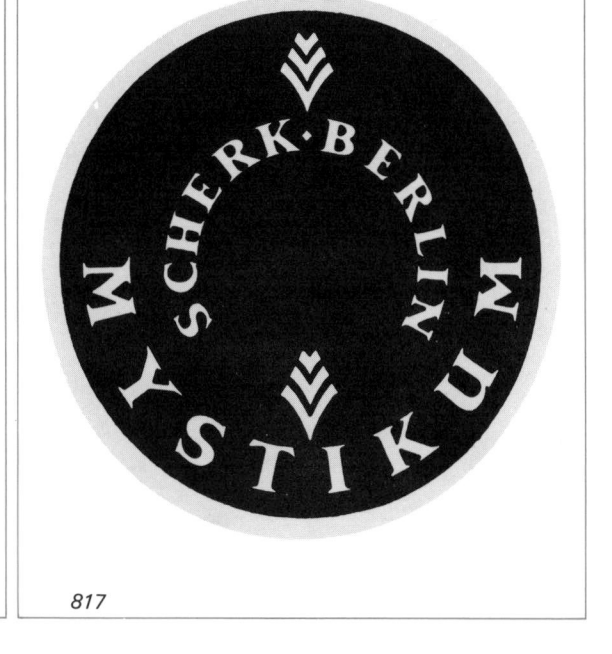

817

813. Perfume. 1 3/4 in. diameter. Letterpress, 3 colours. Design, E. Blankenburg. Germany, 1924.
814. Perfume. 1 11/16 in. diameter. Letterpress, 3 colours. Design, E. Blankenburg/ Schwerdiner. Germany, 1924.
815. Perfume. 1 3/4 in. diameter. Letterpress, 3 colours. Design, E. Blankenburg. Germany, 1924.
816. Face cream. 1 15/16 in. diameter. Letterpress, monochrome. Design, E. Blankenburg. Germany, 1924.
817. Perfume. 1 11/16 in. diameter. Letterpress, 3 colours. Design, E. Blankenburg/ Schwerdiner. Germany, 1924.

813. Parfum. Diam. 4,5 cm. Typo trois coul. Créat. E. Blankenburg. Allemagne, 1924.
814. Parfum. Diam. 4,3 cm. Typo trois coul. Créat. E. Blankenburg/Schwerdiner. Allemagne, 1924.
815. Parfum. Diam. 4,5 cm. Typo trois coul. Créat. E. Blankenburg. Allemagne, 1924.
816. Parfum. Diam. 5 cm. Typo une coul. Créat. E. Blankenburg. Allemagne, 1924.
817. Parfum. Diam. 4,3 cm. Typo trois coul. Créat. E. Blankenburg/Schwerdiner. Allemagne, 1924.

813. Parfüm. Durchmesser 4,5 cm. Buchdruck, drei Farben. Urheber: E. Blankenburg. Deutschland, 1924.
814. Parfüm. Durchmesser 4,3 cm. Buchdruck, drei Farben. Urheber: E. Blankenburg/ Schwerdiner. Deutschland, 1924.
815. Parfüm. Durchmesser 4,5 cm. Buchdruck, drei Farben. Urheber: E. Blankenburg. Deutschland, 1924.
816. Parfüm. Durchmesser 5 cm. Buchdruck, eine Farbe. Urheber: E. Blankenburg. Deutschland, 1924.

817. Parfüm. Durchmesser 4,3 cm. Buchdruck, drei Farben. Urheber: Blankenburg/ Schwerdiner. Deutschland, 1924.

818

819

820

821

822

818. Wine. 4 ³/₄ × 4 in. Offset, 4 colours and gold. Italy, 1967.
819. Fire-crackers. 2 ¹⁵/₁₆ × 3 ¹/₂ in. Litho, 4 colours. USA, 1929.
820. Toffees. 4 ³/₈ × 2 ¹⁵/₁₆ in. Litho, 2 colours, on yellow paper. England, 20th century.
821. Liqueur. 3 ³/₄ × 4 ¹³/₁₆ in. Litho, 3 colours and embossed gold. Italy, 1971.
822. Hair oil. 3 ¹⁵/₁₆ × 3 ¹/₂ in. Copper plate engraving, monochrome. England, 19th century.

818. Vin. 12 × 10,2 cm. Offset quatre coul. et or. Italie, 1967.
819. Pétards. 7,5 × 8,8 cm. Litho quatre coul. U.S.A., 1929.
820. Caramels. 11 × 7,5 cm. Litho deux coul., papier jaune. Angleterre, XXᵉ siècle.
821. Liqueur. 9,5 × 12,2 cm. Litho trois coul. et or gaufré. Italie, 1971.
822. Huile pour les cheveux. 10 × 8,8 cm. Gravure sur cuivre une coul. Angleterre, XIXᵉ siècle.

818. Wein. 12 × 10,2 cm. Offset, vier Farben und Gold. Italien, 1967.
819. Feuerwerkskörper. 7,5 × 8,8 cm. Lithographie, vier Farben. U.S.A., 1929.
820. Karamel. 11 × 7,5 cm. Lithographie, zwei Farben, gelbes Papier. England, XX. Jahrhundert.
821. Likör. 9,5 × 12,2 cm. Lithographie, drei Farben und Prägung in Gold. Italien, 1971.
822. Haaröl. 10 × 8,8 cm. Kupferstich, eine Farbe. England, XIX. Jahrhundert.

823

824

825

826

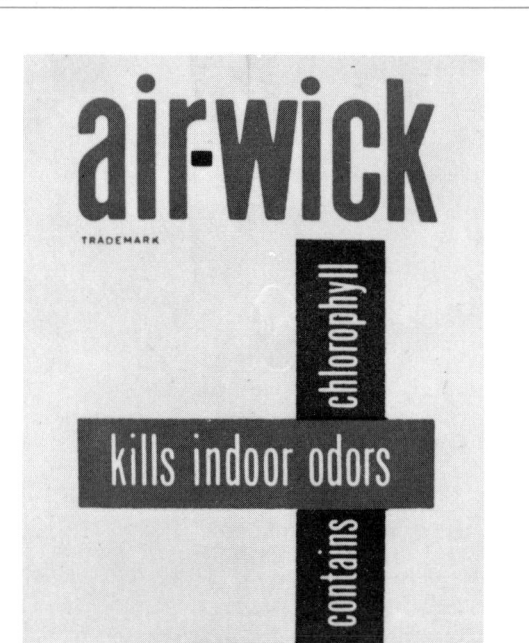

827

823. Advertising agency. 2 $^1/_4$ × 3 $^1/_2$ in. Offset, monochrome and embossing. Design, Herb Lubalin, New York. USA, 1971.
824. Cigarette papers. Letterpress, monochrome. France, early 20th century.
825. Investment fund. 2 $^3/_8$ × 2 $^3/_8$ in. Silkscreen, monochrome. Printing, P. Terbois, Geneva. International, 1968.
826. Sports clothes. 4 $^{13}/_{16}$ × 1 $^5/_8$ in. Letterpress, gold. Design, J. Van der Wal, Geneva. Switzerland, 1969.
827. Air freshener. 1 $^9/_{16}$ × 3 $^1/_8$ in. Offset, 2 colours. Design, Paul Rand, New York. USA, 1944.

823. Publicité. 5,8 × 8,9 cm. Offset une coul. et gaufrage. Créat. Herb Lubalin, New York. U.S.A., 1971.
824. Papier à cigarettes. Typo une coul. France, début du XXᵉ siècle.
825. Fonds de placement. 6 × 6 cm. Sérigraphie une coul. Imp. P. Terbois, Genève. International, 1968.
826. Vêtements de sport. 12,2 × 4,2 cm. Typo or. Créat. J. Van der Wal, Genève. Suisse, 1969.
827. «Air freshener». 4 × 8 cm. Offset deux coul. Créat. Paul Rand, New York. U.S.A., 1944.

823. Werbung. 5,8 × 8,9 cm. Offset, eine Farbe und Prägung. Urheber: Herb Lubalin, New York. U.S.A., 1971.
824. Zigarettenpapier. Buchdruck, eine Farbe. Frankreich, Beginn des XX. Jahrhunderts.
825. Investitionsgelder. 6 × 6 cm. Siebdruck, eine Farbe. Druckerei P. Terbois, Genf. International, 1968.
826. Sportkleidung. 12,2 × 4,2 cm. Buchdruck, Gold. Urheber: J. Van der Wal, Genf. Schweiz, 1969.

827. «Air freshener». 4 × 8 cm. Offset, zwei Farben. Urheber: Paul Rand, New York. U.S.A., 1944.

828

829

830

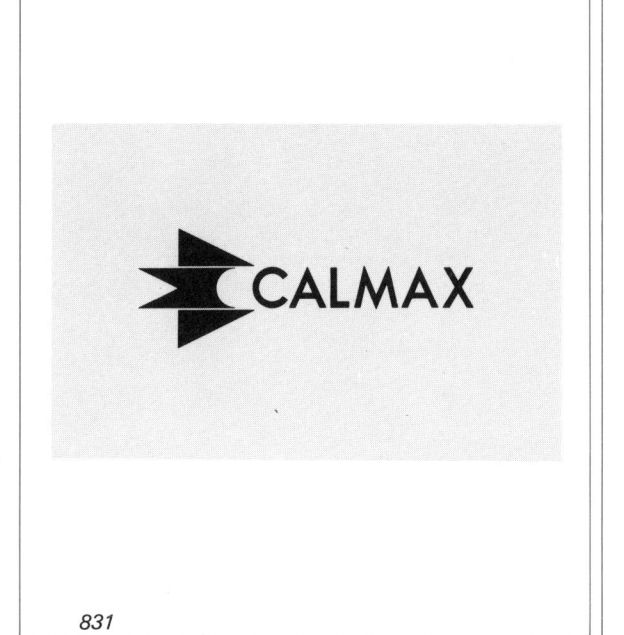

831

832

828. Records, radio, TV. $1\,^{7}/_{16} \times 2\,^{1}/_{4}$ in. Offset, monochrome and silver. Design, J. Van der Wal, Geneva. Switzerland, 1970.
829. Address label. $4\,^{9}/_{16} \times 3\,^{3}/_{8}$ in. Offset, 3 colours. Design, Push Pin Studios Inc./Milton Glaser, New York. USA, 1971.
830. 'Artis'. $1\,^{7}/_{8} \times 1\,^{1}/_{4}$ in. Offset, monochrome. Design, T. Vellve, Barcelona. Spain, 1968.
831. Precision engineering. $2\,^{1}/_{2} \times \,^{13}/_{16}$ in. Offset, monochrome. Design, T. Vellve, Barcelona. Spain, 1970.
832. Airline. $3\,^{1}/_{8} \times 2\,^{5}/_{8}$ in. Offset, monochrome, on green paper. Switzerland, 1971.

828. Disques, radio, TV. 3,7 × 5,8 cm. Offset une coul. et argent. Créat. J. Van der Wal, Genève. Suisse, 1970.
829. Etiquette-adresse. 11,6 × 8,5 cm. Offset trois coul. Créat. Push Pin Studios Inc., Milton Glaser, New York. U.S.A., 1971.
830. «Artis». 4,7 × 3,2 cm. Offset une coul. Créat. T. Vellve, Barcelone. Espagne, 1968.
831. Mécanique de précision. 6,4 × 2,1 cm. Offset une coul. Créat. T. Vellve, Barcelone. Espagne, 1970.
832. Compagnie aérienne. 8 × 6,6 cm. Offset une coul., papier vert. Suisse 1971.

828. Schallpaltten, Rundfunk, Fernsehen. 3,7 × 5,8 cm. Offset, eine Farbe und Silber. Urheber: J. Van der Wal, Genf. Schweiz, 1970.
829. Adressenetikett. 11,6 × 8,5 cm. Offset, drei Farben. Urheber: Push Pin Studios Inc., Milton Glaser, New York. U.S.A., 1971.
830. «Artis». 4,7 × 3,2 cm. Offset, eine Farbe. Urheber: T. Vellve, Barcelona. Spanien, 1968.

831. Feinmechanik. 6,4 × 2,1 cm. Offset, eine Farbe. Urheber: T. Vellve, Barcelona. Spanien, 1970.
832. Fluggesellschaft. 8 × 6,6 cm. Offset, eine Farbe, grünes Papier. Schweiz, 1971.

833

834

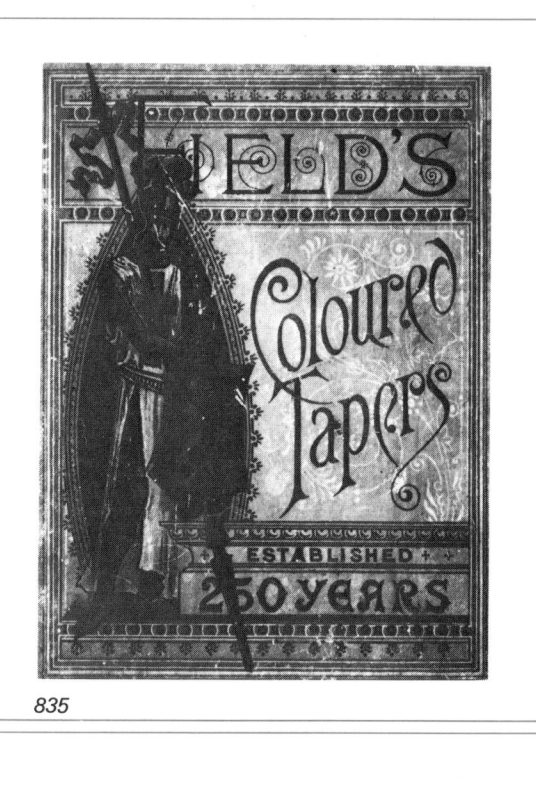

835

833. Bookseller. 4 ³/₈ × 6 ¹/₈ in. Copper plate engraving, monochrome. England, 1730.
834. Rice starch. 4 ³/₁₆ × 5 ³/₈ in. Litho, 7 colours. England, late 19th century.
835. Tapers. 4 ³/₈ × 5 ³/₄ in. Litho, 5 colours. England, early 20th century.
836. Matches. 4 ¹/₈ × 2 ¹³/₁₆ in. Litho, monochrome. Sweden, early 20th century.
837. Sauce. 5 ¹/₄ × 4 ¹/₈ in. Litho, 7 colours. England, 1860–1870.

833. Librairie. 11 × 15,5 cm. Gravure sur cuivre une coul. Angleterre, 1730.
834. Amidon de riz. 10,6 × 13,6 cm. Litho sept coul. Angleterre, fin du XIXᵉ siècle.
835. Cierges. 11 × 14,6 cm. Litho cinq coul. Angleterre, début du XXᵉ siècle.
836. Allumettes. 10,5 × 7,2 cm. Litho une coul. Suède, début du XXᵉ siècle.
837. Sauce. 13,3 × 10,5 cm. Litho sept coul. Angleterre, 1860–1870.

833. Buchhandlung. 11 × 15,5 cm. Kupferstich, eine Farbe. England, 1730.
834. Reisstärke. 10,6 × 13,6 cm. Lithographie, sieben Farben. England, Ende des XIX. Jahrhunderts.
835. Kerzen. 11 × 14,6 cm. Lithographie, fünf Farben. England, Beginn des XX. Jahrhunderts.
836. Streichhölzer. 10,5 × 7,2 cm. Lithographie, eine Farbe. Schweden, Beginn des XX. Jahrhunderts.
837. Sosse. 13,3 × 10,5 cm. Lithographie, sieben Farben. England, 1860–1870.

836

837

838

838. Matches. 1 ⁵/₈ × 2 ³/₁₆ in. Litho, 4 colours. England, late 19th century.

838. Allumettes. 4,2 × 5,6 cm. Litho quatre coul. Angleterre, fin du XIXᵉ siècle.

838. Streichhölzer. 4,2 × 5,6 cm. Lithographie, vier Farben. England, Ende des XIX. Jahrhunderts.

839

840

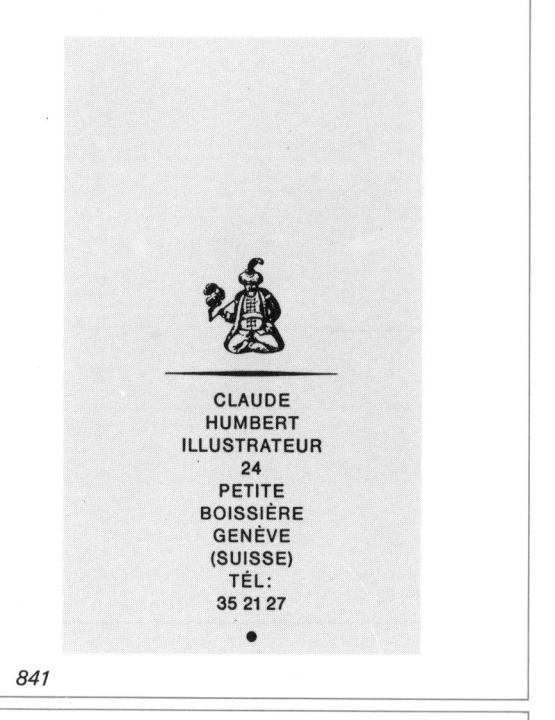

841

839. Polishing paste.   5 $^1/_8$ × 1 $^{15}/_{16}$ in. Letterpress, monochrome, on light blue paper. England, 20th century.
840. Personal label.   Offset, monochrome. Design, Herb Lubalin, New York. USA, 1971.
841. Personal label.   1 $^{11}/_{16}$ × 2 $^1/_{16}$ in. Offset, monochrome.   Design, C. Humbert, Geneva.   Switzerland, 1966.
842. Address label.   3 $^1/_{16}$ × 6 in.   Offset, monochrome.   Design, Herb Lubalin, New York.   USA, 1971.
843. Photosetting.   3 $^5/_8$ × 4 $^1/_4$ in.   Offset, monochrome.   Printing, Impressa SA, Geneva.   Switzerland, 1971.

839. *Pate à polir. 13 × 5 cm. Typo une coul., papier bleu clair. Angleterre, XXe siècle.*
840. *Etiquette personnelle. Offset une coul. Créat. Herb Lubalin, New York. U.S.A., 1971.*
841. *Etiquette personnelle. 4,3 × 5,3 cm. Offset une coul. Créat. C. Humbert, Genève. Suisse, 1966.*
842. *Etiquette-adresse. 7,8 × 15,2 cm. Offset une coul. Créat. Herb. Lubalin, New York. U.S.A., 1971.*
843. *Photocomposition. 9,2 × 10,8 cm. Offset une coul. Imp. Impressa S.A., Genève. Suisse 1971.*

839. Polierpaste. 13 × 5 cm. Buchdruck, eine Farbe, hellblaues Papier. England, XX. Jahrhundert.
840. Persönliches Etikett. Offset, eine Farbe. Urheber: Herb Lubalin, New York. U.S.A., 1971.
841. Persönliches Etikett. 4,3 × 5,3 cm. Offset, eine Farbe. Urheber: C. Humbert, Genf. Schweiz, 1966.

842

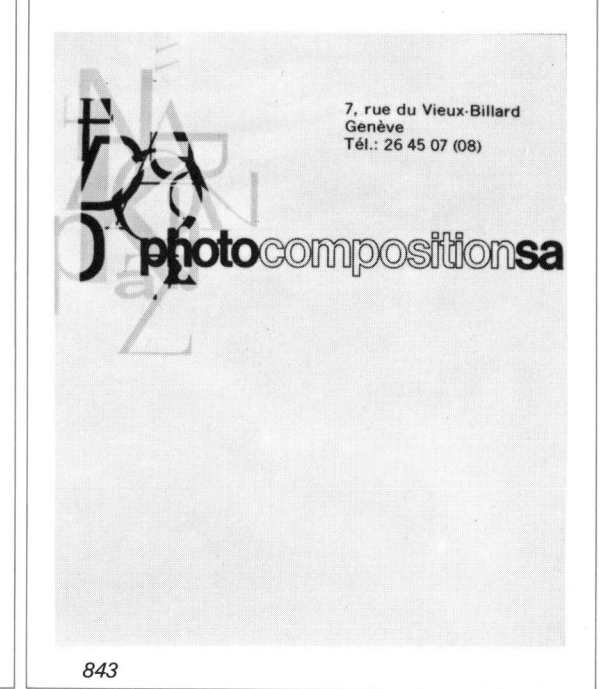

843

842. Adressenetikett. 7,8 × 15,2 cm. Offset, eine Farbe. Urheber: Herb Lubalin, New York. U.S.A., 1971.
843. Fotokomposition. 9,2 × 10,8 cm. Offset, eine Farbe. Druckerei Impressa S.A., Genf. Schweiz, 1971.

844

845

846

847

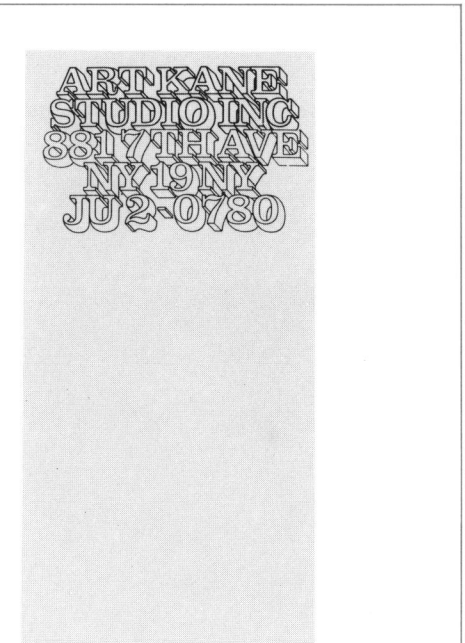

848

844. Cigarette papers. 1 $^{3}/_{4}$ × 3 $^{5}/_{16}$ in. Litho, monochrome and gold.   Spain, early 20th century.
845. Cigars. 7 $^{5}/_{8}$ × 6 $^{3}/_{8}$ in.   Letterpress, 3 colours.   Design, Prof. C. O. Czeschka, Hamburg. Germany, 1924.
846. Wine. 3 $^{7}/_{8}$ × 3 $^{1}/_{4}$ in.   Offset, 2 colours, on deep yellow paper.   Design, E. Poncy, Geneva. England, 1962.
847. Anchovies. 4 $^{3}/_{4}$ × 3 $^{15}/_{16}$ in.   Litho, 6 colours and embossed gold. Spain, 1971.
848. Address label. 3 $^{1}/_{2}$ × 7 in. Offset, 3 colours.   Design, Herb Lubalin, New York. USA, 1971.

844. Papier à cigarettes. 4,5 × 8,4 cm. Litho une coul. et or. Espagne, début du XXe siècle.
845. Cigares. 19,4 × 16,2 cm. Typo trois coul. Créat. prof. C.O. Czeschka, Hambourg. Allemagne, 1924.
846. Vin. 9,8 × 8,2 cm. Offset deux coul., papier jaune foncé. Créat. E. Poncy, Genève. Angleterre, 1962.
847. Anchois. 12 × 10 cm. Litho six coul. et or gaufré. Espagne, 1971.
848. Etiquette-adresse. 8,9 × 17,8 cm. Offset trois coul. Créat. Herb Lubalin, New York. U.S.A., 1971.

844. Zigarettenpapier. 4,5 × 8,4 cm. Lithographie, eine Farbe und Gold. Spanien, Beginn des XX. Jahrhunderts.
845. Zigarren. 19,4 × 16,2 cm. Buchdruck, drei Farben. Urheber: Professor C.O. Czeschka, Hamburg. Deutschland, 1924.
846. Wein. 9,8 × 8,2 cm. Offset, zwei Farben, dunkelgelbes Papier. Urheber: E. Poncy, Genf. England, 1962.
847. Sardellen. 12 × 10 cm. Lithographie, sechs Farben und Prägung in Gold. Spanien, 1971.

848. Adressenetikett. 8,9 × 17,8 cm. Offset, drei Farben. Urheber: Herb Lubalin, New York. U.S.A., 1971.

849

850

851

852

853

849. Dates. 8 ⁹/₁₆ × 2 ¹/₂ in. Litho, 4 colours.
Printing, Soc. Azémard Cousins, Nîmes.
France, 20th century.
850. Beer. 7 ⁵/₈ × 4 ³/₈ in. Offset, 2 colours
and gold. Germany, 1971.
851. Dates. 8 ⁹/₁₆ × 2 ¹/₂ in. Litho, 4 colours.
Printing, Soc. Azémard Cousins, Nîmes.
France, 20th century.
852. Pasta. 10 ⁵/₈ × 3 ¹/₁₆ in. Offset, 4 colours. Italy, 1971.
853. Lychees. 10 ³/₈ × 4 ¹/₈ in. Offset, 4 colours. Hong Kong, 1971.

849. Dattes. 21,7 × 6,3 cm. Litho quatre coul.
Imp. Soc. Azémard Cousins, Nîmes. France,
XXᵉ siècle.
850. Bière. 19,3 × 11 cm. Offset deux coul. et or.
Allemagne, 1971.
851. Dattes. 21,7 × 6,3 cm. Litho. quatre coul.
Imp. Soc. Azémard Cousins, Nîmes. France,
XXᵉ siècle.
852. Pâtes alimentaires. 27 × 7,7 cm. Offset
quatre coul. Italie, 1971.
853. Lychees. 26,3 × 10,5 cm. Offset quatre
coul. Hong-Kong, 1971.

849. Datteln. 21,7 × 6,3 cm. Lithographie, vier
Farben. Druckerei Firma Azémard Cousins,
Nîmes. Frankreich, XX. Jahrhundert.
850. Bier. 19,3 × 11 cm. Offset, zwei Farben und
Gold. Deutschland, 1971.
851. Datteln. 21,7 × 6,3 cm. Lithographie, vier
Farben. Druckerei Firma Azémard Cousins,
Nîmes. Frankreich, XX. Jahrhundert.
852. Teigwaren. 27 × 7,7 cm. Offset, vier Farben.
Italien, 1971.
853. Lychees. 26,3 × 10,5 cm. Offset, vier Far-
ben. Hongkong, 1971.

854

855

856

857

858

854. Cold cream. 1 1/2 × 1 5/8 in. Letterpress, 3 colours. Design, E. Blankenburg/ Schwerdiner. Germany, 1924.
855. Instant coffee. 2 1/2 × 2 15/16 in. Offset, 4 colours. Italy, 1971.
856. Matches. 2 1/2 × 1 7/8 in. Offset, monochrome, on brown paper. Italy, 1967.
857. Cigars. 9 1/16 × 4 7/8 in. Letterpress, 3 colours. Design, Prof. C..O. Czeschka, Hamburg. Germany, 1924.
858. Wine. 3 11/16 × 3 7/8 in. Litho, monochrome. Spain, 1969.

854. Crème de beauté. 3,8 × 4,2 cm. Typo trois coul. Créat. Blankenburg/Schwerdiner. Allemagne, 1924.
855. Café en poudre. 6,4 × 7,4 cm. Offset quatre coul. Italie, 1971.
856. Allumettes. 6,3 × 4,8 cm. Offset une coul., papier brun. Italie, 1967.
857. Cigares. 23 × 12,4 cm. Typo trois coul. Créat. prof. C.O. Czeschka, Hambourg. Allemagne, 1924.
858. Vin. 9,3 × 9,8 cm. Litho une coul. Espagne, 1969.

854. Schönheitscreme. 3,8 × 4,2 cm. Buchdruck, drei Farben. Urheber: Blankenburg/ Schwerdiner. Deutschland, 1924.
855. Pulverkaffee. 6,4 × 7,4 cm. Offset, vier Farben. Italien, 1971.
856. Streichhölzer. 6,3 × 4,8 cm. Offset, eine Farbe, braunes Papier. Italien, 1967.
857. Zigarren. 23 × 12,4 cm. Buchdruck, drei Farben. Urheber: Professor C.O. Czeschka, Hamburg. Deutschland, 1924.
858. Wein. 9,3 × 9,8 cm. Lithographie, eine Farbe. Spanien, 1969.

859

860

861

859. Address label. 5 × 3 in. Offset, 2 colours.
Design, Push Pin Studios Inc./S. Chwast,
New York. USA, 1971.
860. Cigarette papers. 1 $^7/_8$ × 1 $^5/_8$ in. Litho,
3 colours. Spain, early 20th century.
861. Cigarette papers. 1 $^{15}/_{16}$ × 1 $^5/_8$ in. Litho,
monochrome. France, early 20th century.
862. Fruit. 8 $^7/_8$ × 9 $^1/_{16}$ in. Litho, 5 colours.
Printing, Woodward & Tierman, St. Louis.
USA, early 20th century.
863. Haberdashery. 9 $^7/_{16}$ × 7 $^3/_{16}$ in. Litho,
7 colours. China, late 19th century.

859. Etiquette-adresse. 12,6 × 7,6 cm. Offset
deux coul. Créat. Push Pin Studios Inc.,
S. Chwast, New York. U.S.A., 1971.
860. Papier à cigarettes. 4,7 × 4,2 cm. Litho
trois coul. Espagne, début du XXe siècle.
861. Papier à cigarettes. 5 × 4,2 cm. Litho une
coul. France, début du XXe siècle.
862. Fruits. 22,5 × 23 cm. Litho cinq coul. Imp.
Woodward & Tierman, St. Louis. U.S.A.,
début du XXe siècle.
863. Mercerie. 24 × 18,2 cm. Litho sept coul.
Chine, fin du XIXe siècle.

859. Adressenetikett. 12,6 × 7,6 cm. Offset, zwei
Farben. Urheber: Push Pin Studios Inc.,
S. Chwast, New York. U.S.A., 1971.
860. Zigarettenpapier. 4,7 × 4,2 cm. Lithographie, drei Farben. Spanien, Beginn des
XX. Jahrhunderts.
861. Zigarettenpapier. 5 × 4,2 cm. Lithographie, eine Farbe. Frankreich, Beginn des
XX. Jahrhunderts.
862. Früchte. 22,5 × 23 cm. Lithographie, fünf
Farben. Druckerei Woodward & Tierman,
St. Louis. U.S.A., Beginn des XX. Jahrhunderts.
863. Kurzwarengeschäft. 24 × 18,2 cm. Lithographie, sieben Farben. China, Ende des
XIX. Jahrhunderts.

862

863

864

864. Product for preserving food. 5 3/16 × 10 1/4 in. Litho, 5 colours. England, 1880.

864. Produit pour la conservation des aliments. 13,2 × 26 cm. Litho cinq coul. Angleterre, 1880.

864. Lebensmittelkonservierungsstoff. 13,2 × 26 cm. Lithographie, fünf Farben. England, 1880.

865

866

865

865. Crème caramel. 4 ³/₄ × 3 ¹/₈ in. Offset, 4 colours. France, 1971.
866. Consumers' association. 4 ³/₄ × 4 ³/₄ in. Offset, monochrome, on pink paper. Switzerland, 1971.

865. *Crème caramel. 12 × 7,9 cm. Offset quatre coul. France, 1971.*
866. *Société de consommatrices. 12 × 12 cm. Offset une coul., papier rose. Suisse, 1971.*

865. Karamelcreme. 12 × 7,9 cm. Offset, vier Farben. Frankreich, 1971.
866. Konsumgesellschaft. 12 × 12 cm. Offset, eine Farbe, Rosapapier. Schweiz, 1971.

V. The appearance of the label in various forms of art

V. Apparition de l'étiquette dans diverses formes de l'Art

V. Auftreten des Etiketts in verschiedenen Kunstformen

This chapter briefly sketches the appearance of the label in the field of art. Here as in other contexts, we find the label providing information and identification, and indications of ownership and use.

Dans ce cinquième chapitre, nous esquissons brièvement l'apparition de l'étiquette dans l'Art. En effet, nous retrouvons ici l'étiquette dans ses fonctions d'information, d'identification, d'appartenance et de destination.

In diesem fünften Kapitel skizzieren wir kurz das Erscheinen des Etiketts in der Kunst. Tatsächlich finden wir hier das Etikett in seinen Funtionen der Information, der Kennzeichnung, der Zugehörigkeit und Bestimmung.

867

868

869

870

871

867. Porcelain bowl with the legend: 'Long life, riches, honours.' China, mid-16th century.
868. Portrait of Michelangelo. Unknown master. Italy, 1560.
869. Publication. Cervantes' *Don Quijote de la Mancha.* Spain, 1605.
870. Wood engraving. Utamaro. Japan, 17th century.
871. Publication. Bossuet's *Histoire universelle.* Printing, Sébastien Mabre, Cramoisy. France, 1681.

867. *Bol en porcelaine. Marque de vœux: «Longue vie, richesses, honneurs.» Chine, milieu du XVIe siècle.*
868. *Portrait de Michel-Ange. Maître inconnu. Italie, 1560.*
869. *Edition.* Don Quichotte de la Manche, *de Cervantès. Espagne, 1605.*
870. *Gravure sur bois. Utamaro. Japon, XVIIe siècle.*
871. *Edition.* Histoire universelle *de Bossuet. Imp. Sébastien Mabre, Cramoisy. France, 1681.*

867. Porzellanschüssel. Wunschzeichen: «Langes Leben, Reichtum, Ehren.» China, Mitte des XVI. Jahrhunderts.
868. Bildnis von Michelangelo. Unbekannter Meister. Italien, 1560.
869. Verlag. *Don Quijote von La Mancha,* von Cervantes. Spanien, 1605.
870. Holzschnitt. Utamaro. Japan, XVII. Jahrhundert.
871. Verlag. *Universalgeschichte* von Bossuet. Druckerei Sébastien Mabre, Cramoisy. Frankreich, 1681.

872

873

874

875

876

872. Wood engraving. Komatsu. Japan, 18th century.
873. Painting, *The Betrothal.* Der Meister des Hausbuches. Germany.
874. Wood engraving. Hiroshige. Japan, 19th century.
875. Wood engraving. Kitagawa Murasakiya. Japan, late 18th century.
876. Publication. Fénelon's *Education des filles.* France, 1687.

872. *Gravure sur bois. Komatsu. Japon, XVIIIe siècle.*
873. *Peinture* Les Fiancés. *Der Meister des Hausbuches. Allemagne.*
874. *Gravure sur bois. Hiroshige. Japon, XIXe siècle.*
875. *Gravure sur bois. Kitagawa Murasakiya. Japon, fin du XVIIIe siècle.*
876. *Edition.* Education des filles, *de Fénelon. France, 1687.*

872. Holzschnitt. Komatsu. Japan, XVIII. Jahrhundert.
873. Gemälde *Die Verlobten.* Der Meister des Hausbuches. Deutschland.
874. Holzschnitt. Hiroshige. Japan, XIX. Jahrhundert.
875. Holzschnitt. Kitagawa Murasakiya. Japan, Ende des XVIII. Jahrhunderts.
876. Verlag. *Töchtererziehung* von Fénelon. Frankreich, 1687.

877

878

879

880

881

877. Wood engraving. Komatsu. Japan, 18th century.
878. Wood engraving. Hiroshige. Japan, 19th century.
879. Wood engraving. Chûrinsha Katsukawa Shunchô. Japan, 1790.
880. Publication. Boileau's *Satires*. France, 1667.
881. Terra cotta. Seal of a Sumerian accoucheur. 12th century BC.

877. *Gravure sur bois. Komatsu. Japon, XVIIIe siècle.*
878. *Gravure sur bois. Hiroshige. Japon, XIXe siècle.*
879. *Gravure sur bois. Chûrinsha Katsukawa Shunchô. Japon, 1790.*
880. *Edition. Satires, de Boileau. France, 1667.*
881. *Terre cuite. Sceau d'un médecin accoucheur sumérien. XIIe siècle av. J.-C.*

877. Holzschnitt. Komatsu. Japan, XVIII. Jahrhundert.
878. Holzschnitt. Hiroshige. Japan, XIX. Jahrhundert.
879. Holzschnitt. Chûrinsha Katsukawa Shunchô. Japan, 1790.
880. Verlag. *Satiren* von Boileau. Frankreich, 1667.
881. Ton. Siegel eines sumerischen Geburtshelfers. XII. Jahrhundert v. Chr.

882

883

884

882. Fresco. Paolo Uccello. Italy, 15th century.
883. Porcelain. Mark of the reign of Wan Li. China, 1573–1619.
884. Lithograph. H. Daumier. France, 1855.
885. Painting. *Le Déserteur.* Switzerland, early 19th century.
886. Painting, *The wife of Jacques Cœur.* French school, 15th century.

882. *Fresque. Paolo Uccello. Italie, XVe siècle.*
883. *Porcelaine. Marque du règne de Wan Li. Chine, 1573-1619.*
884. *Lithographie. H. Daumier. France, 1855.*
885. *Peinture.* Le Déserteur. *Suisse, début du XIXe siècle.*
886. *Peinture,* La femme de Jacques Cœur. *Ecole française du XVe siècle.*

882. Freske. Paolo Ucello. Italien, XV. Jahrhundert.
883. Porzellan. Merkmal der Wan Li-Herrschaft. China, 1573–1619.
884. Lithographie. H. Daumier. Frankreich, 1855.
885. Gemälde. *Le Déserteur.* Schweiz, Beginn des XIX. Jahrhunderts.
886. Gemälde. *Die Frau des Jacques Cœur.* Französische Schule des XV. Jahrhunderts.

885

886

887

888

889

890

891

887. Copper plate engraving. Guillaume Le Testu's cosmography. France, 1555.
888. Wood engraving. Utamaro. Japan, 17th century.
889. Painting. *Le Déserteur*. Switzerland, 1830.
890. Wood engraving. Utamaro. Japan, 17th century.
891. Mosaic. Palatine Chapel, Palermo. Italy, 12th century.

887. *Gravure sur cuivre, cosmographie de Guillaume Le Testu. France, 1555.*
888. *Gravure sur bois. Utamaro. Japon, XVIe siècle.*
889. *Peinture. Le Déserteur. Suisse, 1830.*
890. *Gravure sur bois. Utamaro. Japon, XVIe siècle.*
891. *Mosaïque. Chapelle Palatine, Palerme. Italie, XIIe siècle.*

887. Kupferstich. Kosmographie des Guillaume Le Testu. Frankreich, 1555.
888. Holzschnitt. Utamaro. Japan, XVII. Jahrhundert.
889. Gemälde. *Le Déserteur*. Schweiz, 1830.
890. Holzschnitt. Utamaro. Japan, XVII. Jahrhundert.
891. Mosaik. Palatinische Kapelle, Palermo. Italien, XII. Jahrhundert.

892

893

894

895

896

892. *Rohan's Grandes Heures.* France, 15th century.
893. Sabre hilt. Mosamitsu Taû. China, 19th century.
894. Lithograph. H. Daumier. France, mid-19th century.
895. Lithographic poster. E. Vuillard. France, 1894.
896. Porcelain with the legend: 'Fine china for the Jade pavilion.' China, early 17th century.

892. *Les Grandes Heures de Rohan. France, XVᵉ siècle.*
893. *Garde de sabre. Mosamitsu Taû. Chine, XIXᵉ siècle.*
894. *Lithographie. H. Daumier. France, milieu du XIXᵉ siècle.*
895. *Affiche lithographique. E. Vuillard. France, 1894.*
896. *Porcelaine. Marque d'appréciation: «Belle vaisselle pour le pavillon de Jade.» Chine, début du XVIIᵉ siècle.*

892. *Die grossen Stunden von Rohan.* Frankreich, XV. Jahrhundert.
893. Schwertwache. Mosamitsu Taû. China, XIX. Jahrhundert.
894. Lithographie. H. Daumier. Frankreich, Mitte des XIX. Jahrhunderts.
895. Lithographisches Plakat. E. Vuillard. Frankreich, 1894.
896. Porzellan. Bewertungskennzeichen: «Schönes Geschirr für den Jade-Pavillon.» China, Beginn des XVII. Jahrhunderts.

897

898

899

900

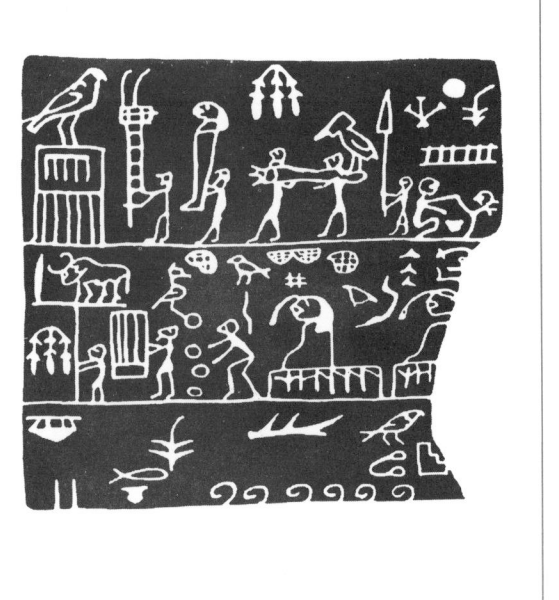

901

897. Copper plate engraving. Albrecht Dürer. Germany, 1515.
898. Porcelain with the legend: 'Fine china for the rich and the honourable.' China, 16th century.
899. Fresco, Sistine Chapel. Michelangelo. Italy, 1508–1512.
900. Publication. The Works of Molière. Claude Barbin. France, 1673.
901. Tablet. Saggarah. Egypt, 4th dynasty.

897. Gravure sur cuivre. Albert Dürer. Allemagne, 1515.
898. Porcelaine. Marque d'appréciation: «Belle vaisselle pour le riche et l'honorable.» Chine, XVIᵉ siècle.
899. Fresque, chapelle sixtine. Michel-Ange. Italie, 1508-1512.
900. Edition. Œuvres de Molière. Claude Barbin. France, 1673.
901. Tablette. Saggarah. Egypte, IVᵉ dynastie.

897. Kupferstich. Albrecht Dürer. Deutschland, 1515.
898. Porzellan. Bewertungskennzeichen: «Schönes Geschirr für den Reichen und Ehrenhaften.» China, XVI. Jahrhundert.
899. Freske. Sixtinische Kapelle. Michelangelo. Italien, 1508–1512.
900. Verlag. Molière's Werke. Claude Barbin. Frankreich, 1673.
901. Täfelchen. Sakkarah. Ägypten, IV. Dynastie.

902

903

904

902. Wood engraving. Hokusai. Japan, late 18th-early 19th centuries.
903. Porcelain. Kia-Tsing. China, 1522–1566.
904. Drawing. Albrecht Dürer. Germany, 1527.
905. Wood engraving. Ichiyusai Kumiteru. Japan, early 19th century.
906. Wood engraving. Ishikawa Toyonobu. Japan, 18th century.

902. Gravure sur bois. Hokusai. Japon, fin du XVIIIᵉ siècle-début du XIXᵉ siècle.
903. Porcelaine. Kia-Tsing. Chine, 1522-1566.
904. Dessin. Albert Dürer. Allemagne, 1527.
905. Gravure sur bois. Ichiyusai Kumiteru. Japon, début du XIXᵉ siècle.
906. Gravure sur bois. Ishikawa Toyonobu. Japon, XVIIIᵉ siècle.

902. Holzschnitt. Hokusai. Japan, Ende des XVIII. Jahrhunderts-Beginn des XIX. Jahrhunderts.
903. Porzellan. Kia-Tsing. China, 1522–1566.
904. Zeichnung. Albrecht Dürer. Deutschland, 1527.
905. Holzschnitt. Ichiyusai Kumiteru. Japan, Beginn des XIX. Jahrhunderts.
906. Holzschnitt. Ishikawa Toyonobu. Japan, XVIII. Jahrhundert.

905

906

907

908

909

A AIX,
chez C. ADIBERT,
Imprimeur du Roi
vis-à-vis le College.
1767.

910

911

907. Wood engraving. Ichieisai Yoshitsuya Gwa. Japan, 19th century.
908. Stained glass. Cartoon by Hans Holbein. Switzerland, 1520.
909. Wood engraving. Hiroshige. Japan, 19th century.
910. Publication. Legal advice. France, 1767.
911. Wood engraving. Hiroshige. Japan, 19th century.

907. *Gravure sur bois. Ichieisai Yoshitsuya Gwa. Japon, XIXᵉ siècle.*
908. *Vitrail. Carton de Hans Holbein. Suisse, 1520.*
909. *Gravure sur bois. Hiroshige. Japon, XIXᵉ siècle.*
910. *Edition. Consultation judiciaire. France, 1767.*
911. *Gravure sur bois. Hiroshige. Japon, XIXᵉ siècle.*

907. Holzschnitt. Ichieisai Yoshitsuya Gwa. Japan, XIX. Jahrhundert.
908. Buntes Fenster. Pappe von Hans Holbein. Schweiz, 1520.
909. Holzschnitt. Hiroshige. Japan, XIX. Jahrhundert.
910. Verlag. Juristische Beratung. Frankreich, 1767.
911. Holzschnitt. Hiroshige. Japan, XIX. Jahrhundert.

912

913

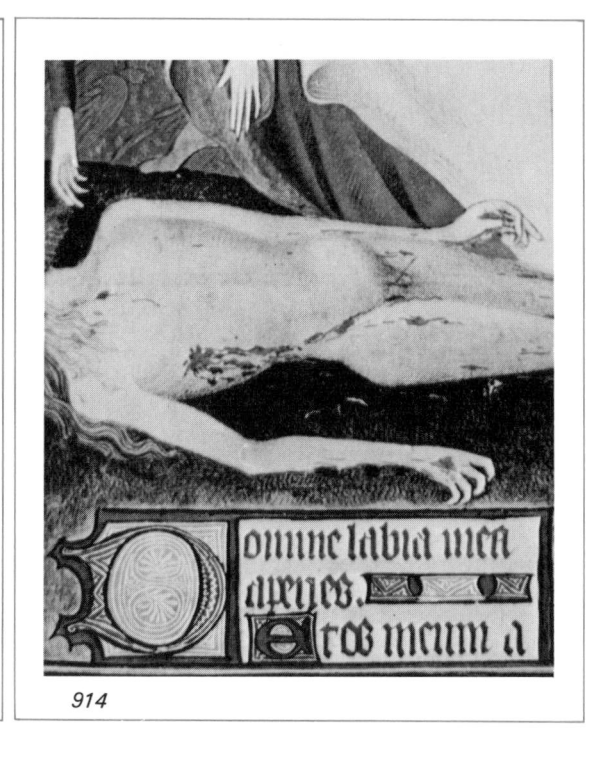

914

912. Porcelain.   Mark of the reign of Wan Li.
     China, 1573–1619.
913. Painting.   French school, 16th century.
914. *Rohan's Grandes Heures.*   France, 15th
     century.

912. *Porcelaine. Marque du règne de Wan Li.
     Chine, 1573-1619.*
913. *Peinture. Ecole française du XVIᵉ siècle.*
914. Les Grandes Heures de Rohan. *France,
     XVᵉ siècle.*

912. Porzellan. Merkmal der Wan Li-Herrschaft.
     China, 1573–1619.
913. Gemälde. Französische Schule des XVI.
     Jahrhunderts.
914. *Die grossen Stunden von Rohan.* Frank-
     reich, XV. Jahrhundert.

VI. The label in the context of international and humanitarian organizations

By way of a conclusion, this chapter is devoted to examples of label design used by international and humanitarian organizations. The examples given enable us to show on the one hand the principle of the functional label, and on the other the varied forms which this takes on an international level.

VI. L'étiquette dans le cadre des Organisations internationales et Humanitaires

Il nous a paru intéressant, en guise de conclusion, de consacrer ce sixième chapitre aux Organisations internationales et Humanitaires. La comparaison des exemples présentés nous permet de définir d'une part le principe de l'étiquette fonctionnelle, et d'autre part, la diversité d'expression sur le plan international.

VI. Das Etikett im Rahmen der internationalen und humanitären Organisationen

Es schien uns interessant, als Abschluß, dieses sechste Kapitel den internationalen und humanitären Organisationen zu widmen. Der Vergleich der aufgeführten Beispiele gestattet uns einerseits, das Prinzip des funktionellen Etiketts, und andererseits die Ausdrucksvielfalt auf internationaler Ebene zu definieren.

915

916

917

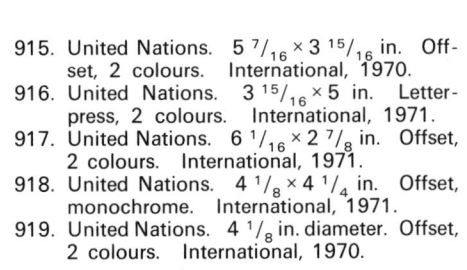
(see below)

918

919

915. United Nations. 5 $^7/_{16}$ × 3 $^{15}/_{16}$ in. Offset, 2 colours. International, 1970.
916. United Nations. 3 $^{15}/_{16}$ × 5 in. Letterpress, 2 colours. International, 1971.
917. United Nations. 6 $^1/_{16}$ × 2 $^7/_8$ in. Offset, 2 colours. International, 1971.
918. United Nations. 4 $^1/_8$ × 4 $^1/_4$ in. Offset, monochrome. International, 1971.
919. United Nations. 4 $^1/_8$ in. diameter. Offset, 2 colours. International, 1970.

915. ONU. 13,8 × 9,9 cm. Offset deux coul. International, 1970.
916. ONU. 10 × 12,6 cm. Typo deux coul. International, 1971.
917. ONU. 15,3 × 7,3 cm. Offset deux coul. International, 1971.
918. ONU. 10,5 × 10,7 cm. Offset une coul. International, 1971.
919. ONU. Diam. 10,5 cm. Offset deux coul. International, 1970.

915. UNO. 13,8 × 9,9 cm. Offset, zwei Farben. International, 1970.
916. UNO. 10 × 12,6 cm. Buchdruck, zwei Farben. International, 1971.
917. UNO. 15,3 × 7,3 cm. Offset, zwei Farben. International, 1971.
918. UNO. 10,5 × 10,7 cm. Offset, eine Farbe. International, 1971.
919. UNO. Durchmesser 10,5 cm. Offset, zwei Farben. International, 1970.

920

921

922

920. United Nations. 4 ³/₁₆ × 6 ⁷/₁₆ in. Letterpress, monochrome. International, 1971.
921. United Nations. 4 ³/₁₆ × 6 ⁷/₁₆ in. Letterpress, 2 colours. International, 1971.
922. United Nations. 3 ¹⁵/₁₆ × 6 ⁵/₁₆ in. Letterpress, 3 colours. International, 1961.
923. United Nations. 2 ¹³/₁₆ × 2 ¹⁵/₁₆ in. Offset, monochrome. International, 1971.
924. United Nations. 4 ³/₄ × 4 ³/₁₆ in. Letterpress, 2 colours. International.

920. ONU. 10,6 × 16,3 cm. Typo une coul. International, 1971.
921. ONU. 10,6 × 16,3 cm. Typo deux coul. International, 1971.
922. ONU. 10 × 16 cm. Typo trois coul. International, 1961.
923. ONU. 7,2 × 7,5 cm. Offset une coul. International, 1971.
924. ONU. 12 × 10,6 cm. Typo deux coul. International.

920. UNO. 10,6 × 16,3 cm. Buchdruck, eine Farbe. International, 1971.
921. UNO. 10,6 × 16,3 cm. Buchdruck, zwei Farben. International, 1971.
922. UNO. 10 × 16 cm. Buchdruck, drei Farben. International, 1961.
923. UNO. 7,2 × 7,5 cm. Offset, eine Farbe. International, 1971.
924. UNO. 12 × 10,6 cm. Buchdruck, zwei Farben. International.

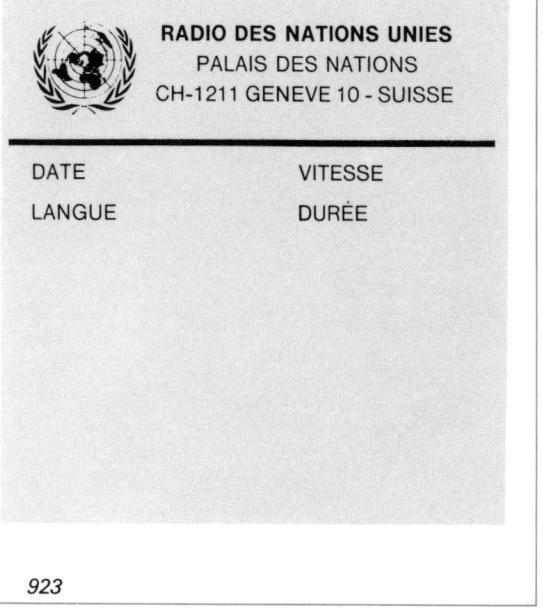

923

924

925

926

BUREAU INTERNATIONAL DU TRAVAIL

CONFIDENTIEL

Ce pli ne doit être ouvert que par le destinataire

A :
To :

DATE   EXPÉDITEUR :
                        SENDER :

To be opened by the recipient only

CONFIDENTIAL

ILO 9 3.62   INTERNATIONAL LABOUR OFFICE

927

Informations du BIT
Information from the ILO
Información de la OIT

Bureau International du Travail
CH — 1211 Genève 22, Suisse

928

BUREAU INTERNATIONAL DU TRAVAIL
INTERNATIONAL LABOUR OFFICE
CH 1211 GENÈVE 22

Operational Equipment Section
Section d'Equipement pour la Coopération technique   ILO 497 4.71

929

925. International Labour Office. 3 $^{9}/_{16}$ × 4 $^{3}/_{8}$ in. Silk-screen, 2 colours and gold. International, 1971.
926. International Labour Office. 4 $^{15}/_{16}$ in. diameter. Offset, 2 colours. International, 1971.
927. International Labour Office. 4 $^{1}/_{8}$ × 4 $^{1}/_{4}$ in. Letterpress, monochrome. International, 1971.
928. International Labour Office. 5 $^{5}/_{16}$ × 3 $^{5}/_{8}$ in. Letterpress, monochrome. International, 1971.
929. International Labour Office. 5 $^{1}/_{8}$ × 3 $^{9}/_{16}$ in. Offset, monochrome. International, 1971.

925. BIT. 9 × 11 cm. Sérigraphie deux coul. et or. International, 1971.
926. BIT. Diam. 12,5 cm. Offset deux coul. International, 1971.
927. BIT. 10,4 × 10,8 cm. Typo une coul. International, 1971.
928. BIT. 13,5 × 9,2 cm. Typo une coul. International, 1971.
929. BIT. 13 × 9 cm. Offset une coul. International, 1971.

925. Internationales Arbeitsamt (IAA). 9 × 11 cm. Siebdruck, zwei Farben und Gold. International, 1971.
926. IAA. Durchmesser 12,5 cm. Offset, zwei Farben. International, 1971.
927. IAA. 10,4 × 10,8 cm. Buchdruck, eine Farbe. International, 1971.
928. IAA. 13,5 × 9,2 cm. Buchdruck, eine Farbe. International, 1971.
929. IAA. 13 × 9 cm. Offset, eine Farbe. International, 1971.

930

931

932

933

934

930. ILO, fuel. 1 $^3/_4$ × 1 $^3/_4$ in. Letterpress, monochrome. International, 1971.
931. ILO, beware of explosion. 1 $^3/_4$ × 1 $^3/_4$ in. Letterpress, monochrome. International, 1971.
932. ILO, danger, inflammable. 1 $^3/_4$ × 1 $^3/_4$ in. Letterpress, monochrome. International, 1971.
933. ILO, corrosive liquid. 1 $^3/_4$ × 1 $^3/_4$ in. Letterpress, monochrome. International, 1971.
934. ILO, poison. 1 $^3/_4$ × 1 $^3/_4$ in. Letterpress, monochrome. International, 1971.

930. *BIT., matière comburante. 4,5 × 4,5 cm. Typo une coul. International, 1971.*
931. *BIT., danger d'explosion. 4,5 × 4,5 cm. Typo une coul. International, 1971.*
932. *BIT., danger d'inflammation. 4,5 × 4,5 cm. Typo une coul. International, 1971.*
933. *BIT., danger de corrosion. 4,5 × 4,5 cm. Typo une coul. International, 1971.*
934. *BIT., danger d'intoxication. 4,5 × 4,5 cm. Typo une coul. International, 1971.*

930. IAA. Brennbarer Stoff. 4,5 × 4,5 cm. Buchdruck, eine Farbe. International, 1971.
931. IAA. Explosionsgefahr. 4,5 × 4,5 cm. Buchdruck, eine Farbe. International, 1971.
932. IAA. Brandgefahr. 4,5 × 4,5 cm. Buchdruck, eine Farbe. International, 1971.
933. IAA. Korrosionsgefahr. 4,5 × 4,5 cm. Buchdruck, eine Farbe. International, 1971.
934. IAA. Vergiftungsgefahr. 4,5 × 4,5 cm. Buchdruck, eine Farbe. International, 1971.

935

936

937

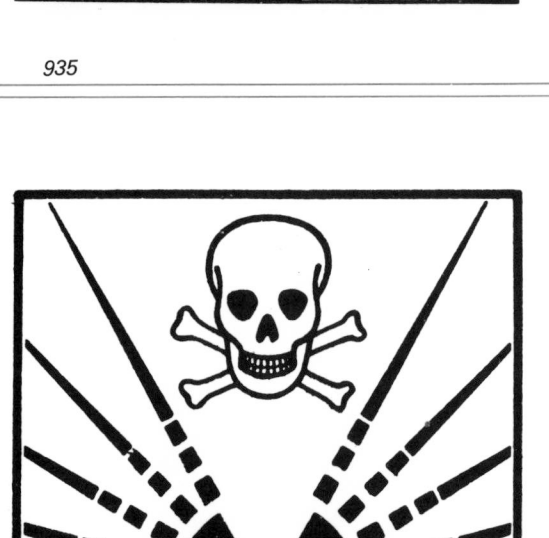

938

939

935. UIT (International Telecommunications Union). $2\frac{5}{16} \times 2\frac{3}{8}$ in. Silk-screen, 2 colours. International.
936. UIT. $4\frac{1}{4} \times 2\frac{3}{4}$ in. Silk-screen, 3 colours. International.
937. UIT. $2\frac{1}{4} \times 2\frac{1}{4}$ in. Silk-screen, 2 colours. International, 1967.
938. ILO, intense radioactivity. $1\frac{3}{4} \times 1\frac{3}{4}$ in. Letterpress, monochrome. International, 1971.
939. ILO, radioactivity. $1\frac{3}{4} \times 1\frac{3}{4}$ in. Letterpress, monochrome. International, 1971.

935. UIT. $5,9 \times 6$ cm. Sérigraphie deux coul. International.
936. UIT. $10,8 \times 7$ cm. Sérigraphie trois coul. International.
937. UIT. $5,8 \times 5,7$ cm. Sérigraphie deux coul. International, 1967.
938. BIT., radioactivité intense. $4,5 \times 4,5$ cm. Typo une coul. International, 1971.
939. BIT., radioactivité. $4,5 \times 4,5$ cm. Typo une coul. International, 1971.

935. Internationale Union der Telekommunikationen (UIT). $5,9 \times 6$ cm. Siebdruck, zwei Farben. International.
936. UIT. $10,8 \times 7$ cm. Siebdruck, drei Farben. International.
937. UIT. $5,8 \times 5,7$ cm. Siebdruck, zwei Farben. International, 1967.
938. IAA. Starke Radioaktivität. $4,5 \times 4,5$ cm. Buchdruck, eine Farbe. International, 1971.
939. IAA. Radioaktivität. $4,5 \times 4,5$ cm. Buchdruck, eine Farbe. International, 1971.

940

941

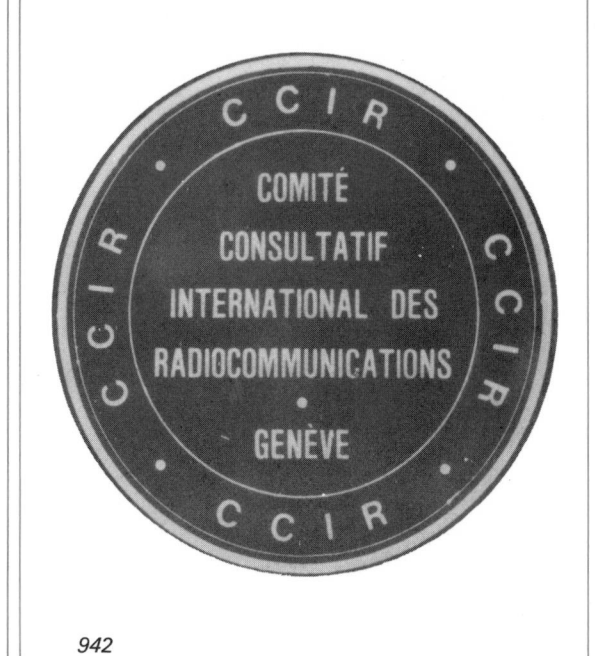

942

940. UIT. 2 $^{15}/_{16}$ in. diameter. Offset, 2 colours. International, 1971.
941. UIT. 2 $^{13}/_{16}$ in. diameter. Offset, monochrome. International.
942. UIT. 2 $^{13}/_{16}$ in. diameter. Offset, monochrome. International.
943. UIT. 1 × $^{3}/_{4}$ in. Offset, monochrome. International, 1963.
944. World Meteorological Organization. 4 $^{3}/_{16}$ in. diameter. Letterpress, monochrome. International, 1971.

940. UIT. Diam. 7,5 cm. Offset deux coul. International, 1971.
941. UIT. Diam. 7,2 cm. Offset une coul. International.
942. UIT. Diam. 7,2 cm. Offset une coul. International.
943. UIT. 2,6 × 1,9 cm. Offset une coul. International, 1963.
944. OMM. Diam. 10,6 cm. Typo une coul. International, 1971.

940. UIT. Durchmesser 7,5 cm. Offset, zwei Farben. International, 1971.
941. UIT. Durchmesser 7,2 cm. Offset, eine Farbe. International.
942. UIT. Durchmesser 7,2 cm. Offset, eine Farbe. International.
943. UIT. 2,6 × 1,9 cm. Offset, eine Farbe. International, 1963.
944. Weltwetterdienst (World Meteorological Organization. WMO.) Durchmesser 10,6 cm. Buchdruck, eine Farbe. International, 1971.

943

944

945

946

ORGANISATION METEOROLOGIQUE MONDIALE

947

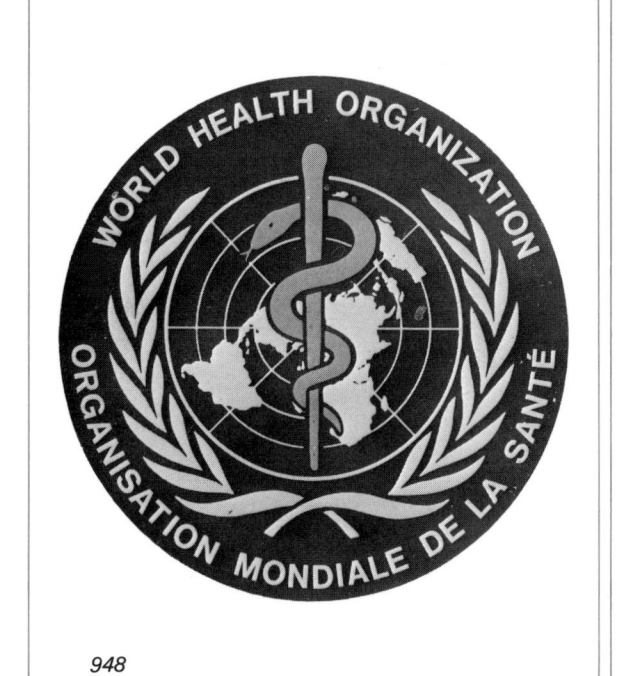

948

949

945. World Meteorological Organization.
$4 \frac{1}{4} \times 5 \frac{7}{16}$ in. Offset, monochrome, on green paper. International, 1971.
946. World Meteorological Organization.
$4 \frac{1}{4}$ in. diameter. Letterpress, monochrome, on green paper. International, 1971.
947. World Meteorological Organization.
$3 \frac{3}{4} \times 3 \frac{15}{16}$ in. Offset, monochrome. International, 1971.
948. World Health Organization. 7 in. diameter. Offset, 2 colours. International, 1971.
949. World Health Organization. $2 \frac{15}{16} \times 1 \frac{7}{8}$ in. Offset, monochrome. International, 1971.

945. OMM. $10,8 \times 13,7$ cm. Offset une coul., papier vert. International, 1971.
946. OMM. Diam. 10,7 cm. Typo une coul., papier vert. International, 1971.
947. OMM. $9,5 \times 10$ cm. Offset une coul. International, 1971.
948. OMS. Diam. 17,8 cm. Offset deux coul. International, 1971.
949. OMS. $7,5 \times 4,7$ cm. Offset une coul. International, 1971.

945. WMO. $10,8 \times 13,7$ cm. Offset, eine Farbe, grünes Papier. International, 1971.
946. WMO. Durchmesser 10,7 cm. Buchdruck, eine Farbe, grünes Papier. International, 1971.
947. WMO. $9,5 \times 10$ cm. Offset, eine Farbe. International, 1971.
948. Weltgesundheitsorganisation (World Health Organization. W.H.O.) Durchmesser 17,8 cm. Offset, zwei Farben. International, 1971.
949. WHO. $7,5 \times 4,7$ cm. Offset, eine Farbe. International, 1971.

950

951

952

950. CICR (International Red Cross Committee, Geneva). International, 1918.
951. CICR. International, 1918.
952. CICR. International, 1916.
953. CICR. 1 ³/₈ × 1 ³/₄ in. Litho, 2 colours. Spain, 1870.
954. CICR. 1 ¹¹/₁₆ in. diameter. Litho, 2 colours. Spain, 1870.

950. CICR. International, 1918.
951. CICR. International, 1918.
952. CICR. International, 1916.
953. CICR. 3,5 × 4,5 cm. Litho deux coul. Espagne, 1870.
954. CICR. Diam. 4,3 cm. Litho deux coul. Espagne, 1870.

950. Internationales Komitee des Roten Kreuzes. International, 1918.
951. Internationales Komitee des Roten Kreuzes. International, 1918.
952. Internationales Komitee des Roten Kreuzes. International, 1916.
953. Internationales Komitee des Roten Kreuzes. 3,5 × 4,5 cm. Lithographie, zwei Farben. Spanien, 1870.
954. Internationales Komitee des Roten Kreuzes. Durchmesser 4,3 cm. Lithographie, zwei Farben. Spanien, 1870.

953

954

955

955. Red Cross. 1 $\frac{1}{2}$ in. diameter. Hungary, 1870—1878.

955. Croix-Rouge. Diam. 3,8 cm. Hongrie, 1870-1878.

955. Rotes Kreuz. Durchmesser 3,8 cm. Ungarn, 1870—1878.

956

957

958

956. Red Cross.   1 $^7/_{16}$ in. diameter.   Litho, 2 colours.   Portugal, 1870.
957. Red Cross.   1 $^3/_8$ in. diameter.   Litho, monochrome.   Serbia, 1870–1878.
958. Red Cross.   1 $^{11}/_{16}$ in. diameter.   Litho, 2 colours.   Mecklenburg, 1870.
959. Red Cross.   1 $^1/_2$ in. diameter.   Litho, 2 colours.   Germany, 1870.
960. CICR.   1 $^1/_2$ in. diameter.   Litho, monochrome.   Trieste, 1878.

956. Croix-Rouge. Diam. 3,6 cm. Litho deux coul. Portugal, 1870.
957. Croix-Rouge. Diam. 3,5 cm. Litho une coul. Serbie, 1870-1878.
958. Croix-Rouge. Diam. 4,3 cm. Litho deux coul. Mecklembourg, 1870.
959. Croix-Rouge. Diam. 3,8 cm. Litho deux coul. Allemagne, 1870.
960. CICR. Diam. 3,8 cm. Litho une coul. Trieste, 1878.

956. Rotes Kreuz. Durchmesser 3,6 cm. Lithographie, zwei Farben. Portugal, 1870.
957. Rotes Kreuz. Durchmesser 3,5 cm. Lithographie, eine Farbe. Serbien, 1870–1878.
958. Rotes Kreuz. Durchmesser 4,3 cm. Lithographie, zwei Farben. Mecklenburg, 1870.
959. Rotes Kreuz. Durchmesser 3,8 cm. Lithographie, zwei Farben. Deutschland, 1870.
960. Internationales Komitee des Roten Kreuzes. Durchmesser 3,8 cm. Lithographie, eine Farbe. Triest, 1878.

959

960

961

962

964

965

961. Red Cross. 1 × 1 ¹/₄ in. Litho, 2 colours. Italy, 1864.
962. Red Cross. 1 ⁹/₁₆ × 1 ³/₄ in. Litho, monochrome. Serbia, 1870–1878.
963. CICR. 1 ⁹/₁₆ in. diameter. Litho, 2 colours. International, 1870–1871.
964. Red Cross. 1 ³/₁₆ × 1 ¹/₄ in. Litho, 2 colours. Spain, 1870–1878.
965. Red Cross. 1 ³/₈ in. diameter. Litho, 2 colours. Russia, 1870–1878.

961. Croix-Rouge. 2,5 × 3,2 cm. Litho deux coul. Italie, 1864.
962. Croix-Rouge. 4 × 4,5 cm. Litho une coul. Serbie, 1870-1878.
963. CICR. Diam. 4 cm. Litho deux coul. International, 1870-1871.
964. Croix-Rouge. 3 × 3,2 cm. Litho deux coul. Espagne, 1870-1878.
965. Croix-Rouge. Diam. 3,5 cm. Litho deux coul. Russie, 1870-1878.

961. Rotes Kreuz. 2,5 × 3,2 cm. Lithographie, zwei Farben. Italien, 1864.
962. Rotes Kreuz. 4 × 4,5 cm. Lithographie, eine Farbe. Serbien, 1870–1878.
963. Internationales Komitee des Roten Kreuzes. Durchmesser 4 cm. Lithographie, zwei Farben. International, 1870–1871.
964. Rotes Kreuz. 3 × 3,2 cm. Lithographie, zwei Farben. Spanien, 1870–1878.
965. Rotes Kreuz. Durchmesser 3,5 cm. Lithographie, zwei Farben. Russland, 1870–1878.

966

967

968

966. Red Cross. 1 $^3/_8$ × 1 $^3/_{16}$ in. Litho, 2 colours. Austria, 1870–1878.
967. CICR. 3 $^5/_8$ × 2 $^1/_4$ in. Offset, 2 colours. International, 1971.
968. Red Cross. 1 $^9/_{16}$ × 1 $^5/_{16}$ in. Litho, monochrome. Serbia, 1870–1878.
969. Red Cross. 1 $^3/_{16}$ × 1 $^3/_4$ in. Offset, 4 colours. Design, Solo Susice. Czechoslovakia, 1961.
970. Red Cross. 6 $^{11}/_{16}$ in. diameter. Litho, 2 colours. Vietnam, 1959.

966. Croix-Rouge. 3,5 × 3 cm. Litho deux coul. Autriche, 1870-1878.
967. CICR. 9,2 × 5,8 cm. Offset deux coul. International, 1971.
968. Croix-Rouge. 4 × 3,3 cm. Litho une coul. Serbie, 1870-1878.
969. Croix-Rouge. 3 × 4,5 cm. Offset quatre coul. Créat. Solo Susice. Tchécoslovaquie, 1961.
970. Croix-Rouge. Diam. 17 cm. Litho deux coul. Vietnam, 1959.

966. Rotes Kreuz. 3,5 × 3 cm. Lithographie, zwei Farben. Österreich, 1870–1878.
967. Internationales Komitee des Roten Kreuzes. 9,2 × 5,8 cm. Offset, zwei Farben. International, 1971.
968. Rotes Kreuz. 4 × 3,3 cm. Lithographie, eine Farbe. Serbien, 1870–1878.
969. Rotes Kreuz. 3 × 4,5 cm. Offset, vier Farben. Urheber: Solo Susice. Tschechoslowakei, 1961.
970. Rotes Kreuz. Durchmesser 17 cm. Lithographie, zwei Farben. Vietnam, 1959.

969

970

971

972

973

974

975

971. Red Cross. 2 $^1/_4$ × 3 $^5/_8$ in. Silk-screen, 2 colours. USA, 1970.
972. Red Cross. 2 $^3/_8$ in. diameter. Offset, 2 colours. Morocco, 1969.
973. Red Cross. 1 $^9/_{16}$ × 1 $^1/_4$ in. Offset, 3 colours. Algeria, 1971.
974. Red Cross. 3 $^{13}/_{16}$ × 3 $^3/_4$ in. Silk-screen, 4 colours. Venezuela, 1959.
975. Red Cross. 4 $^1/_8$ × 3 $^{15}/_{16}$ in. Litho, 3 colours. Indonesia, 1965.

971. Croix-Rouge. 5,8 × 9,2 cm. Sérigraphie deux coul. U.S.A., 1970.
972. Croix-Rouge. Diam. 6 cm. Offset deux coul. Maroc, 1969.
973. Croix-Rouge. 4 × 3,2 cm. Offset trois coul. Algérie, 1971.
974. Croix-Rouge. 9,7 × 9,5 cm. Sérigraphie quatre coul. Venezuela, 1959.
975. Croix-Rouge. 10,5 × 10 cm. Litho trois coul. Indonésie, 1965.

971. Rotes Kreuz. 5,8 × 9,2 cm. Siebdruck, zwei Farben. U.S.A., 1970.
972. Rotes Kreuz. Durchmesser 6 cm. Offset, zwei Farben. Marokko, 1969.
973. Rotes Kreuz. 4 × 3,2 cm. Offset, drei Farben. Algerien, 1971.
974. Rotes Kreuz. 9,7 × 9,5 cm. Siebdruck, vier Farben. Venezuela, 1959.
975. Rotes Kreuz. 10,5 × 10 cm. Lithographie, drei Farben. Indonesien, 1965.

976

977

978

976. Red Cross. 1 ³/₈ × 1 ³/₄ in. Offset, 2 colours.   Switzerland, 1963.
977. Red Cross. 1 × 1 ³/₁₆ in. Offset, 2 colours and gold.   Norway, 1971.
978. Red Cross. 1 ³/₁₆ × 1 ³/₁₆ in. Offset, 2 colours.   Yugoslavia, 1961.
979. Red Cross. 1 ⁵/₁₆ × 1 ¹³/₁₆ in. Offset, 3 colours.   Design, Solo Susice. Czechoslovakia, 1959.
980. Red Cross. 1 ⁹/₁₆ × 1 ¹/₄ in.   Offset, 3 colours.   International, 1969.

976. Croix-Rouge. 3,5 × 4,4 cm Offset deux coul. Suisse, 1963.
977. Croix-Rouge. 2,5 × 3 cm. Offset deux coul. et or. Norvège, 1971.
978. Croix-Rouge. 3 × 3,1 cm. Offset deux coul. Yougoslavie, 1961.
979. Croix-Rouge. 3,3 × 4,6 cm. Offset trois coul. Créat. Solo Susice. Tchécoslovaquie, 1959.
980. Croix-Rouge. 4 × 3,2 cm. Offset trois coul. International, 1969.

976. Rotes Kreuz. 3,5 × 4,4 cm. Offset, zwei Farben. Schweiz, 1963.
977. Rotes Kreuz. 2,5 × 3 cm. Offset, zwei Farben und Gold. Norwegen, 1971.
978. Rotes Kreuz. 3 × 3,1 cm. Offset, zwei Farben. Jugoslawien, 1961.
979. Rotes Kreuz. 3,3 × 4,6 cm. Offset, drei Farben. Urheber: Solo Susice. Tschechoslowakei, 1959.
980. Rotes Kreuz. 4 × 3,2 cm. Offset, drei Farben. International, 1969.

979

980

981

NETGIRAF

DANSK RØDE KORS

982

ČEST
ZASLOUŽILÝM
DÁRCŮM KRVE

983

COLABORADOR
ASAMBLEA PROVINCIAL DE BARCELONA

984

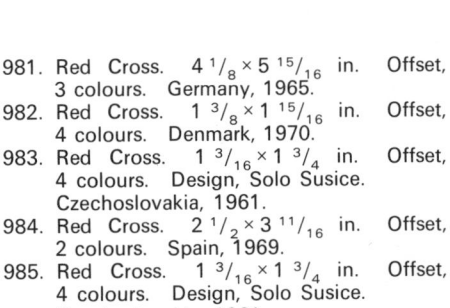

PRACUJTE

V ZDRAVOTNICKÝCH
HLÍDKÁCH
ČSČK

985

981. Red Cross. 4 $1/8$ × 5 $15/16$ in. Offset, 3 colours. Germany, 1965.
982. Red Cross. 1 $3/8$ × 1 $15/16$ in. Offset, 4 colours. Denmark, 1970.
983. Red Cross. 1 $3/16$ × 1 $3/4$ in. Offset, 4 colours. Design, Solo Susice. Czechoslovakia, 1961.
984. Red Cross. 2 $1/2$ × 3 $11/16$ in. Offset, 2 colours. Spain, 1969.
985. Red Cross. 1 $3/16$ × 1 $3/4$ in. Offset, 4 colours. Design, Solo Susice. Czechoslovakia, 1961.

981. Croix-Rouge. 10,5 × 15 cm. Offset trois coul. Allemagne, 1965.
982. Croix-Rouge. 3,5 × 5 cm. Offset quatre coul. Danemark, 1970.
983. Croix-Rouge. 3 × 4,5 cm. Offset quatre coul. Créat. Solo Susice. Tchécoslovaquie, 1961.
984. Croix-Rouge. 6,4 × 9,4 cm. Offset deux coul. Espagne, 1969.
985. Croix-Rouge. 3 × 4,5 cm. Offset quatre coul. Créat. Solo Susice. Tchécoslovaquie, 1961.

981. Rotes Kreuz. 10,5 × 15 cm. Offset, drei Farben. Deutschland, 1965.
982. Rotes Kreuz. 3,5 × 5 cm. Offset, vier Farben. Dänemark, 1970.
983. Rotes Kreuz. 3 × 4,5 cm. Offset, vier Farben. Urheber: Solo Susice. Tschechoslowakei, 1961.
984. Rotes Kreuz. 6,4 × 9,4 cm. Offset, zwei Farben. Spanien, 1969.
985. Rotes Kreuz. 3 × 4,5 cm. Offset, vier Farben. Urheber: Solo Susice. Tschechoslowakei, 1961.

986

987

988

986. Red Cross. 1 $^3/_{16}$ × 1 $^3/_4$ in. Offset, 3 colours. Czechoslovakia, 1959.
987. Red Cross. 1 $^3/_{16}$ × 1 $^3/_4$ in. Offset, 3 colours. Czechoslovakia, 1959.
988. Red Cross. 1 $^3/_{16}$ × 1 $^3/_4$ in. Offset, 3 colours. Czechoslovakia, 1959.
989. Red Cross. 2 $^1/_4$ × 3 $^5/_{16}$ in. Offset, 5 colours. Denmark, 1970.
990. Red Cross. 2 $^3/_4$ × 4 $^1/_4$ in. Offset, 4 colours. Czechoslovakia, 1962.

986. Croix-Rouge. 3 × 4,5 cm. Offset trois coul. Tchécoslovaquie, 1959.
987. Croix-Rouge. 3 × 4,5 cm. Offset trois coul. Tchécoslovaquie, 1959.
988. Croix-Rouge. 3 × 4,5 cm. Offset trois coul. Tchécoslovaquie, 1959.
989. Croix-Rouge. 5,8 × 8,4 cm. Offset cinq coul. Danemark, 1970.
990. Croix-Rouge. 7 × 10,7 cm. Offset quatre coul. Tchécoslovaquie, 1962.

986. Rotes Kreuz. 3 × 4,5 cm. Offset, drei Farben. Tschechoslowakei, 1959.
987. Rotes Kreuz. 3 × 4,5 cm. Offset, drei Farben. Tschechoslowakei, 1959.
988. Rotes Kreuz. 3 × 4,5 cm. Offset, drei Farben. Tschechoslowakei, 1959.
989. Rotes Kreuz. 5,8 × 8,4 cm. Offset, fünf Farben. Dänemark, 1970.
990. Rotes Kreuz. 7 × 10,7 cm. Offset, vier Farben. Tschechoslowakei, 1962.

989

990

991

992

993

994

ZEBRA

DANSK RØDE KORS

995

991. Red Cross. 3 15/16 × 3 15/16 in. Letter-press, monochrome, on silver paper. Switzerland, 1971.
992. Red Cross. 1 5/16 × 1 15/16 in. Offset, 3 colours. Design, Solo Lipnik. Czechoslovakia, 1960.
993. Red Cross. 3 1/8 × 3 3/8 in. Offset, 3 colours and gold. Australia, 1964.
994. Red Cross. 1 1/4 × 2 in. Offset, 4 colours. Sweden, 1970.
995. Red Cross. 1 3/8 × 1 15/16 in. Offset, 4 colours. Denmark, 1970.

991. *Croix-Rouge. 10 × 10 cm. Typo une coul., papier argent. Suisse, 1971.*
992. *Croix-Rouge. 3,3 × 5 cm. Offset trois coul. Créat. Solo Lipnik. Tchécoslovaquie, 1960.*
993. *Croix-Rouge. 7,9 × 8,5 cm. Offset trois coul. et or. Australie, 1964.*
994. *Croix-Rouge. 3,2 × 5,1 cm. Offset quatre coul. Suède, 1970.*
995. *Croix-Rouge. 3,5 × 5 cm. Offset quatre coul. Danemark, 1970.*

991. Rotes Kreuz. 10 × 10 cm. Buchdruck, eine Farbe, Silberpapier. Schweiz, 1971.
992. Rotes Kreuz. 3,3 × 5 cm. Offset, drei Farben. Urheber: Solo Lipnik. Tschechoslowakei, 1960.
993. Rotes Kreuz. 7,9 × 8,5 cm. Offset, drei Farben und Gold. Australien, 1964.
994. Rotes Kreuz. 3,2 × 5,1 cm. Offset, vier Farben. Schweden, 1970.
995. Rotes Kreuz. 3,5 × 5 cm. Offset, vier Farben. Dänemark, 1970.

996

997

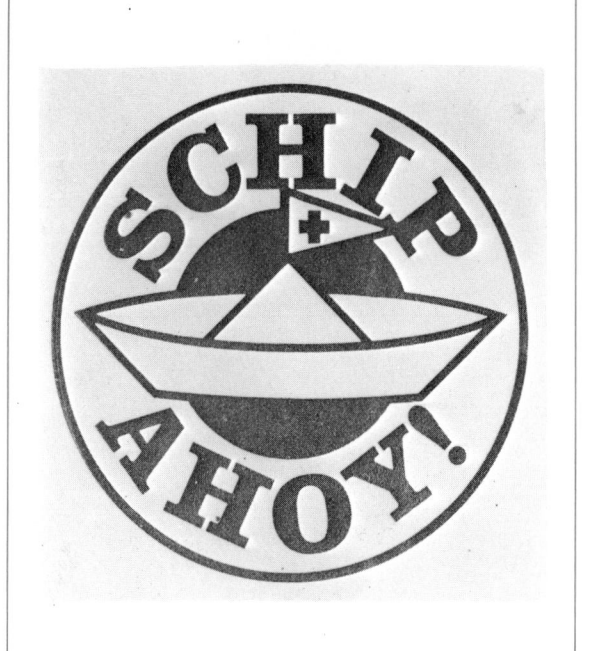

998

996. Red Cross. 4 $^5/_{16}$ × 4 $^9/_{16}$ in. Silk-screen, 2 colours. Venezuela, 1963.
997. Red Cross. 7 $^5/_{16}$ × 6 $^5/_{16}$ in. Letter-press, monochrome. Venezuela, 1970.
998. Red Cross. 4 $^3/_8$ × 4 $^3/_8$ in. Litho, monochrome. Netherlands, 1970.
999. Red Cross. 3 $^{15}/_{16}$ × 3 $^3/_4$ in. Letter-press, 3 colours. Indonesia, 1961.
1000. Red Cross. 1 $^5/_{16}$ × 1 $^3/_8$ in. Offset, 3 colours. International, 1970.

996. Croix-Rouge. 10,9 × 11,6 cm. Sérigraphie deux coul. Venezuela, 1963.
997. Croix-Rouge. 18,5 × 16 cm. Typo une coul. Venezuela, 1970.
998. Croix-Rouge. 11 × 11 cm. Litho une coul. Pays-Bas, 1970.
999. Croix-Rouge. 10 × 9,5 cm. Typo trois coul. Indonésie, 1961.
1000. Croix-Rouge. 3,4 × 3,5 cm. Offset trois coul. International, 1970.

996. Rotes Kreuz. 10,9 × 11,6 cm. Siebdruck, zwei Farben. Venezuela, 1963.
997. Rotes Kreuz. 18,5 × 16 cm. Buchdruck, eine Farbe. Venezuela, 1970.
998. Rotes Kreuz. 11 × 11 cm. Lithographie, eine Farbe. Niederlande, 1970.
999. Rotes Kreuz. 10 × 9,5 cm. Buchdruck, drei Farben. Indonesien, 1961.
1000. Rotes Kreuz. 3,4 × 3,5 cm. Offset, drei Farben. International, 1970.

999

1000

Index

Index

Register

COLLECTIONS

COLLECTIONS

SAMMLUNGEN

This book was printed in September 1972 by Imprimerie Paul Attinger S.A., Neuchâtel
Photolithos by Gravor S.A., Bienne
Binding by Mayer & Soutter S.A., Renens
Layout by Claude Humbert, Geneva
Printed in Switzerland